The Best of
ASK ED®

Your Marijuana
Questions Answered

Ed Rosenthal

Quick American

The Best of Ask Ed
Copyright © 2003 Ed Rosenthal
ISBN: 0-932551-57-2
      978-0-932551-57-3

Project Editor: S. Newhart
Cover Photo: Pepper Design
Hemp shirt on cover: Island Hemp Wear, www.islandhemp.com
Cover & Interior Design: Lightbourne
Printed in the US by Publishers Express Press

Publisher's Cataloging-in-Publication
(Provided by Quality Books, Inc.)

Rosenthal, Ed.
      The best of ask Ed : your marijuana questions
answered / Ed Rosenthal.
            p. cm.
            Includes index.
            ISBN 0-932551-57-2

            1. Cannabis.   2. Marijuana.   I. Title.
      SB295.C35R67 2003   633.7'
                        QBI33-1600

Thanks to all of the readers who contributed questions to Ask Ed® and
submitted photos for the Bud, Plant and Garden of the Month® contests.
All photos were received from readers unless otherwise indicated.

Ask Ed®, Bud of the Month®, Plant of the Month® and Garden of the Month®
is a registered trademark of Edward Rosenthal and is Registered in the US
Patent & Trademark Office.

Lyrics from The Golden Road To Unlimited Devotion by the Grateful Dead,
copyright Ice Nine Publishing Company. Used with permission.

EVERYBODY'S DANCING IN A RING AROUND THE SUN
NOBODY'S FINISHED, WE AIN'T EVEN BEGUN
SO TAKE OFF YOUR SHOES AND TAKE OFF YOUR HAT,
TRY ON YOUR WINGS AND FIND OUT WHERE IT'S AT.

FROM "THE GOLDEN ROAD TO UNLIMITED DEVOTION"
BY THE GRATEFUL DEAD

CONTENTS

TWENTY YEARS.

TO QUOTE THE DEAD, "WHAT A LONG, STRANGE TRIP IT'S BEEN."

I NEVER ANTICIPATED THE longevity of the Ask Ed column. When I first suggested it to my editors in January 1983, they thought it might last three months. They put a little blurb soliciting letters in a spring issue of *High Times*, and the first column appeared in the magazine in August of that year. The letters have never stopped.

The most fascinating part of my work has been the breadth of interests and the depth of understanding and complexity that you, my readers have presented. You direct the "Ask Ed" column. It's reader driven. In a way, we've written this book together.

I'd like to take this opportunity to thank you for allowing me to serve you. You provided me with the time to do research and the resources to seek out the answers. You allowed me to remain a student all these years. It has been an adventure and a great way to spend my time.

You have taken me down avenues that I never would have explored—on hidden trails and invisible highways. Once again, I thank you. I hope I've answered some of your questions and you find this collection an enjoyable and satisfying read.

The questions that appear in this book were all sent in by readers over the span of the column. Some things have changed over the years; for instance, new products, new varieties and new methods of cultivation have emerged. I have revised and updated the answers that appear here in order to give the most up-to-date, current information available about marijuana and its cultivation. Although the book is a twenty-year collection, it has the answers you need now.

BASICS:

THE FREQUENTLY ASKED QUESTIONS

AS YOU CAN IMAGINE, some questions get asked more often than others. Here are the top 12 questions asked by readers. I have listed them here to point you to the section in the book you're looking for. If you don't find your question here, try the alphabetic list that follows the FAQs, the table of contents or the index.

1. How do you set up a garden?
2. Where can I get seeds?
3. My plants/seedlings are stretching, what do I do?
4. What lights should I use?
5. Is it better/easier to grow hydro or soil method?
6. How can I tell a male from a female?
7. How do you force flowering?
8. How can you tell that plants are ripe?
9. Does CO_2 work? How do you use it?
10. The bottom leaves are yellowing, what do I do?
11. How do I get rid of mites/powdery mildew?
12. How can I minimize the telltale smell of my garden?

FAQ 1 ▶ HOW DO YOU SET UP A GARDEN?

HERE ARE A FEW questions and answers that address this very general, very frequently asked question.

ADVICE TO BEGINNERS

I am looking for tips on how to grow my own. I don't know anything about it. What should I do?

M., Carteret, New Jersey

BEFORE YOU PLAN A garden or buy any equipment you should read at least one book on growing marijuana. There are a number of good books out there by several authors. Although the techniques described in the books differ, all of them will improve your success rate.

Rather than attempting to start a garden using trial and error techniques, which often results in buying expensive but unnecessary equipment, use others' expertise to create a productive garden the first time. Information is the cheapest, most effective equipment you can buy. Think of it as software for your garden. Even with equipment worth thousands of dollars, the garden cannot be run well without knowledge of how to do it.

The Best of Ask Ed supplements grow guides and growing websites. You can also write to me by e-mail or snail mail, just follow the instructions on page 392. Information about equipment and set-ups for indoor gardens are discussed in chapter 2 and chapter 4. For outdoor gardening, see chapter 5.

In addition, before starting the project, you should acquaint yourself with the repercussions of the laws should an accident occur. Chapter 8 on Stealth and Safety discusses the law.

SETTING UP INEXPENSIVELY

How can I set up an inexpensive closet garden?

BUD JONES, Internet

PLANTS REQUIRE LIGHT, WATER, nutrients, CO_2 and mild temperatures. As long as these needs are met, and the plants have good genetics, the garden will produce a plentiful yield of potent bud. The cheapest way of doing anything is to read the instructions before beginning.

Questions and answers about lighting equipment are in chapter 2. For lighting amount and the light regimen, see chapter 6. CO_2 is covered in chapter 3. Watering and nutrients are covered in chapter 4. Chapter 6 discusses the plant's needs as it matures.

LEARNING TO GROW

> I know nothing about growing. Do you believe I could learn about it if I went to Amsterdam? Would a grower really show me how to do it, if offered to pay to learn? I hope we meet in the future to smoke some Brazilian Homegrown!
>
> ROBERTO, Rio de Janeiro, Brazil

YOU DON'T HAVE TO go to Amsterdam or anywhere else to learn how to grow marijuana. There are many books available on cultivation, Some of them are written specifically for the personal cultivator. You can order them through the internet and learn all you need to grow a successful crop in the privacy of your own home. Seeds are also available on the internet, and chapter 1 discusses obtaining seeds.

FACTORS FOR KILLER WEED

> What's the most important factor with growing killer weed? Would it be soil, temperature, nutrients, or something else?
>
> BUD LOVER, Internet

THE MOST IMPORTANT FACTOR that affects the quality of the weed you are growing is the plant's genetics. No matter how well a plant is grown, it can only reach its genetic potential. The cheapest way to improve your garden is to find better varieties. Chapter 1 discusses seeds and sources for good genetics. Chapter 11 discusses plant genetics, differences between sativa and indica and different varieties. Finally, chapter 7 talks about how to create mothers in order to maintain a reliable stock for continuous gardening.

Environmental conditions enhance the potential of your crop, or rather, they can hinder your plants from reaching their full potential if the plants' basic needs are not met. Light is foremost: lighting equipment and the best lights to use are discussed in chapter 2, and temperature is also discussed here. The light regimen and dark period are discussed in chapter 6. Soil, nutrients and other factors are covered in chapter 4.

FAQ 2 ▸ WHERE CAN I GET SEEDS?

IT IS ILLEGAL TO possess or sell seeds anywhere in the US. Any domestic company which advertises is either a rip-off of some kind, or a set-up, in either case a losing situation.

Several other countries with more relaxed laws have seeds available for sale, but as a policy, most companies claim that they do not ship to the US. You are taking your chances by ordering seeds through the mail.

Some resources for seeds are suggested in chapter 1. Other ways of acquiring seeds or perpetuating a garden are discussed in chapter 7.

It may also be possible to acquire or produce clones. Clone basics are discussed in chapter 1. Learning how to create clones may eliminate the need to buy additional seeds, thus lowering risk. If you are interested in selection and breeding to develop your own specific variety of killer weed, you can find questions and answers about it in chapter 11.

It is illegal to import seeds into the US. People who are caught with them can face severe penalties although seizure usually results in a fine. There is a small chance that an individual will be caught. Be sure to know your rights. Legal questions are included in chapter 8 on stealth and safety.

FAQ 3 ▸ MY PLANTS/SEEDLINGS ARE STRETCHING, WHAT DO I DO?

THE PLANTS ARE PROBABLY suffering from insufficient light. This is a common problem.

You can read about seedling and plant stretching in chapter 9 on troubleshooting, which allows you to look up many problems by their symptoms. Then follow the cross-references to find solutions. Additional problems, such as pests, are described in chapter 10.

In the case of stretching, if you suspect that insufficient light is the problem, find out about the type and amount of light you should be using in your space in chapter 2.

FAQ 4 ▶ WHAT LIGHTS SHOULD I USE?

OUTDOORS, MARIJUANA LIKES FULL sun. Indoors its growth rate and yield are sensitive to the amount of light it receives. Although marijuana may grow and flower using as little as 20 watts per square foot, the yield increases with each increase to the light. However, the more light in the garden, the more heat that is generated which must be dissipated.

Read about the different lighting equipment, including the types of lights and reflectors and the amount of light to use in chapter 2. Ways to manage heat are covered in chapter 3.

FAQ 5 ▶ IS IT BETTER/EASIER TO GROW HYDRO OR SOIL METHOD?

EACH METHOD HAS ITS advantages. Compare methods in chapter 4, Indoor Environment, which elaborates on how various setups work and what types of problems people encounter.

FAQ 6 ▶ HOW CAN I TELL A MALE FROM A FEMALE?

THIS IS THE MOST-ASKED question in my 20 years of writing the column. Marijuana is an unusual annual plant since the plants have separate male and female sexes. The part of the plant that growers prize is the ripened, unpollinated female buds. In order to keep the female unpollinated, males are removed from the garden.

The female reacts to this by producing more flowers, which eventually "ripen," that is, the stigma of the pistil recedes into the ovary, forming a false seed pod. Since they have not been pollinated, these females produce no seeds and are called "sinsemilla."

Male plants are easily distinguished from females if you know what you are looking for. Males produce little rounded buds, which open in clusters of white or yellow flowers. The female flower consists solely of pairs of pistils protruding from the ovary. See photos in chapter 6 for a visual identification, which also covers how to recognize males, and when and how to sex the plants.

Marijuana plants ordinarily produce male and female flowers on separate plants. If they produce both male and female buds, they're called hermaphrodites. These plants are often unwanted, but they can have some use in breeding. To find out about hermaphrodites and their use in breeding, see chapter 11.

FAQ 7 ▸ HOW DO YOU FORCE FLOWERING?

MARIJUANA IS CALLED A SHORT DAY plant because it flowers in response to a long night cycle. The plant measures the number of hours of darkness each night by producing a hormone. When this hormone builds to a critical level, the plant is triggered into flowering. The hormone is destroyed by the presence of light, even for a few short moments. Then the plant starts its count over. When the gardener intentionally alters the plants' environment to include the critical period of uninterrupted darkness in each 24-hour cycle, it is called "flower forcing."

When and how to force flowering is discussed primarily in chapter 6, which covers the growth cycle from young plant to full bloom, including changes to lighting, which are the key to flower forcing. It covers critical changes to nutrients and other environmental conditions that optimize flower growth. This chapter also addresses some problems you might encounter, including advice on how to visit your garden during the dark period. Chapter 5 covers flower forcing outdoors.

FAQ 8 ▸ HOW CAN YOU TELL THAT PLANTS ARE RIPE?

PLANTS RANGE IN HOW long they take to ripen based on their variety and the conditions provided. Ripeness can be recognized when the ovaries recede and swell to bulging with THC. Specifics on how to recognize ripeness, ripening problems and techniques for harvesting and returning plants to vegetative growth (called revegetating or regenerating) are all discussed in chapter 7.

FAQ 9 DOES CO$_2$ WORK? HOW DO YOU USE IT?

CO$_2$ (CARBON DIOXIDE) IS an inert gas composed of carbon and oxygen. Plants use light energy to combine water with CO$_2$, which produces sugar and releases free oxygen in a process called *photosynthesis*.

The growth rate climbs in a linear ratio to the presence of CO$_2$. Find out about CO$_2$ levels, when to run CO$_2$, and various ways to supply CO$_2$ to your garden (and a few ways not to use for supplementing CO$_2$) in chapter 3.

FAQ 10 THE BOTTOM LEAVES ARE YELLOWING, WHAT DO I DO?

THE PLANTS ARE LIKELY suffering from nitrogen (N) deficiency. To build tissue, the plant uses N. When there is a deficiency, the plant moves the N from old growth to the new growth. The solution is to add a high N fertilizer. Nitrogen, phosphorus and potassium are always listed in fertilizer packages in the same order, commonly known as the fertilizer's N-P-K.

To find out about potential deficiencies, see the troubleshooting section, chapter 9. In this chapter, you can look up the problem you are experiencing by common symptoms to identify the specific culprit causing the problem and get solutions.

Since yellowing plants are caused by nutrient deficiency, you may want to see information on fertilizers in chapter 4, and how to change nutrients for flowering plants' needs in chapter 6.

FAQ 11 HOW DO I GET RID OF MITES/POWDERY MILDEW?

MITES ARE COMMON INDOOR pests. These and other pests are listed by name in chapter 10. Powdery mildew and other molds, bacteria and viruses are also discussed in this chapter.

If you aren't sure what the problem is, you can try to identify the problem based on symptoms by browsing through chapter 9.

FAQ 12 ▸ **HOW CAN I MINIMIZE THE TELLTALE SMELL OF MY GARDEN?**

IN CHAPTER **8** LEARN about the different equipment that reduces odor and get tips to make sure you don't accidentally reduce the taste and smell of your buds in the process. It is worth the time and effort to consider stealth measures: making sure there are no light leaks, minimizing smell, being discreet when ordering goods and understanding detection technology, which are all covered in chapter 8.

BASICS:

FREQUENT TOPICS

IF YOU DIDN'T FIND your question in the FAQ, you can check in this alphabetical list of frequent topics. Also, see the index at the back of the book for more extensive listings.

PHOTO DIRECTORY:

READER PHOTOS:

Thanks to readers who have sent photos for Bud, Plant and Garden of the Month® contests: 27, 42, 46, 49, 52, 60, 65, 69, 76, 79, 83, 105, 116, 123, 127, 146, 151, 170, 173, 176, 187, 191, 192, 197, 198, 210, 215, 217, 223, 228, 235, 244, 258, 264, 320, 324, 326, 335, 354, 372, 379

Readers also send photos to accompany questions. The following photos were also sent in from readers: 17, 35, 44, 72, 97, 132, 142, 148, 165, 251, 256

1 SEEDS & CLONES

A. SEEDS

1. SEEDS & GENETICS
2. OBTAINING SEEDS
3. GERMINATING & SEEDLING CARE
4. STORING SEEDS

B. CLONES

1. CLONING METHODS
2. CLONES & POTENCY
3. TRANSPLANTING CLONES

RELATED TOPICS

Problems with seedlings and clones: chapter 9
    Troubleshooting, section A.
Clones and viruses: chapter 10 Pests & Diseases.
Regeneration: chapter 7 Harvest.
Breeding: chapter 11 Genetics & Breeding.
Selecting varieties: chapter 12 Varieties.

MORE ABOUT

Genetics: chapter 11 Genetics & Breeding; chapter 12
    Varieties.
Clones and taking cuttings: chapter 7 Harvest, section C
    Revegetation & Mothers; chapter 11 Genetics & Breeding.
Young plants' lighting requirements: chapter 2 Lighting
    Equipment; chapter 6 Plant Life Cycle.
Growing conditions: chapter 4 Indoor Environment; chapter
    6 Plant Life Cycle.

A . SEEDS

SEED QUALITY

Are expensive seeds necessary to grow good weed? For instance, some of the seed companies advertise in *Cannabis Culture* magazine. Can you get a plant to look like the ones featured in the magazine from any kind of seeds?

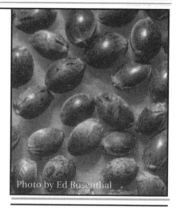

Photo by Ed Rosenthal

POOR GROWER, Morrilton, Arkansas

THE FAST ANSWER TO this question is maybe, or perhaps. Just because a seed or variety is high priced doesn't mean that it has great qualities. However, expensive seed is more likely to produce high quality buds.

The most important factor in determining a plant's appearance, rate of maturation, yield, potency and taste is the plant's genetic make-up. So, the choice of variety affects the quality of the bud. No matter how well the garden grows, the plant's genetics will determine the quality of the crop. For this reason it is very important to start with the best seeds or clones.

You have probably noticed that seed prices vary greatly. The high or low cost of seed is not necessarily a determinant of its quality. Prices are determined as a result of marketing strategy. It is true that as a variety gets popular, its seeds go up in price. Popularity is often determined by winning contests. These factors may be an indication of its quality.

While commercial seed usually has more uniformity, some seed breeders do not use standard breeding techniques. They make hybrids of hybrids that have not been inbred for stability. As a result, there is quite a bit of variation within their strains. Growers do best by taking clones of each of the plants they grow from seed. After harvest, when the yields and quality have been compared, the best plants are selected and their clones are reproduced for future cultivation.

An alternative solution is to select clones if they are available. These plants have already been selected for their superior qualities so you don't have to go through the selection process. The clones have exactly the same genetic qualities as their clone mother.

The quality of the plants' environment does have an effect on the yield, potency and appearance of the bud. Plants that have their needs met in terms of light, nutrients, water, temperature and space will grow better quality buds. However, no matter how good the garden, only plants with quality genetics will produce great bud.

For more about genetics and specific varieties, see chapters 11, 12.

USING STASH SEEDS

I have seeds that I have saved from only the best sinsemilla buds I've smoked in the last two years. Will these seeds produce good plants and buds or would I be better off driving to Vancouver for good seeds? I'm planning on growing a three- or four-plant indoor garden under a 400-watt high pressure sodium (HPS) light.

RINGO, Alberta, Canada

PLANTING SEED FROM STASH is a lot like rolling dice. You don't know what will come up. You have some idea of the quality, but know nothing of the plants' growing habits, ripening time or other characteristics. The plant was probably a hybrid, like most plants grown from commercial seed or their descendents. If that's the case, the seeds are second generation (F2) hybrids and the characteristics sort out. Expect some range in size, growing habits, ripening time and morphology. It could be a great experience, but may not be.

Sinsemilla means "without seeds," so the seeds that you saved from sinsemilla buds may be suspect. The grower may have started with clones that were all females. How did all-female plants produce seeds? There are three possibilities: they were pollinated by a hidden male plant, a hermaphrodite plant that produced some male flowers, or by stray pollen riding the wind. The plant may not be desirable.

Commercial seed has more uniformity. You know what to expect and the chances are you'll get it or at least close variations on a theme. There are not supposed to be any wild cards in the batch. This is very convenient if the gardener wants a specific variety.

When commercial growers start, they often germinate hundreds of seeds, and then choose just a few plants. These are cloned. Cloning your best plants is a good way to avoid continually putting yourself at risk by purchasing seeds. If you can acquire clones known to be of high quality, that is probably the best way to get started.

SEED SIZE

I harvested some seeds from a bud. Although they are all mature, they vary in size . . . some are twice as large as others. Will this affect plant size? Mucho grassias.

T.H., Ann Arbor, Michigan

THE SIZE OF THE SEEDS from a particular bud vary for one of two reasons. The first may be genetic—some wild Kush seeds are extremely small, just a little bit larger than carrot seeds. Hemp seeds are sometimes as large as a small peppercorn.

The second reason is environmental. Seeds from a sparsely pollinated bud grow larger than those from a heavily seeded bud because they have less competition for nutrients. Some seeds in a particular bud may have had a better environment than others.

In any case, seed size and plant size are not necessarily related.

SEXING SEEDS

Is there an easy way to determine the sex of a seed?

H., East Aurora, New York

NOT TO MY KNOWLEDGE.

> *For info on sexing plants, see chapter 6, section A.*

READER TIP ▶ SEXING SUCCESS

I have been growing some great smoke for five years. The reason I am writing to you is because readers often ask, "How can you tell a male seed from a female seed?" I think I may have found the answer everyone is looking for.

First, germinate the seeds. Look to see where the sprout comes out of the seeds. If it comes out on top or on either end, I've found that the plant will be female. If it comes out on the side, it will be a male.

I know that this sounds crazy, but I've had over 90% success with this method and so have friends of mine.

I hope this is of some help to your readers.

R. L., Tipton, Missouri

EXPERIMENT VERIFIED

You asked readers to get back to you about detecting sex depending on where the first sprout appears, on the side, top, or middle of the seed. Well, I tried this method and it works. I kept track of the ones that sprouted out of the top or the bottom and every one turned out to be a female. I would like to thank R. L. a lot for this info.

K. M., Land of Goshen

A. 2. OBTAINING SEEDS

GETTING SEEDS/CLONES

Where can I get decent seeds or clones?

WANNABE GROWER, Unknown

EXCEPT UNDER MEDICAL CIRCUMSTANCES in a few states, marijuana is a felony to grow in every state and territory in the US. It is also a federal crime. Rather than loosening, both arrests and penalties are increasing at a steady pace. There are also harsh federal laws against possession, cultivation and sale. Federal arrests are also rising dramatically, and seed importing is subject to smuggling charges. So, before you even consider growing in the US, think of the possible consequences to you and your loved ones. This is a very serious matter and should be thought through.

Seeds are readily available in Canada and Holland. They are

advertised in *High Times* and *Cannabis Culture* magazines as well as on the internet. Holland used to be the main seed producing and selling nation with many established companies. However, many Dutch companies refuse to ship to the US and depend on Americans coming to them. An increasing percentage of their sales are within Europe.

Canada has a progressive attitude toward marijuana. Thanks to the brave efforts of Mark Emery, seeds are readily available. There are quite a few Canadian companies willing to ship to the US. The 3,000-plus-mile Canadian-US border is quite porous so hundreds of seed buyers risk the border daily. Very few are caught.

Clones are a very efficient way of starting a garden. Clones are cuttings taken from a female plant that has been selected for its superior qualities. It takes the arduous work to select plants from seeds. The only way to get clones in the US is through a friend or associate. They are worth paying for if they carry good genes.

LOCATING SEED COMPANIES

Could you give me a list of Dutch and Canadian seed companies?

JOHNNY, Victoria, BC, Canada

IT IS EASY TO LOCATE seed companies on the internet. That's the best place to look for seeds. Some sites that discuss the seed companies are:

- Green Man has been giving out seedbank ratings and providing links to seedbank websites since 1998: www.seedbankupdate.com.

- Marc Emery's website is the clearinghouse for Dutch and Canadian Seeds in British Columbia: www.emeryseeds.com.

- Most seed companies have websites, so if you know the names of reputable seed companies, you can usually find them with relative ease on the web. The company websites give physical addresses and other contact information.

> *For info on specific strains, see chapter 12.*

A. 3. GERMINATING & SEEDLING CARE

BEST GERMINATION METHOD?

I've set up my garden, and received seeds from three Canadian seed companies. Now I'm confused. One company's directions say to soak the seed for 24 hours in a cup of water to hasten germination, and then to put the seeds in planting mix or block $1/2$-inch deep. Another company's directions say to fold a paper towel into quarters, wet it, place the seeds on it and fold it over. They recommend placing a piece of plastic or a plate over the paper towel to keep it moist. Then as soon as the plant breaks through the shell, place it $1/2$-inch deep in medium using tweezers. What do you think?

JOSEY SEMILLA, Potstown, Pennsylvania

BOTH METHODS WORK. I prefer to plant directly in the planting medium without soaking first or soaking in a $1/2$% hydrogen peroxide solution (one part in six for 3% hydrogen peroxide) for only a day and then plant it. I don't like to disturb the emerging plant. Once in the medium, the seed orients itself and immediately begins to interact with the environment. In a paper towel, the seedling isn't oriented the way it will be in the medium, and it may be damaged while it is being moved, especially if you're clumsy like me. Also, the seeds have to be watched several times a day to catch them at optimal planting stage. The time constraints may not be convenient, especially if you have a life.

The best way to assure a successful germination is to make sure everything is clean and sterile. The planting medium should be new, sterile and fine grained. The water should be fresh. You might put some SuperThrive® or Hormex® in the water. Both of these products have vitamins and plant stimulants that promote root growth. When the seedlings emerge, gently water them with room temperature water and a dilute flowering formula such as 10-30-20. The high potassium (K) formula will encourage root growth.

The two greatest dangers to seedlings are inadequate light and attack by fungi and bacteria. Stretched seedlings, which grow thin stems that do not support the tops, indicate a lack of light intensity. From the start, the plants do well with intense light, which encourages stout sturdy stems. Fungi and bacteria are most likely to attack when the plants are kept a little on the cool side with inadequate light.

If the seedlings are already suffering from stretched stems, support them using wooden cooking skewers and twist-ties and increase the light intensity. The new growth will reflect the environmental changes. When the young plant is repotted in a week or two, the thin portion of the stem can be placed in the planting medium.

After it has grown five sets of true leaves, the seedling can be transplanted to larger quarters.

For info on container size, see chapter 4, section A.3.
For more on stretching seedlings, see chapter 9, section A.

Photo by Ed Rosenthal

READER TIP ▷ **GERMINATION**

I have found a good way to germinate seeds. Rather than using a hot pad or finding a warm safe place for your seeds, purchase a "Baby Wipe Warmer." It is economical, and holds temperature and moisture well. I have had good success rates. However, you do have to watch for drying out.

BUDDY, Colorado

THANKS FOR THE GROWING tip, Buddy.

WHEN IS SEED MATURE?

How long does it take for a seed to mature after it comes off the plant?

DON'T KNOW, Internet

ONCE THE SEED HAS turned a deep shade of brown and is off the plant, it is capable of germination. There is no dormancy period or other natural process the seed must experience.

FROM FREEZER TO GROWING MEDIUM

I've had some seeds stored in my freezer for ten years. What's the procedure for going from freezer to growing medium? I have read that if you soak the seeds in nutrient water, viability will be improved. What do you think?

GANJA KING, Erie, Pennsylvania

OLDER SEEDS TAKE LONGER to germinate than young ones. The germination rate goes down after a few years, about 5-10% per year, but that partly depends on the seeds and the way they were stored. The germination rate of these seeds is unpredictable. It could be only 10% or it could be as much as 60%. Soaking them in nutrient water is a good way to improve viability.

Soak the seeds in lukewarm water mixed with flowering fertilizer at ¼-strength, liquid kelp at the recommended strength for germination, and ½% hydrogen peroxide solution (two parts water to one part 1% hydrogen peroxide, or six parts water to one part 3% hydrogen peroxide). Soak the seeds for 24 hours in this solution to improve the germination rate and help to prevent infection.

Once they have been soaked, the seeds should be placed in a sterile medium such as pasteurized planting mix, Oasis® or rockwool cubes. They should be kept moist and warm using a heating mat or heating cables. These are then placed under the planting tray so that it is kept at about 70-75° F. If the seeds are viable, they will germinate within ten days.

SEEDS PER CONTAINER

How many seeds should I plant in each container? I plan to grow in 20-liter pots.

STEVIE, Internet

START EACH SEED IN an individual container. Rather than germinating the seeds in the large containers, use 2-inch to 4-inch pots so that many seeds can be sown. Then the best plants can be selected to grow in the large pot.

For more on containers, see chapter 4, section A.3.

LIGHT NEEDS FOR SEEDLINGS

What is the proper amount of light for a seedling indoors?

GROW-CURIOUS, Columbia, South Carolina

SEEDLINGS SHOULD RECEIVE A light input of 30 to 60 watts per square foot (psf)—close to or equal to the light input a larger plant receives. Some people start their seedlings under fluorescents and then transfer them to stronger lights. I think this practice stresses the plants when they are transferred.

Seedlings that receive low light levels grow long thin stems. Plants growing under adequate light grow sturdy stems, which support subsequent growth.

> *For info on lighting equipment, see chapter 2.*
> *For info on lighting regimen, see chapter 6, section D.*
> *For info on stretched seedlings, see chapter 9, section A.*

STARTING SEEDS FOR OUTDOORS

I am going to start some seed for planting outdoors in a few months. I was planning to start them under a 500-watt halogen lamp. Is this the right light to use? I have a limited budget.

QUINCY'S DREAM, Byron Bay, NSW, Australia

THE BEST INDOOR LAMPS to use for seed germination are metal halide (MH) and high pressure sodium (HPS) lights. They provide good light spectrums for vegetative growth, and are quite efficient at converting electricity to light. They also provide an intensity that promotes sturdy stems and fast growth.

If metal halides cost more than your budget allows, use fluorescent tubes. An input of about 40 watts per square foot would assure good growth. That comes to four tubes in a one-foot width. The spectrum of the tube is important. A tube such as a cool-white, or natural-white, with a Kelvin of between 4,000-5,000 is a good choice. Inexpensive screw-in compact fluorescent lamps may be a more convenient way to light the starter garden than fluorescent tubes. Fluorescent tubes sold for lighting reptile tanks have up to 7% UV light. This desensitizes the plants to sunlight. These tubes can be used in place of standard fluorescents for the entire germination process to help the plants make their eventual move to the outdoors.

Rather than giving the seedlings continuous light, they should be on a light regimen of 17-18 hours of light and 6-7 hours of darkness in a regular cycle each day. Using a light cycle rather than continuous light prevents plants from being shocked when they are transplanted. If they are grown under continuous light, they may start to flower when placed outdoors, where they receive only 15 or 16 hours of light each day.

Before placing the plants out in the full sun, they should be acclimated to the outdoors, especially the ultraviolet light, which causes sunburn in humans and also burns unacclimated plant leaves. They should be introduced to outdoor light by placing them in shade and working up to full sun over a week-long period. Even then, many of the indoor leaves may die. The new growth will be healthy.

For more on specialized lights, see chapter 2, section B.

A. 4. STORING SEEDS

STORING SEEDS LONG TERM

What is the best way to store seeds for a long time? I'd like to store some for five years. Can you freeze them?

T., Whites Creek, Tennessee

THE BEST WAY TO store seeds for long a time is to make sure they are extremely dry and place them in a vacuum-sealed container inside a glass jar in a freezer. Keep them frozen until they are to be used. Freezing and unfreezing weakens the seeds a bit. If it happens a lot, they lose viability.

READER TIP SEED READINESS

I have found that as long as viable seeds have dried completely, they will have no problem germinating. It doesn't matter if they are dried in the bract or not, as long as they are completely dried. Seeds removed from a wet bud should be dried for about a month. Seeds that are not dried completely have a much lower germination rate.

RICK BUDMASTER, Lynn, Massachusetts

THANKS FOR YOUR TIP, Rick.

SEED AGE & GERMINATION RATE

You have written that seeds can be planted right after harvest and they will germinate as well as seeds that have been stored for several months. I have found that stored seeds germinate more robustly than fresh ones.

FIAT LUX, USA

I RECENTLY HAD A conversation with a grower who said that he had the same experience. It could very well be, though I have seen no research on this matter. One breeder who I spoke with told me that in certain varieties he found the germination rate of fresh seeds to be lower than that of two- to three-month-old seeds. However, he noticed no difference in the growth rate of the seedlings.

For info on planting seeds after they've been stored, see section 1. C. in this chapter.

Photo by Ed Rosenthal

B. CLONES

1. CLONING METHODS

HOW TO TAKE CUTTINGS

What is the easiest way for me to take and root cuttings? I have a small garden with only four plants, all from clones a friend gave me. I really like two of the plants and want two cuttings from each of them to replace the plants I'm about to flower. What should I do?

REYNALDO, Santa Fe, New Mexico

TAKE FOUR CUTTINGS FROM each plant in case some do not survive. Cut them from minor underbranches, where few buds grow. Leave only a few top leaves on the 4-5-inch branch. Dip them in a rooting compound according to the directions on the rooting compound package. Using Oasis® cubes, rockwool or sterile planting mix, place the cutting in the medium. Cover the cutting with a transparent top that will incubate it, and illuminate using cool-white fluorescent tubes, metal halides (MH) or high pressure sodium (HPS) lamps that are not too bright. Keep the cubes moist with water adjusted to a pH of 6.2. After 3 days, remove the top and irrigate with a very dilute, $1/4$-strength, water–nutrient solution made from flowering fertilizer. The cuttings should be rooted in 7-15 days.

It takes 60-90 days for the buds to mature once the lights are turned down to 12 hours daily. If the clones root 15 days after they are taken, this leaves 45-75 days to keep the plants in a holding pattern. It may be convenient to let them develop for 2-4 weeks, but beyond that time, they are likely to get too large. One solution is to let the plants grow, but to prune them back to the size and shape you want while they continue in vegetative growth.

For more on taking cuttings, see chapter 7, section C.

WHEN TO TAKE CUTTINGS

Is it best to take cuttings in the vegetative or flowering cycle? If a plant is budding can I take clones off it? Should I return the plant to vegetative cycle to make it into a clone mother?

N.R.P., Nashville, Tennessee

CUTTINGS ARE USUALLY TAKEN from plants in the vegetative cycle. However, they can be taken from flowering plants at almost any stage of development. One grower claims that his cuttings root faster when they are taken from plants that are a week into flowering.

EARLY CLONING

I am growing plants indoors from seed. When my plants get about four weeks old can I take clones from them?

COLA DUDE, Cincinnati, Ohio

YES. THEN THE CLONE can be forced to flower. The clone and the plant will have the exact same genetics and will react similarly to the environment.

> *For more on plants that are being cloned, see chapter 7, section C.*

OASIS® CUBES

Photo by Ed Rosenthal

CLONES ANYWHERE

I am planning to take a lot of cuttings from my plants for cloning. Are side shoots as good as cuttings from the main stem?

ED THE HEAD, Virginia

CLONES FROM SIDE SHOOTS have the same genetic qualities as the ones from the main stem. Robert Clarke claims that shoots shaded while on the plant root more easily because they have more stored carbohydrates. However, clones from the top of the plant, exposed to direct light, have no problem rooting.

READER TIP ▸ PROPER CLONING TECHNIQUE

I read the letter in your column regarding senescence of clones. The writer failed to describe the appearance of the clones as they died or failed to root.

I've had about an 80% success rate taking cuttings from outdoor plants and then rooting them inside under fluorescents. Without a description of the clones as they died, there are two possible causes:

1. Shock — high intensity light outside, lower light conditions under fluorescents.
2. Improper cloning technique.

My guess from prior experience is that both are the cause for his no-success rate. The following methods work very well for me.

1. The cuttings should have three nodes. The bottom two nodes should have the leaves removed.
2. Use a pre-diluted rooting solution formulated for soft tissue plants.
3. Insert the cutting into the medium so that the lower two nodes are beneath the soil line.
4. Keep the medium moist, but not soggy. I use one part each perlite and Pro-Mix.
5. Cover with plastic wrap or a transparent dome cover.
6. Air and mist daily.
7. After one week, add a dilute solution of high phosphorus (P) nutrients. A typical formula might be 10-50-10.
8. If the cut turns yellow, reduce the humidity.
9. If they wilt or lose vigor, increase the humidity (assuming no pathogens are present).
10. If a green mold appears, air more often and decrease humidity. Add $1/2$% hydrogren peroxide to the water (1 pint 3% hydrogen peroxide to 5 pints water).

11. For a foot-wide tray, use two fluorescent tubes.

It's an all-time high,

PROPAGATION PRO, Illinois

THANKS FOR YOUR INFO, Pro.

CLONING MADE EASY

What is an easy method of getting the clones to root quickly?

DONALD III, Unknown

CUTTINGS ROOT QUICKLY IF they are prepared correctly and kept under ideal conditions. Cuttings have no roots, so they have a limited ability to obtain water. To prevent a water shortage, which causes wilting and ultimately, death, the plants should be well trimmed. The cutting should be 3-5 inches tall. All leaves except for the crown should be removed. The crown leaves should be trimmed to 1 or 1 1/2 inches in diameter.

A temperature of 72-74° F is ideal for both roots and tops. High humidity, moist rooting medium and moderate intensity of light high in blue spectrum encourage fast root growth.

First trim the cuttings. Contrary to rumor, they can be cut with scissors and don't need to be cut under water. Then, line them up by their crowns in groups of ten, and make a final cut on the ends of the stems so that the cuttings are of equal height. Dip them in a rooting solution or gel, then immediately place them in sterile planting medium in 1 1/2- to 2-inch square pots, or 1 1/2-inch square

Oasis® or rockwool cubes.

They are placed in a tray and kept moist using a clear plastic top. If the shelf surface is cold, a Styrofoam sheet can be used to insulate the tray so the medium maintains the same temperature as the surrounding air. If the air temperature is low, a horticultural heating mat may be needed.

After three days the top should be removed and the plants irrigated using a watering can. Hydrogen peroxide should be added at the strength of $1/2$%. They should be watered with unfertilized water the first time. The second and third times, they should be fertilized with a flowering formula such as 15-30-15 or 5-8-3 or a similar high phosphorus formula (the middle number, or P, on the fertilizer denotes the percentage of phosphorus) at $1/4$-strength or a concentration of 400 parts per million (ppm). After that, use a vegetative formula such as 18-18-21 or 16-16-16 at regular strength.

Illuminate the garden with 5,000 Kelvin fluorescent tubes such as GE Chroma or similar tubes. Space them so there is one tube per foot of width. A cloning space that measures 1'x 4' would be illuminated by a single 4-foot tube. If you are using compact fluorescents, use one 13-watt lamp per square foot.

After a week to ten days, the roots should be visible. Increase the concentration of the vegetative formula to 800 ppm. If the clones are to wait around for planting, keep the lights at 10 watts per square foot. The plants will grow slowly. To increase the growth rate, increase the number of tubes to two tubes per foot of width. After a week of this regimen, the plants will have vigorous new vegetative growth.

For more on lighting amounts and types, see chapter 2, section D. For more on environmental conditions, see chapter 4.

READER TIPS   CLONING TIPS FROM AROUND THE GLOBE

I have found a way to make clones root faster and better. First I soak the stems in Dip 'N Grow™ for an hour. Then I use a powdered rooting hormone before I place them in

pumice (similar to lava or hydro-corn). I find rockwool too fussy to use.

PHIL, Northland, New Zealand

To root clones, I dip the stems in Baby Bio Roota™, a liquid rooting hormone, then place them in individual peat pots filled with a mix of perlite and store-bought sterilized compost. The pots go into a heated propagator. When the roots poke through the peat pot, the plant is ready to be repotted.

LAURETTE, Bristol, England

I've been cloning plants for several years. I've tried various techniques, but I get closest to 100% success when I put the cuttings in water, the same as I do with houseplants. For top results, I let the water sit for a day so the chlorine evaporates and then I put four or five 3-inch cuttings in the 8-ounce cup and place that under a fluorescent light so that the tops of the cuttings are about 4 inches from the tube.

First, I trim the sun leaves from the cuttings, and all of the leaves from the bottom 2 inches so that only the stems are in the water. I change the water every 2 days using aged water. After 4 days, I add 2 eye-dropper-drops of fish emulsion fertilizer. At 70° F, the cuttings root in 1-2 weeks.

D. J., Hershey, Pennsylvania

CLONING FROM BUDS

Is it possible to clone buds?

MICKIE, Cincinnati, Ohio

YES, A BUD CAN be cloned by treating it much like any other cutting. It should be placed in a rooting medium after using a rooting hormone on the bottom of the stem.

B. 2. CLONES & POTENCY

PRESERVING CLONE POTENCY

I recently received some prized clones. My source takes clones from his plants as he puts them into harvest. He kills the budded mothers as they ripen.

I have thought of keeping these original clones in vegetative growth and just cloning off of these. I want to preserve the genetics that I now have. Will one method be more likely than the other to lead to changes in taste, potency or yield?

PHRED, Internet

SINCE A CUTTING HAS the same genetic code as the plant from which it is taken, the clone and clone mother should have the same characteristics. So a clone taken from a clone should have the same characteristics as the original plant. However, other factors may play a part in the equation.

While a cutting is an exact duplicate of the plant from which it was taken, in a given group of clones from a single plant, there are subtle differences in vigor and morphology. When these clones are cloned, their progeny often retains these differences, indicating that there are slight evolutionary divergences. If this is so, one must be careful in choosing each generation of clones. This is often hard to do, since quality and yield is determined only after harvest.

Keeping the original mother alive and producing for as long as possible is the best way to preserve the original characteristics of the plant.

For more about regeneration, see chapter 7.
For more about specific problems over generations, see chapter 9, section F, chapter 10, section B. 1. and chapter 11, section D.

CLONE POTENCY OVER GENERATIONS

**A friend of mine had a clone, and he let it grow in vegeta-
tive growth until it was about 3 feet tall. He then took cuttings from the plant, and later took cuttings from the
clones. How many times can you repeat this process and
does it affect the potency of the weed?**

PENNIAC, Fredericton, NB, Canada

SEEDS ARE THE RESULT of sexual reproduction and are a random
combination of the characteristics of the two parents. No two plants
from seeds will be the same because there are so many possibilities.

When cuttings are taken, there is no recombination of genes.
Clones are the most reliable way of assuring high quality plants
because they are exact duplicates of the clone mother. They will
have the same growth habits and eventually the same type of buds,
taste and potency as the original plant. Cuttings from clones contain the same gene package. Thus cloning from clones continues
the genetic line without variance. Some clone lines have been
maintained for more than fifteen years.

Occasionally a clone's characteristics change. For instance, one
group of clones exhibited poor potassium uptake, and the leaves
had a slight twist unlike their parent. This characteristic grew more
problematic over time. When a plant from this clone line was
placed in a hydroponic system with another line and the two
shared water, the second clone started to exhibit the same characteristics. Curiously, this problem did not appear when clones were
grown in planting mix, which may have been the result of actions of
mycorrhiza in the organic mix. My conclusion was that a virus
infected the first plant line, which then spread to the other line.

The main problem with long-lived plants or generational
clones is the chance of infection with a virus. One of the advantages
that annual plants have is that viruses don't migrate into the seed,
so the germinating plant starts off life uninfected but faces chal-
lenges from the environment. Once a plant is infected, the disease
spreads throughout its tissue. It may be transferred to other plants
through the media, water or even air, depending on the virus. The

longer a plant lives, the greater its chance of becoming infected.

Clones short-circuit cannabis' anti-infection strategy. Instead of living just a few months, the plant may live for years through its clones. With the passage of time, there is more chance of a virus infecting the plant. Some of these viruses are non-specific, that is, they attack many varieties of plants. Examples of non-specific viruses include the mosaic and ring viruses.

Although the passing of time favors infections, I have seen gardens of potent, healthy clones that are generations removed from original seeds that were started years before. The growers claim that there has been no change in the plants over the generations.

Some changes are caused by mutations, but the vast majority is the result of viral infections. Once a plant is infected, there is no way of eliminating the virus. It is best to eliminate it and wipe down the area with a sterilizing agent such as hydrogen peroxide or Zero Tolerance®.

If the clones look healthy and are performing as well as ever, the plants are probably not infected with a damaging virus. However, subtle changes may occur that may not be apparent at once. For this reason it would be wise to keep sampling amounts of the original bud to test against subsequent harvests from clones.

For more about identifying viruses, see chapter 10.
For info about identifying a virus problem, see chapter 9, section F.

B. 3. TRANSPLANTING CLONES

LONG CLONES

> I was a grower for a long time, but gave it up to travel for a
> while. When I got back my friend gave me clones from the
> genetics I gave him. The plants he gave me are rooted, but
> they are about 8 inches long with no leaves except a little
> crown on top. Should I plant them only as deep as the
> plants are in the growing cube or can I also bury part of
> the stem?
>
> GEORGE, Seattle, Washington

YOU CAN BURY THE root system and the stem deep into the soil. This
will provide support for the healthy plant. In addition, some of the
nodes where leaves had grown may grow roots.

> For info on stem stretching, see chapter 9, section A.

CLONES IN ROCKWOOL

> I plan on rooting clones in one-inch rockwool cubes, and
> then transplanting them to my drip system, which uses
> expanded clay pellets. Should I remove the clone from the
> rockwool or can I just place the cube with rooted clone an
> inch below the surface of the pellets? I don't want to dam-
> age the fragile roots during transplanting.
>
> SNACKMAN, Lakeland, Florida

LEAVE THE ROOTS IN the cube when you transplant, whether it's to
soil or hydroponic system. The roots will grow from the rockwool to
the new medium. Removing the roots from the cube will damage
them and set the plant back.

2

LIGHTING EQUIPMENT

A. TYPES OF LIGHT
1. HIGH PRESSURE SODIUM/ METAL HALIDE
2. FLUORESCENTS

B. CONVERTERS/ SPECIALIZED LIGHTS

C. LIGHTING SUPPLEMENTALS

D. AMOUNT OF LIGHT

E. REAL SPACES: LIGHTING SCENARIOS

F. LIGHTS & ELECTRICITY

RELATED TOPICS
Light cycles for different phases of plant growth: chapter 6
    Plant Life Cycle.
Heat created by lights: chapter 3 Ventilation & CO_2.

MORE ABOUT
Air-cooled lights: chapter 3 Ventilation & CO_2, section A.2.

A.TYPES OF LIGHT

WHICH TYPE OF LAMP?

What is the best type of light to use, fluorescent, metal halide (MH), or high pressure sodium (HPS)?

JOSH, Pensacola, Florida

OF THE THREE TYPES of lamps mentioned, fluorescent lights are the least efficient, and produce the least amount of light per unit of electricity. Metal halide (MH) lamps emit almost twice as much light per unit of electricity. Further, they come in much larger wattages, so they produce a much more intense light than fluorescents. MH lamps produce a white light. They are used to illuminate sports fields and other large areas. Most of this light is produced in the orange, yellow and green spectrums. High pressure sodium (HPS) lamps produce about 20% more light than MH lamps and the spectrum is skewed to the orange and red. Some companies now market a brighter HPS lamp with more blue light. Results using these specialty lamps are mixed.

During photosynthesis, special organs in the leaf and stem cells (chloroplasts), which contain the green pigment chlorophyll, use water from the planting media and carbon dioxide (CO_2) from the air to create sugars. This process is fueled by light. The more light the plants receive in spectrums absorbed efficiently by chlorophyll, the more sugar they produce. Chlorophyll absorbs light most efficiently in two spectrums, red and blue. It uses virtually no green light. As the spectrum migrates from yellow to orange to red, the chloroplasts' efficiency increases. Blue light is not used as efficiently as red light. Light in the yellow and green spectrums is mostly reflected. That's why plants look green; they reflect the green part of the spectrum while absorbing the rest of it.

The more intense the compatible light the plants receive, the more sugars they produce. These sugars are used for energy for cell functioning (metabolism) and with the addition of nitrogen (N) to create tissue. HPS lamps, which produce the most light per electrical unit and the most light in the red spectrum, are the most efficient for the garden, resulting in more vigorous plants with higher yield.

Buds grown under conventional fluorescent tubes are skimpy and weaker as compared with buds grown under intense light. The introduction of compact fluorescents that screw into conventional incandescent lamp sockets has changed the equation. The bulky fixtures of yesteryear can be eliminated using these lamps.

A new generation of compact fluorescents is available in high wattages including 105 watts, which emits 6,500 lumens, or almost 65,000 if 10 lamps were used. This light would be more evenly distributed. For a small garden, these lamps could be a problem solver. Even if they aren't as efficient as an HPS or MH lamp, they may be much less hassle.

I am not suggesting that anyone with a large garden switch from an HPS to fluorescents except for experimental purposes. Still, for some gardeners, it may be the most convenient way to move forward.

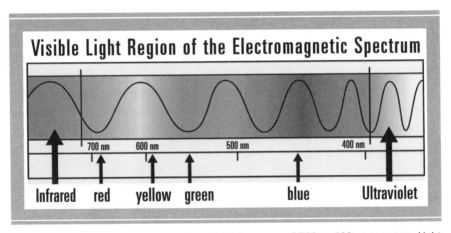

The visible light spectrum has a wavelength in the range of 700 to 400 nanometers. Light beyond this range is not visible to the human eye. The visible spectrum moves from red light at 700-650 nm, to orange (600 nm), yellow (580 nm), green (550 nm), blue (450 nm) and violet (400). When the wavelength is longer than 700 nm, the light is infrared; when it is shorter than 400 nm, it is ultraviolet.

Plants use red and blue light most efficiently for photosynthesis. They use very little yellow and green light, so the leaves reflect that light. That's why plants look green.

A. 1. HIGH PRESSURE SODIUM / METAL HALIDE

DIFFERENT LAMPS FOR VEG & FLOWERING?

I purchased a 400-watt metal halide (MH) lamp. The sales-man told me that the lamp could be used for both vegeta-tive and flowering. However, a fellow grower told me that the MH would be a waste of time and a high pressure sodi-um (HPS) lamp should be used instead. What do you think?

BABY BUDS, Quebec, Canada

WHICH LAMP FOR SINGLE LIGHT GARDEN?

In a single-light garden is it better to use an enhanced spectrum HPS lamp such as a Son Agro 430-watt bulb as opposed to a regular HPS to emit more light in the blue spectrum?

C. WALSH, Amityville, New York

MH LAMPS CONTAIN MORE blue light and less red light than HPS. HPS lamps produce more total light than MH lamps and more light in the red spectrum, which is used more efficiently than blue light, powering a faster rate of photosynthesis. In addition, red light helps in flower development.

The only reason to use an MH lamp rather than an HPS is to avoid the suspicion that a weird-colored light may arouse. Using metal halide lamps in any stage of growing is a waste of time and money. More total light that is useable by the plant is produced by HPS than MH lamps, so plants grow faster using HPS lamps alone.

The plants don't need the extra blue light offered by the Son Agro. Enhanced blue light doesn't increase production. Although plants use blue light for photosynthesis, they use more red light. In rooms with mixed lights (MH and HPS), the plants between the two lights, which were receiving a mixture didn't perform quite as well

41

as the plants directly under the HPS lamps, but yielded slightly more than those under the MH. You could see the "wave effect."

The solution to the ballast problem is to replace the MH bulb with an MH-to-HPS conversion lamp. This bulb will fit into your system and is powered by the same ballast as an MH but it emits an HPS spectrum.

Vertical lamp using inefficient reflector loses light to walls.

METAL HALIDE UV A HAZARD?

Our area is often overcast. The grow room, with its 1,000-watt metal halide lamp, is like our own little bottle of sunshine. It's also the warmest room in the house, and we use it for reading and making love. Is this a dangerous practice? Is UV light emitted? We did get a slight sunburn on the forehead while harvesting one evening. Is there a danger of the bulb exploding, fire hazards, et cetera, or are the warnings on the package just obligatory legalese?

TANNING, Seattle, Washington

METAL HALIDE LAMPS DO emit UV-A and UV-B light, which cause tanning and can damage the skin or make one more susceptible to various cancers. UV is also harmful to the eyes. While the amount of UV emitted is small, some precautions should be taken. Always wear glasses that filter out UV light. If you are close to the bulb (less than 4 feet away), always wear protective clothing or use sunscreen.

The warnings on the box are real. If the lamp is hot, the glass bulb will explode on contact with water. The safest fixtures have a glass barrier over the bulb, which stops many accidents and protects you from flying debris should one occur.

For more on UV light, see section B in this chapter.

A. 2. FLUORESCENTS

FLUORESCENT LIGHTS

I've read that fluorescent lighting will produce as well as HPS will. This sounds tempting due to purchase and operating costs; however, I want killer buds for my effort. I trust your expertise. How should I equip my first garden?

FUTURE FARMER OF AMERICA, Antioch, Tennessee

FLUORESCENT TUBES HAVE BEEN used to cultivate and flower marijuana. However buds grown under these lights are usually fairly small and loose. The reason for this is that the intensity of the light—that is, the amount of light that is produced by fluorescent tubes—is relatively low. In addition, the light is produced over a large area. The result is a lower amount of light spread out over a large area so the amount reaching the plants is a small fraction of the amount the plants receive from a metal halide (MH) or high pressure sodium (HPS) lamp. Self-ballasted high-watt compact fluorescent lamps screw into incandescent sockets. They are useful in lighting small gardens. They emit intense light from a small area.

Fluorescent tubes are more expensive than HPS lamps, too. The initial cost of a fluorescent is less than an HPS. However, when the cost of electricity is considered, the overall cost picture changes. HPS lamps emit about two to three times the amount of light per unit of energy consumed. The efficient HPS lamp is much cheaper over its life than a fluorescent tube, giving much more light to the garden per unit of electrical energy. Although you can grow marijuana using a fluorescent, you will produce a much higher yield of better grade grass cheaper and easier if you use an HPS lamp instead of a fluorescent.

A 1,000-watt lamp emits about 130,000 lumens, a 72-watt, 8-foot fluorescent emits 3,200 lumens and a compact fluorescent emits 6,800. That comes to 130 and 45 and 65 lumens per watt, respectively. When the cost of electricity is considered, the fluorescent is the high priced option.

Standard fluorescent tubes distribute their light over a long distance, usually 4 or 8 feet. Compact fluorescents and HPS lamps have small point sources, about 5 and 9 inches, respectively. The standard area that gardeners use to power gardens is usually about 4'x 4'. It is impossible to get that intensity of light using standard fluorescents.

Convenience should also play a part in your decision. It would require thirteen 8-foot fluorescents or 16 compacts to equal the light capacity of one 1,000-watt HPS. Adjusting one light is much easier than messing with three or four fluorescent fixtures.

COMPACT FLUORESCENTS

I'm designing a small growth chamber with compact fluorescent tubes. How effective are these lamps?

FARMER JACK, Internet

COMPACT FLUORESCENTS ARE MORE efficient than standard fluorescent tubes. Further, they can be placed close to each other to increase light intensity. Most of the tubes in these lamps have a "warm-white" spectrum. This spectrum is suitable for the vegetative growth stage and is excellent for flowering. The buds produced will be potent and filled with crystals.

High-wattage compact fluorescents can be used to supply ample light to a small garden and the electric bill may not be significantly higher. A single 250-watt HPS lamp emits 28,000 lumens. To get the same light intensity from compact fluorescents, four 105-watt and one 55-watt compacts would be required. They would use almost twice the electricity as the HPS. At 10 cents per kilowatt-hour, the cost of running the HPS lamp per month is about $21 during vegetative growth and $10.50 during flowering. The cost of running the four 105-watt and one 55-watt compact fluorescents is $34 a month during vegetative growth and $17 during flowering. It's only a few dollars more each month so the difference might not matter to you. With larger gardens, it becomes more significant.

HPS lamps and their ballasts are notorious for the amount of heat that they emit. That's because they use large amounts of electricity. That energy is turned into either light or heat. A 250-watt HPS unit uses a total of about 300 watts of energy per hour. The fluorescents use 475 watts per hour. They produce more heat than the HPS lamp for two reasons. They are using more electricity and a higher percentage is turned into heat rather than light.

That being said, compact fluorescents are suitable for small gardens and are very convenient. They warrant further investigation. Although HPS lamps emit about twice the light, warm-white fluorescents emit a higher percentage of red light than HPS lamps. The plants use mainly red and blue light, so the amount of light useable to the plant is probably closer than the useable light figure would indicate.

HALOGENS

Is it possible to use cheap department store 300-watt halogen lamps for indoor cultivation?

TAWDAY, Isla Vista, California

HALOGEN LAMPS ARE NOT very efficient light producers, While high pressure sodium (HPS) lamps emit about 60% of the energy input as light, and metal halides, (MH), slightly less, halogens emit only about 15%. When the cost of electricity is figured in, halogens are really more expensive than HPS lamps.

Halogens produce high amounts of red light and a little blue light. The plants will stretch a bit, but they will grow and flower quickly. However, for just a little bit higher initial cost, you could move to fluorescents and produce considerably more useable light per watt.

B. CONVERTERS/ SPECIALIZED LIGHTS

BLACK LIGHTS

A grower I know supplemented her fluorescent lights with black lights during the dark period. People said it was fantastic. What do you think?

DYIN' TO BE TRYIN', Mobile, Alabama

THERE HAS BEEN RESEARCH on UV-B light that showed its addition to a regimen increased THC content of plants in a linear ratio.

I know of no controlled research on the effect of UV-A, which is the light emitted from black lights, but I have received a number of reports from growers who think that black light supplements have increased the potency of their plants.

UV LIGHT

I have heard conflicting stories about the effect of UV light on cannabis. Does it change the plant's stoniness?

GROWER X, Whereabouts Unknown

ULTRAVIOLET (UV) LIGHT IS found in the bands between 300 and 400 nanometers. It's invisible to the human eye, but it is the spectrum of light that affects our pigments and causes us to tan. It affects plants in various ways, too. Apples will not redden without UV, and some plants use this spectrum to regulate functioning.

UV-B light changes the quality of the bud. Anecdotally, buds grown at high altitude are considered to be better quality than lowland products. The difference in conditions between these locations is the amount of UV-B light they receive. It is filtered out by the atmosphere so it is more intense at higher altitudes than at lower. In a controlled experiment, it was shown that the percentage of THC increases in linear ratio to the increase of intensity in this spectrum. Adding reptile lights, which emit 10% UV-B, or tanning lights, which emit even higher amounts would increase the stoniness of the garden.

This is also an argument in favor of forcing flowering early outdoors. The amount of UV-B light reaching earth is much higher in the summer than the fall. June 22 is the strongest day. If plants are forced early outdoors the buds will receive more of these powerful rays and produce more cannabinoids.

> *For more on outdoor growing, see chapter 5.*

THE PERIL OF GREEN LIGHT

> **I wish to give your readers some advice from sad experience. I was given some green lights by a friend and tried using them to grow my plants, Within days half the crop was dead. Green fiberglass has the same effect as the green lights.**
>
> **Why did this happen?**
>
> No Green with Green, Internet

PLANTS DON'T USE GREEN light, they reflect it. That's why they look green. To plants, a green light is like no light at all. The plants weren't hurt by the green light, but by the lack of light in the spectrums they use, primarily red and blue. Plants under a green canopy are also red and blue spectrum deprived.

Green lights can be used safely in the garden during the dark period without affecting the plants.

> *For more on the dark period, see chapter 6, section D.3.*

LIGHTLESS GROW POSSIBLE?

A coworker recently told me that a plant could flourish and bud with minimal or no light and the correct dose of nitrogen. Is this true?

BONGADIDDLE, Dallas, Texas

GREEN PLANTS PRODUCE FOOD through photosynthesis. In this process, plants use light energy to build sugar from water and carbon dioxide while releasing oxygen. Nitrogen is combined with the sugar to build tissue. Without light, plants cannot produce the sugars that are used to power respiration for energy as well for growth.

C. LIGHTING SUPPLEMENTALS

LIGHT TRACKS

I am using a 1,000-watt HPS lamp in a 32-square-foot space. I am thinking of getting a light track that moves the light back and forth to better distribute the light. What should I expect to gain from this?

PMAN, Los Angeles, California

RIGHT NOW, THE STATIONARY light is in the middle of the garden, so the plants on the periphery of the garden receive considerably less light than the ones closest to the center. These plants grow more slowly and yield less. A light mover will even out light distribution by moving the light over the entire garden. As a result, plant growth will be more uniform.

Another advantage of moving lights is that they can be placed closer to the canopy because the heat they produce is not constantly directed to one area. Placing the light closer gives the plants more intense lighting.

There are several models of light movers. Some move the light faster and others slower. All of them work well at distributing the light. I haven't noticed a significant difference in plant growth depending on model.

PARABOLIC REFLECTOR LIGHTS

I am considering buying a parabolic light system, but was wondering if it is as efficient as the other types of reflectors.

GANGA LOVER, Internet

PARABOLIC REFLECTORS HOLD HPS and MH lamps vertically. The bulbs are long and run much of the length of the lamp. The light is emitted horizontally. If there were no reflector, most of the light

50

would not get to the garden, it would hit the wall. The reflector redirects the light down toward the garden. The shape of the reflector has a lot to do with its efficiency. If the reflector is not as deep as the lamp, it cannot work efficiently. The best horizontal reflectors meet the light at an angle that produces a fairly uniformly lit spot directly under the reflector or at a very light angle out. A vertical unit can be very effective as a single light over a small garden.

Horizontal reflectors hold the lamp horizontally. Much more of the light shines on the garden directly, and most of the rest is reflected down. There are many models of horizontal reflectors, and their efficiency and the light patterns they create vary widely. They are smaller than parabolic reflectors and many models are air-cooled. Horizontal reflectors outperformed parabolics in actual tests.

REFLECTIVE SURFACE

Will reflective surfaces in a grow space enhance plant growth?

FLAVEMAN, Calgary, AB, Canada

ANY LIGHT THAT DOES not reach the garden is wasted. Reflectors vary widely in the light pattern they create. Usually areas directly under the light get the greatest intensity. The light is less intense to the sides. Some of the light is sent to areas outside the garden. To increase plant growth, this light should be reflected back so the plants can use it. Mylar reflects more than 90% of the light, while mirrors reflect 70% or less. Aluminum foil reflects about 75%; flat white paint reflects about 85%; and semi-gloss white about 80%. Clean Styrofoam reflects nearly 100%.

READER TIP ▶ **REFLECTIVE MATERIAL**

The finest reflective material I have found is an exterior sheathing called "Thermo-Ply." It comes in 4'x 8' sheets and is 1/8-inch thick. Thermo-Ply is foil-faced and contains

a vapor barrier inside. It is extremely reflective. It is available at building supply houses.

GURU, Tullaham, Tennessee

THANKS FOR THE INFO, Guru.

MIRRORS FOR REFLECTION

I have access to enough mirrors to completely cover the walls of my room. Is it a good idea to use them?

J.M., Hampton, Virginia

MIRRORS REFLECT ABOUT 75% of the light, so they are not as effective as Mylar or Styrofoam. They disperse light in hot spots, which radiate unevenly on the plants. They would be especially effective in a space with light movers so the bright spots are constantly changing.

An all-mirrored grow room would be a spacey experience.

D. AMOUNT OF LIGHT

HOW BRIGHT THE LIGHT?

How much light should I use in my garden? Should I spread it out or concentrate it?

WANNABUD, Mattoon, Illinois

USE A MINIMUM OF 30 watts HPS input per square foot (psf). If it is realistic to deliver 60-80 watts per square foot, both the growth rate and the quality of the produce increase. There is a considerable difference in yield and quality between plants grown under lower wattages and those grown under more intense light. Buds grown under intense light mature faster and are tighter, larger and covered with resin glands. The yield increases in direct ratio with light input as long as the plants receive enough water, nutrients and CO_2.

WATTS PER SQUARE FOOT

I am growing plants under 65 watts per square foot (psf) using air-cooled lights and light movers. I was thinking of spreading the plants out over a larger area so that they would receive about 50 watts psf. One expert said I should switch to 600-watt HPS lamps. Should I use them or stick with the 1,000's? If the buds get too large will they become leafy and less potent?

DEAD ANSLINGER, Internet

IF YOU WANT TO add space, add more lighting to the garden. Replacing 65 watts psf with 50 watts psf, a 23% reduction in light, will slow growth and lead to leafier, fluffier buds. They might total the same weight as the buds grown under the brighter light, but they will be looser and lower quality.

Plants growing under the more intense lighting regime will grow denser, heavier buds. These buds are higher quality than the looser buds grown under less intense lighting. Buds become dense by growing a large amount of flowers in a small area. As the flowers squeeze together, they become densely packed. These tight flowers are more potent than looser flowers, which don't produce as many glands.

The expert probably advised you to use 600-watt lamps rather than 1,000's because of their slightly higher light-producing efficiency. They do have several drawbacks, however. It is more difficult to deliver intense light to the plants using smaller wattage lamps. You would require more fixtures, and the fixtures and bulbs are more expensive. On the other hand, more smaller wattage lamps distribute the light more evenly to the garden.

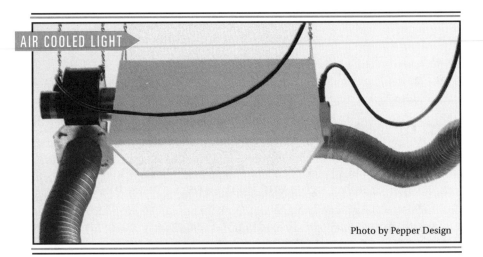

AIR COOLED LIGHT

Photo by Pepper Design

EFFECTS OF REDUCED LIGHT

During the peak flowering stage, I had 4,000 watts lighting a 60-square-foot garden and a few of the tops burned. We removed two of the lights and the burning stopped. Will the garden be affected from less light for these last two weeks?

LES DEVINE, Tulsa, Oklahoma

THE TOPS WERE NOT burning from too much light, but from the heat generated by the lights, which stressed the plants. In severe cases, such as your garden, this burns the tissue. The input in your garden was about 67 watts per square foot (psf). This was not too much light for the plants to use, especially if the air was enriched with CO_2. Cutting the wattage down to 33 watts adversely affects bud growth. Tissue growth and development occur in a linear ratio to the energy (light) input.

The most obvious solution is to raise the lamp so there is more space to ventilate the air beneath the light. Strong ventilation helps but does not completely solve the problem because a good proportion of the heat is radiated as infrared radiation. This is turned into heat when it hits the leaf surface.

Another solution is to use air- or water-cooled lights. Air-cooled lamps ventilate the lamp with a steady stream of unheated air supplied with an intake tube and then removed from the growing space with an out-take tube. A sheet of glass held by the reflector keeps the air enclosed in the system. Water-cooled lights do the same thing, but more efficiently because of water's higher mass. Using either of these cooling methods, the lights can be placed closer to the plants to increase the intensity.

For more on managing heat created by lamps, see chapter 3.

SPACE BETWEEN PLANTS & LAMP

How far above my plants should I put my 1,000-watt and my 400-watt high pressure sodium lamps?

DAVE, Internet

THE AMOUNT OF LIGHT emanating from a 1,000-watt horizontal HPS lamp measured at 24 inches above the plants equals about half of the light on a cloudless day in early July at the 38th parallel. It equals the light in early September at noon at the 38th parallel. The problem that people sometimes have with high-wattage bulbs comes from the heat that they generate. Heat from the lights caus-es the buds to "run." Instead of blocky buds on compact stems, the branches stretch and new growth appears.

The height of the 400-watt lamp from the top of the plant canopy depends on the light and how it is used. Lamps with air-cooled reflectors can get closer to the canopy than reflectors with-out a heat barrier. Moving lights can be placed closer than stationary ones. A stationary, unprotected 400-watt lamp reflector needs a minimum distance of 20 inches from the top of the canopy to dissipate the heat generated by the lamp. A 1,000-watt lamp should be placed about 30 inches away.

Air-cooled reflectors enclose the heat so that lights can be placed closer to the plant tops.

The lights create heat in two ways. First, heat is caused when opaque objects absorb light, mostly from the infrared (below red) spectrum, which is invisible to humans. This is the type of light emitted by heat lamps. When it hits a solid object, light from this part of the spectrum turns into heat, so it is especially damaging to plant tissue. The second source is air that comes in contact with the hot lamp, is heated, and is forced down the sides of the reflector.

Once it escapes the sides of the reflector, some of the heat rises away from the garden, but much of it reaches the plants. Its dissi-pation is affected by the size and shape of the reflector and the air current. Swift circulation/ventilation systems can be set up to move heated air away from the canopy and out of the area. This works best when there is a constant source of cool air. For instance, in Holland, which has cool air most of the time, heated air is replaced with a constant flow of filtered street air. In large spaces, the air draft results in a low roar of white noise.

Air- and water-cooled reflectors enclose the heat so that it has less effect on the canopy or the room temperature. Air-cooled lights can be placed about one-third closer to the plants, about 14 inches for the 400 watt and 20 inches for the 1,000-watt lamp. Water-cooled lights can be placed at half the distance, 10 and 15 inches, respectively.

A reflector and a bottom glass plate enclose air-cooled lights. Most of the lamp's heat remains enclosed. Using 4-inch duct tubing powered by an inline fan, cool air is drawn in from outside the space to cool the light. Heated air is pushed out through the exhaust duct on the other side of the reflector. This air has never been in contact with the garden; it has no odor, just heat. It can be used to heat a living space or can just be vented to the outdoors.

Water-cooled lights bathe the lamp in a thin stream of water that removes the heat directly from the lamp. Although the bulb is touching water, the units are generally considered safe. Water is more effective than air at transferring heat, so these units are very efficient. Water-cooled lamps require plumbing and a unit to cool the water or a continuous source of water.

Stationary lights shine continuously on the leaf tissue. Lights on movers are intense but give the leaf respite and the tissue time to cool before it receives another burst of bright light and heat. Moving lights can be placed a few inches closer to the plants than ones that don't move.

ALTERNATE SUN & LAMPLIGHT?

I'm growing four plants under a 150-watt high pressure sodium lamp. They are now two weeks old and are growing a treat!

I live in a part of the UK that's fairly cloudy. When we do get a glorious sunny day, I place my plants in the window to get as much of the natural light spectrum as possible. And when it gets dark or cloudy, they go back on the lamps. I just read an article that says moving plants from one light source (sun) to another (lamps) could kill them as they need to stick with what they have become used to. Is this true?

ANT, United Kingdom

THE PLANTS MAY HAVE a problem if they are placed in the window only once or twice weekly. If the plants are used to a certain intensity of light, and then are exposed to a much higher intensity, the leaves will suffer and may die. If the sun through your window is very bright it may be much more than what the plants are used to. The leaves will get a sunburn, resulting in a major setback to the plants. If the plants are under the lamp and sun on a more or less daily basis so the leaves are used to sunlight, the plant will appreciate the extra intensity. Window glass filters most UV light, so the plants will still not be acclimated to outdoor life.

> *For more on indoor/outdoor light, see chapter 5.*

FROM FLUORESCENT TO HPS

I recently transplanted my plants from fluorescent lights to a 1,000-watt HPS light. They are growing in an air-conditioned 2'x 6' closet with the door open and a fan blowing. The edges on the upper leaves on my plants are curling up in a cylindrical fashion, but are otherwise fine. What am I doing wrong?

FIRST TIME INDOOR GROWER, Pullman, Michigan

WHEN THE PLANTS WERE placed under the 1,000-watt HPS after being grown under fluorescents they had a problem handling the intensity of the new light. Although these leaves are damaged, the new growth, which has grown under the high intensity light, will not have this problem. In the meantime raise the light to lower the intensity and prevent further damage.

> *For other troubleshooting on curling leaves, see chapter 9, section B.*

E. REAL SPACES:
LIGHTING SCENARIOS

LIGHTING A TEENSY GARDEN

I have a small space, 18' x 24', where I am trying to grow some bud. I am using a 75-watt incandescent bulb and a 15-watt fluorescent desk lamp, (a total of 90 watts, 30 watts per square foot). Small fans from old Apple computers circulate and exhaust the air. I am planning to line the walls with Mylar to enhance the light. Should I use a different light? I heard that there was a HPS 70-watt model. Do you have any other advice?

CPT, Internet

THE INCANDESCENT BULB IS a very inefficient source of light. The fluorescent is more efficient, but not as good as a high pressure sodium (HPS) lamp. Your garden could be lit by a 100-watt high pressure sodium lamp, which will produce a lot more light than the combination you have now. These lights are available at indoor garden shops. You could also use two smaller watt HPS lamps. These are available in hardware stores, sold for use as outdoor security lights.

Another possibility is using two 105-watt compact fluorescent lamps. These screw into standard incandescent sockets. The warm-white spectrum bulbs will carry the garden through both vegetative and flowering.

LIGHTING A TINY CLOSET

What kind of light source would you recommend for optimum growth and potency in a garden just 2'x 3'? We have a lot of vertical space and the entire surface is reflective. Ventilation is not a problem.

KA-BLOOIE, Address Unknown

THE AREA IS A total of 6 square feet. A 250-watt lamp would provide an electrical input of more than 40 watts per square foot (psf). A 400-watt lamp would be using about 66 watts psf. Either of these lamps would work. The larger wattage would support faster growth and bigger buds. It would generate more heat, so it would require more ventilation.

SMALL GARDEN

I want to grow a 2'6" x 4' closet, which is 6 feet high. What lighting and hydroponic systems do you recommend? Or would you recommend soil? What about Emily's Garden? Is it real or a joke?

J.R., THE NOVICE, Los Angeles, California

THE TOTAL AREA OF your garden is a little more than 10 square feet. You could use either a 400 or 600-watt high pressure sodium (HPS) lamp. The 400 would supply an input of 40 watts per square foot (psf) to the garden, while the 600 would supply 60 watts psf. The yield would differ both quantitatively and qualitatively. The higher wattage lamp would produce about 50% more buds, which will be tighter and have a bit more potency.

For so few plants I would recommend either a planting mix that is hand watered or watered using a wick system, or a recirculating system using hydrostones (baked clay pellets) as the planting medium. All are easy to set up and maintain and will produce a large yield.

I developed "Liz's Garden" for HydroFarm. They renamed it Emily's Garden after a big drug scare in the US. I am not associated with the product commercially now. This system works very well, too and is also easily constructed. Imagine a tray with sides about 6 inches high. Six-inch planting containers, preferably square, are placed in the tray in rows touching each other. They are filled with grow rocks. Water is placed in the container to a level of two inches. Voila! The reservoir hydro-garden is ready. Maintain the water level by adding solution as needed, which may be daily. This system works very well. However, the addition of a small pump and a dripper or constant flow of water will increase growth and yield.

> *For info on hydro system setups, see chapter 4, section C.1.*

LIGHTING A MEDIUM SIZE GARDEN

The space available for my garden is 5'x 4'x 7', a total of 20 square feet. I would like to use at least 40 watts per square foot (psf). What should I use?

DEDICATED READER, Dragon, South Carolina

YOU COULD USE A 1,000-watt lamp, which would provide 50 watts input per square foot (psf), or two or three 400-watt lamps, which would provide you with 800 or 1,200 watts, exactly 40 or 60 watts.

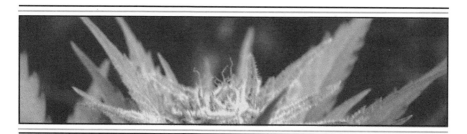

MEDIUM GARDEN II

I am trying to start a garden and I am looking for some pointers. I have a 4'x 4' area that is about 5 feet tall. I was wondering if you could provide me with a few suggestions on lights for that space size. How many plants could I grow there? How much yield should I expect?

C. HAYES, Norman, Oklahoma

A 4'x 4' AREA IS 16 square feet. Cannabis thrives on a high-light diet. An electrical input of 50-70 watts per square foot (psf) of high pressure sodium light provides the kind of intense rays that promote growth and flowering. A 1,000-watt lamp over a 16 square foot area has an input of 62.5 watts psf. This is the right size lamp for the space. Place the light on a 2- or 3-foot track light mover. Use an air-cooled light so the plants can grow closer to it without burning from the heat.

Use a shallow container for planting medium, such as a rockwool slab in a tray or a tray of horticultural clay pebbles. The plants should be low growing indica varieties that branch out but stay under 3 feet tall. Place the plants in flowering when they have reached the height of 12-20 inches tall.

> For more on the shift from vegetative to flowering phase, see chapter 6.

LIGHTING A LARGE SPACE

Are two 1,000-watt metal halide lamps on light rails enough light for a grow room that is 3 meters wide and 4.4 meters long?

MICK, Brisbane, Australia

THE GROW ROOM IS 13 square meters (about 130 square feet). A 1,000-watt metal halide is most efficient at lighting a space of about

1.5 meters. Together, the two lamps will only adequately light an area of 3 meters. If the room was maximized, it would have two planting areas. Each space would be 4.4 meters long and 1 meter wide, with a meter-wide walkway between the gardens. Each garden would use three 1,000-watt lamps.

I would change over to high pressure sodium conversion bulbs to get the most efficient use of the lighting. The new ballasts should all be HPS.

If you were running all the lights at the same time, they would produce more than 20,000 BTU's of heat. Air-cooled reflectors keep the lights cool using cool air enclosed in reflectors and tubing so that the heat never gets into the room. This eliminates more than half of the heat that the lights generate. Keeping the ballasts in an area separate from the garden will also eliminate thousands of BTU's. The ballast area can be cooled using intake and outtake fans.

Devising a curtain system would allow you to run one-half of the garden at a time during flowering. Only half the heat would be generated at any time, so it would be easier to keep the room cool.

Photo by Ed Rosenthal

F. LIGHTS & ELECTRICITY

ELECTRICAL USAGE

How much electricity does a 1,000-watt metal halide or high pressure sodium light use?

ROLLA'S LITTLE BOGOTA, Anchorage, Alaska

A 1,000-WATT UNIT, ballast and lamp uses about 1.2 kilowatts per hour. If it is on constantly for 30 days, it uses 1.2 x 24 x 30 =864 kilowatts. If it's on 12 hours a day, it uses half that, 432 kilowatts. If the power costs 10 cents per kilowatt it would cost $86 and $43 per month, respectively.

In northern California, electricity costs about 17 cents per kilowatt-hour off-peak and 31 cents during peak (Monday-Friday, excluding holidays, from 12-6 pm). It costs about $172 a month to run a light continuously. If you were running it eighteen hours daily, eliminating peak period, it would cost $110 a month. If you were running it just 12 hours daily, it would cost $73 a month.

> *For info on the light cycle, see chapter 6.*

220 VOLTS

If a 1,000-watt HPS lamp using 110 volts were switched to 220 volts, thus using fewer amps, how would you figure out the amount of electricity saved?

HIGH ELECTRIC, Iowa

THE FORMULA FOR FIGURING watts, the unit the electric company measures, is:

$$\text{Amperes x Volts} = \text{Watts}$$

Another permutation of this formula is:
Amperes = Watts/Volts

Amperes, or amps, are the current flow, voltage is the pressure and wattage is the resulting work produced. A good analogy is a garden hose. The diameter of the hose is equal to the amperage. The water pressure is equal to the voltage. The resulting amount of water is the wattage. So, if the water were turned down (the pressure decreased) or the hose were squeezed (the amperage lowered) the amount of water, or work is altered.

A 1,000-watt lamp uses 1,000 watts, or 1 kilowatt. The ballast uses additional electricity, say 200 watts. That is a total of 1,200 watts. Divided by standard American voltage (110),

A	V	W
10.9	x	120	= 1200
5.45	x	220	= 1200

it uses about 10.9 amperes of electricity. Running at 220 volts (European voltage), only half as much electricity is needed to do the same work, so the system uses about 5.68 amperes. Either way, each hour, it uses 1,200 watts or 1.2 kilowatt-hours, which is the unit by which electrical bills are typically figured.

3

VENTILATION & CO_2

A. CONTROLLING THE TEMPERATURE

1. OPTIMUM TEMPS

2. HEAT

3. COLD

B. CO_2

1. HOW CO_2 HELPS

2. TYPES OF CO_2 ENRICHMENT

3. CO_2 HOW-TO

RELATED TOPICS

Temperature in outdoor gardens: chapter 5 Outdoors & Greenhouse.

A. CONTROLLING
THE TEMPERATURE

1. OPTIMUM TEMPS

OPTIMAL TEMPS FOR VEG & FLOWERING

What are the best temperatures for vegetative and flowering rooms?

420'ERS, Ontario, California

THE MAXIMUM GROWTH RATE is achieved when the temperature ranges from 70-74° F during the lit period, with a drop of about 10 degrees (but no lower than the high 50's) during the dark period. When temperatures are lower during the lit period, photosynthesis slows. When the temperature rises, photosynthesis proceeds at a stable rate, but the metabolism rate increases, using up much of the sugar produced during photosynthesis.

When CO_2 enrichment is used and light intensity is high, the plants function better at a higher temperature—in the mid-80's F during the day and the mid-70's F during the dark period. The higher temperature is often helpful to growers, since heat from lights and other equipment must often be managed.

For more on CO_2, see section B in this chapter.
For more on conditions for vegetative and flowering phases, see chapter 6, sections D and E.

READING PLANT TEMPERATURE

Where should I take the temperature of my grow area, at the top of the plant, the middle of the plant, or at the bottom of the plant?

BIG AL, Internet

THERE ARE TWO RELEVANT temperatures. The first is the canopy temperature, which shows what the plant leaves are experiencing. The other is the temperature of the soil, because it is at the root level. Each affects the plant. Generally, cannabis does best with a temperature in the mid 70's F (low 20's C) for both leaves and roots. When the roots are cool, the leaves can withstand warmer temperatures and vice versa. For instance, with roots cooled to 62° F (16° C) the leaves would do best with a temperature around 85° F (29° C).

ROOT ZONE TEMPERATURE

I was wondering more about "root zone temperature." What is it exactly and what would the ideal temperature be for the roots in the rockwool? And one more question: what is the ideal temperature for the reservoir in a hydroponic system?

HYDRO HO, Internet

THIS IS THE TEMPERATURE in the area of the roots. Marijuana thrives when its roots are kept at room temperature, about 72° F. When the air temperature remains at 72° F and the root zone is cool, which often happens when containers are placed on a cold floor, the roots do not work as efficiently as they do at higher temperatures.

Root zone temperature can be used as an environmental variable in relationship to air conditions. If the air temperature is too hot, for instance 85° F, which is 10-13 degrees above the ideal, and the water temperature is lowered to the low 60's using an aquarium-grade water chiller, the cool and the warm seem to cancel each other out. Perhaps there is a heat exchange going on within the plant. Conversely, cool air temperatures can be ameliorated using warm root zone temperatures.

For more on hydroponic setups, see chapter 4, section C.1.

A. 2. HEAT

HOW TO TURN DOWN THE HEAT

We are growing in an enclosed room under a single 1,000-watt high intensity discharge (HID) lamp. We are struggling to keep the temperature under 90° F with fans going continually and an open door during lighted hours. We have an air conditioner in the room, but after 30 minutes it just spews out hot air. We've read that cooling the roots may be the answer to our problem. What do you suggest we do? Will the plants survive in 90° F conditions?

RAOUL, Internet

HIGH TEMPERATURES WILL NOT kill the plants as long as the roots are kept moist. However, it will ruin the flowers, which will be loose and sparse along a stretched stem. Therefore it is essential to keep the room in the low to mid 70's F (about 24° C) with unenriched air and below 82° F (27° C) when the air is enriched with CO_2.

An easy way to eliminate the heat would be to stop it from getting in the room. An air-cooled light vents most of the hot air created by the bulb. This air never enters the room. It is drawn from outside through a tube, is heated in the reflector and removed through a second tube. It has no conspicuous odor and can be freely vented.

A single 1,000-watt lamp creates about 3,200 BTUs of heat. A

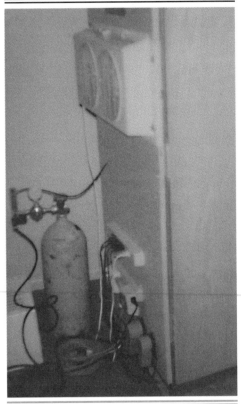

room air conditioner (the kind that goes into a window) can be used to move the heat out of the room, either outdoors or to another space, such as a room or hallway. For convenience, a portable air conditioner can be rolled into the space when needed. It vents heat out through a 4-inch tube.

Changing the light cycle so the lights are on at night and off during the day can be a solution. Depending on the area and season, nighttime temperatures may be much cooler than daytime temperatures. Cool outside air could be vented into the space and hot air removed.

There are many reports about cooling or heating roots to counteract above-ground temperatures. If the canopy temperature were 85° F (29° C), the roots would need to be cooled to 65° F to counteract the hot air. In a hydroponic garden, this can be accomplished using an aquarium water chiller. However, there is a learning curve involved.

KEEPING COOL

I have a 1,000-foot space with 15-foot ceilings, which I have divided, into three rooms using polyethylene. Each has 100 square feet under cultivation and the internal ceilings are about 9 feet high. Each room has 4 lights, a total of 12 lights. It is very hot, 90-100° F in the spaces, and my plants are wilting and look weak. I have an ebb-and-flo system, a tube-based water system and some larger plants in 5-gallon containers of planting mix.

During the winter, the cool bottom air from a low vent kept the place cool. Now that summer's here, I'm boiling. What can I do to stop this situation? A friend gave me a high-capacity water chiller with copper coils. Can I use it?

KENNY, Mission, California

THE ROOM CEILINGS COULD be opened up. Even though they were probably designed to hold in the CO_2 there is no reason to have them. CO_2 coming from a tank is cooler than the surrounding air and also heavier. As soon as the ceilings are removed, the hot air will rise, providing relief.

With CO_2, the plants can take a temperature in the room in the mid-80's. However, climbing to 90-degree-plus tempratures creates stress for the plant. Also, hydroponic systems probably have oxygen problems because the warmer the water gets, the less oxygen it holds. As temperatures climb, oxygen levels fall precipitously.

Using the copper-coiled water cooler will result in copper toxicity. Instead, change the tubes to stainless or plastic. If this cannot be done, use the chiller with a homemade heat exchanger. A simple one can be built using a Styrofoam container. In closed water systems, water is run through a circuit, which includes a tube coiling through a Styrofoam container filled with salt water. Water going to the tubes should also circuit in tubes through the Styrofoam container. The chiller water cools the salt water, which cools the irrigation water.

One way to cool the ebb-and-flo table is by using a small oscillating fan blowing on the table. This evaporates water and cools the medium. Regulate the fans with a thermostat placed in the medium to make sure it doesn't get too cool. Seventy-two degrees F is an ideal temperature for the medium.

If resources are available, and you can have the job done safely, the rooms should be cooled using a central furnace/air conditioner on a thermostat or room air conditioners, which are really heat exchangers. They would pull the heat from the grow rooms into the hallways or through 12-inch-diameter air ducts to the roof, where it is blown out by a fan.

> For more on cooling solutions, see "Lighting a Large Space" in chapter 2, section E.
>
> For more on ebb-and-flo systems, see chapter 4, section C.1.

SWAMP COOLER IN THE DESERT

When growing indoors in a hot, dry climate, can an evaporative swamp cooler be used effectively or would it be harmful? I use a flood-and-drain hydroponic system.

DESERT DWELLER, Las Vegas, Nevada

A SWAMP COOLER COULD cool your heat problems. Swamp coolers work by drawing hot dry air through a wet pad. The water evaporates, cooling and humidifying the air. Swamp coolers cool the air for the cost of running a fan rather than an air conditioner.

The drier the air is, the more effective the swamp cooler will be. The space should be ventilated so that humidity doesn't get too high.

THE RIGHT AIR CONDITIONER

I have a garden that supplies a local medical buyer's club. It has three flowering rooms, each with four or five lights as well as a mother garden and clone hall. My problem is heat. As you can imagine there is a tremendous heat build-up, so I purchased a 90,000 BTU air conditioning unit, figuring that each light produced about 3,200 BTU's of heat, so the system would never function near capacity. However, I didn't realize that the unit was controlled by only one thermostat, resulting in only one room kept at ideal temperature. I investigated temperature controlled

registers but they are impractical. What can I do to correct the situation?

HIGHLAND GROWER, Albany, California

THE BEST THING TO do is to tear out this unit and install a more appropriate system. You could use the unit for the largest room, but the unit would be running inefficiently at a small fraction of its capacity.

Barring redesign of the system, there are several changes that you could try. Perhaps thermostat-controlled registers could be installed. These would probably have to be custom made, since they do not seem to be made commercially. An A/C thermostat in each room could control shutters. The A/C thermostat would be placed in the warmest room, but should be on a long line so it can be moved from space to space. The warmest room would function with open shutters. The shutters in the other rooms would close when the air temperature lowers to a pre-determined level.

If you had it to do it all over again, there would be two ways to go. The first would be to place room air conditioners in each room so the heat is exchanged into the hallway. This hot air passes through an electrostatic precipitator to remove odor as it vents out of the building. This kind of system has a lot of flexibility and does not cause entire panic if one malfunctions. Furthermore, the appliances are relatively inexpensive and easy to replace.

A well-installed central A/C with individually controlled stations is a no-brainer and a delight to use. Set it and forget it.

HOT ROOM

We grow in a 5' x 6' room with an 8-foot ceiling, but no windows. We use a 12-inch fan to blow air out a vent, yet the temperature in the room stays in the 90's. We wanted to take the ballast out of the room, but the extension cord is too short. How can we get it down 72° F?

UPSTATER, Rochester, New York

THERE ARE SEVERAL THINGS that you can do to reduce temperatures. First, remove the ballast. To do this, cut the cord and put male and female plugs on the ends, then use an extension cord.

Although the ballast generates some of the lamp's heat, an air-cooled lighting system will capture most of the heat. The reflectors have glass shields on the bottom. A fan sends cool air through a tube to cool the lamp. The tube vents from the other side of the reflector carrying the heated, unscented air out, so it never heats the room. The hot air can be vented out or into another room or the central heating system since it is odorless.

These two steps would bring the temperature down to a near acceptable range. Another step you can take would be to place an air intake vent with a fan near the floor so that there is better air flow than having just the vent fan pumping air out.

By adding bottled CO_2 with a regulator and increasing the CO_2 levels in the air to 1,500 parts per million (ppm) or higher, the plants can function well with temperatures in the low 80's.

Air-cooled Horizontal Reflectors

KEEPING BASEMENT GARDEN COOL

I am currently designing my grow room. It will be in a base-ment but will only incorporate a space with dimensions of 2'x 5'x 6' (an area of 10 square feet) using a 400-watt high pressure sodium (HPS) lamp.

I have most of the technical aspects worked out except for two things.

1) I need a method of temperature control especially in the summer.

2) I want to enhance the enclosed atmosphere with CO_2. Would the exhaust from the nearby water heater suffice if I diverted a portion of it into the growing closet?

THE WHITE PUNK, San Jose, California

THERE ARE SEVERAL THINGS you can do to keep the temperature within the 70-85° F range. The main heat contributor is the lamp. An air-cooled reflector eliminates most of the heat before it ever gets into the room.

Even with an air-cooled reflector, the garden will gather heat. The easiest way to cool the space is to install a window or portable air conditioner. These units do not exchange air, just heat. This helps keep CO_2 in the space. The exhaust from the water heater can be used to enrich the air with CO_2. Even so, the plants will grow significantly faster if the air is enriched con-stantly during the lit period. This is accomplished most easily using a CO_2 tank with online meter and regulator. This unit measures the amount of CO_2 in the air and adjusts the flow valve on and off accordingly.

ATTIC GARDEN

The only space I have to grow in is my attic. Here in cen-tral Florida the attic can become quite warm in the sum-mers and cold in the winters. How should I construct my

**garden? The attic is a large stand-up space and I would
have no trouble working up there.**

WANTING TO GET STARTED, Daytona, Florida

BUILD A ROOM INSIDE the attic using 2'x 4's for framing and plas-
terboard walls. Insulate it with batting type insulation material.
Cool it using a window air conditioner. Ventilate it using squirrel
fans. Use air-cooled lamps to keep the room free of the lights' heat.
Vent the tubing directly to the attic outflow, so the heated air never
gets into the attic. Of course during the winter, it could be vented
into the living space to keep it cozy. The light ballasts, which create
a lot of heat, should be installed outside the room. The air conditioner will exchange heat with the rest of the attic, so a blower or
ventilator should be installed to remove the hot air from the attic.

Even during the hottest weather the room will maintain moderate temperatures. The insulation will slow the heat creeping into
the room. The air-cooled lights will not contribute more than a
couple of thousand BTU's per hour. The air conditioner and squirrel fans will remove the heat.

A. 3. COLD

WARMING UP THE BASEMENT

**I live in Montana and I'm having a little trouble keeping
heat in my basement garden. With minus 40° F temperatures outdoors, my basement only gets up to 45-50° F. Will
this decrease potency? The plants (30 females) are growing nicely.**

R. L., Somewhere in Montana

THE GROW ROOM TEMPERATURES are low. Low temperatures slow
plant growth. Perhaps some insulating material would hold in the

heat. The garden floors and walls can be insulated with Styrofoam. Placing the planters on pallets protects the containers from losing heat. Another way of solving the problem is by heating the medium using heat coils or mats made for this purpose. If the roots are kept warm, plants tolerate lower air temperatures better. Gas heaters serve a dual purpose; heating the room and creating carbon dioxide (CO_2).

B. CO_2

IMPORTANCE OF CO_2

> **How important is CO_2 to indoor plants? Can I grow beautiful home smoke with the regular space or do I need to add CO_2 containers or yeast product to get a nice luscious bud, or does CO_2 just affect the size of the yields?**
>
> JAH RASTA MON, Alameda, California

PLANTS USE CO_2 AS an ingredient of photosynthesis. Using light to fuel the complex chemical reaction, plants take hydrogen from water and carbon dioxide (CO_2) from the air to create sugar. Oxygen is also released in the process. The formula reads: $6(H_2O) + 6(CO_2) = C_6H_{12}O_6 + 6O_2$. This is the basis of plant growth because plants manipulate sugar as the building block for tissue. Since plants don't photosynthesize during the dark period, CO_2 levels are not critical during the dark period.

Under high light conditions, plants such as cannabis that produce C3 chlorophyll, can photosynthesize more quickly when high amounts of CO_2 are present. Conversely, photosynthesis slows when CO_2 becomes scarce. In a well-ventilated space in which new air is constantly introduced and used air is blown out, the plants obtain enough CO_2.

The average CO_2 level in the air is about 350 parts per million (ppm). In spaces that are not well ventilated, CO_2 levels are quickly depleted when plants are photosynthesizing. When the level drops to about 200 ppm, photosynthesis stops. Under bright lights, as the CO_2 level rises, the plant's photosynthesis rate increases in a linear ratio. In very bright spaces, plants can use CO_2 levels as high as 2,000 ppm, which increases the growth rate and yield significantly.

After the first HPS light, the next investment in the garden should be a CO_2 system consisting of a CO_2 meter that measures the parts per million of CO$_2$, a CO$_2$ tank with pressure regulator and solenoid switch that opens a valve that opens the CO$_2$ gas tank valve.

CAN CO$_2$ HELP?

> I am growing in a fiberboard box 6 feet high with inside dimensions of 5'x 5', a 25 square foot area. The top of the box is open, but covered with fiber mesh. It also has a front door and bottom vents in the back with 4-inch blade fans inside that pull in fresh air. The inside is lined with aluminum foil that reflects the light from a 1,000-watt HPS horizontal lamp mounted on the top. Would CO$_2$ help?
>
> DUANE, Fredonia, New York

YES, FOR TWO REASONS. Adding CO$_2$ will increase the rate of photosynthesis resulting in shorter times between harvests and increased yields. Second, CO$_2$ would give the plants more tolerance to warmer temperatures.

Inject the CO$_2$ under the canopy and let it get pulled through the canopy by rising air. Although you may lose a lot of CO$_2$ with the system, because of the constant ventilation, the cost-benefit ratio remains high. The system can be improved easily by switching to an air-cooled reflector and thermostat-controlled fans.

B. 2. TYPES OF CO$_2$ ENRICHMENT

DRY ICE FOR CO$_2$

Is dry ice a good way to deliver CO$_2$ to cannabis plants?

ICE MAN, Jackson, Michigan

DRY ICE IS FROZEN carbon dioxide, which normally exists only in gaseous and solid state, not liquid. It evaporates as it warms. The evaporative process takes some time, so the CO_2 is released gradually. One pound of dry ice evaporates into 8.7 cubic feet of gas. To figure out how much you need to evaporate, find the cubic size of the room (length x width x height) and multiply that number by 0.0015. For instance, a room 9.5 feet high, 13 feet long and 9 feet wide contains 1,111 cubic feet. Multiply 1,111 by 0.0015 and you get 1.66 lbs, about 26 ounces. This amount must be evaporated in a room without ventilation to add 1,500 ppm CO_2 to the area. The amount of evaporation required to maintain that level depends on the plant's use and the amount lost to ventilation. Perhaps a CO_2 sensor and regulator could be used to operate a valve that releases CO_2 only when the plants need it.

MANUAL CO_2

I am using a 1,000-watt lamp and a hydroponic setup. I want to add CO_2. Would it be possible to saturate the area with CO_2 every few hours rather than buying a CO_2 regulator set-up?

B.V., Fort Worth, Texas

SATURATING THE ROOM WITH CO_2 is an inefficient way to provide it to the plants. Most of the CO_2 will escape the room before the plants can use it. A regulator set-up controlled by a ppm meter will assure the garden a continuous supply of CO_2 at the proper concentration.

Although CO_2 regulators may seem expensive, they are well worth the money. The increase in growth rate will pay for the device in increased yield the first crop. An automatic system makes CO_2 enrichment an easy process, not subject to your schedule.

Carbon dioxide at the concentration advantageous to plants is not harmful to humans, but the body uses CO_2 concentrations to regulate our breathing automatically. A very high concentration may not be healthful.

CO₂ TANK OR GENERATOR?

I currently use bottled CO_2. Would a CO_2 generator cause me problems with excess heat in my grow room?

SKUNK BREEDER, Occidental, California

WHEN USING CO_2, THE temperature in the grow room can be raised from an ideal of 70-73° F to the low 80's F. Less ventilation may be needed. The CO_2 from the tank actually lowers the temperature slightly.

CO_2 generators burn propane or natural gas to produce CO_2. This produces heat. If the grow space stays on the cool side it would be appropriate to use a CO_2 generator. However, if heat is a problem in the space, only tanks should be used.

Both tanks and generators are inexpensive to use. The big expense is up-front, buying the equipment.

GERBILS FOR CO$_2$

I grow buds in a 4'x 3'x 6' closet. If I kept a cage with my
two gerbils in the room would their exhaust CO$_2$ help the
garden?

TOKER, Dallas, Texas

YES. THE GERBILS WOULD produce significant amounts of CO$_2$,
which would help plant growth. The extra oxygen would keep the
gerbils energetic.

SELTZER FOR CO$_2$

I grow in a closet using a 430-watt HPS lamp. I mist the
plants with seltzer water several times a day. Should I continue to do this when the plants start to flower?

CURIOUS CANNABIS CULTIVATOR, Tulare, California

SELTZER WATER IS CARBONATED water with no salt added. It is sometimes used to provide CO$_2$ to small plants since it is an economical
way to get CO$_2$ to them. As the plants grow, it becomes cheaper to
provide CO$_2$ using a tank or by burning natural gas. It also gets
harder to reach the vegetation and to spray as often as the plants
can use it.

During the first three or four weeks of flowering, seltzer water
increases bud growth. After that, it is not a good idea to get the
bud wet.

If seltzer water is used, it should be sprayed on the plants at
the beginning of the light cycle so that it dries off entirely before
the dark period. Moist buds in the dark provide a good environment for molds.

SELTZER FOR OUTDOOR CO$_2$

I misted my plants daily with a spray bottle containing unsalted carbonated water (seltzer). They grew very fast. Will this also help when I move them outdoors in late spring?

CURIOUS, Wellston, Ohio

YES. CARBONATED WATER DELIVERS high quantities of CO$_2$ to the plants. Misting them with it under bright light conditions will increase the plants' growth. Of course, this could be expensive since for best results the CO$_2$ should be replenished every hour or so.

CO$_2$ FIRE HAZARD

Can you use an oil lamp filled with regular lamp oil to provide CO$_2$ in the grow room?

STUNMASTER, London, ON, Canada

A BURNING LAMP OR candle will supply a small grow room with CO$_2$, but it is definitely not worth the risk. Having an open flame in an unattended space is a recipe for disaster. The slightest accident can instead become a disaster. Don't even think about using fire in your grow space.

B. 3. CO$_2$ HOW-TO

CO$_2$ DISCHARGE

Should I set up my CO$_2$ to discharge above the tops of the plants or at the base? I am using a tank and regulator.

SETTING UP, Camino Real, California

IT DEPENDS. IF AIR is being pulled up and out, you should place the tubes under the plant canopy, near the top of the containers or hydroponic unit. If the air is circulating within the grow space, place the emitter tube just above the tops of the plants. The gas is heavier and cooler than the air, so it will drop onto the leaves.

CO$_2$ & WATERING

I recently installed a CO$_2$ tank. Now I have to water every two to three days rather than every five to seven days. Is this increase normal?

INDOORS & LOVING IT, Modesto, California

YES. THE PHOTOSYNTHESIS RATE of the plants has increased. The plants are transpiring more water and use it as a source of hydrogen for building sugars, so they need more of it now that they are larger and their photosynthesis rate has increased.

TEMPERATURE WITH CO$_2$ ENRICHMENT

What is the maximum temperature for a flowering chamber using CO$_2$?

SYLVIA, New York City

WITH THE USE OF CO$_2$, photosynthesis proceeds at a much faster rate than normally occurs (as long as the plant receives sufficient quantities of light, water and nutrients). This rate is not affected much by temperatures in the range of 65-90° F.

Temperature does affect the plant's metabolic rate, which is the rate at which the cell and ultimately the plant, functions. Much like cold-blooded animals, the warmer the temperature, the faster life processes, such as conversion of food to energy and tissue growth, take place. Without CO$_2$, the optimum temperature range for cannabis is from the high 60's to the mid-70's F. At this temperature range, metabolism and plant growth are well balanced. When temperatures fall below 68° F, metabolism slows, increasing the storage of sugar, which plants use for energy. But the growth rate slows. Above the mid-70's, the metabolism rate increases, so the plant uses sugars to fuel metabolism, leaving less sugar for creating tissue. This lack of sugar slows tissue growth.

With CO_2 enrichment, production of sugars increases dramatically, so the plant uses more water and nutrients under comparable lighting conditions. In addition, the plant can use more light. With increased temperature, in the range of 80-85° F, the plant's metabolism rate increases, but so does the plant's rate of tissue building. Because the plant is producing more sugar, there is still a greater amount available for tissue growth, even with more being used for metabolism. This results in faster tissue growth.

CO$_2$ AT RIPENING?

Why do people reduce the use of CO_2 during the last week or two of ripening?

PROFESSOR AFGHANI, Staten Island, New York

PEOPLE THINK THAT THE odor and the potency are reduced if CO_2 is used during the last stages of flowering.

Morphological changes are apparent in CO_2-treated plants; the leaves and stems are thicker, the color is often darker and sativa leaves often become squatter, looking more like Afghanis. The stomata are also affected. I haven't seen any studies describing changes in the odor or taste of herbs or flowers and have not noticed differences myself. The growth of new tissue slows as the flowers ripen so CO_2 loses some of its effectiveness during the final stages.

For more on the ripening phase, see chapter 7.

RENEW CO$_2$?

I was using a generator and had to kill my CO$_2$ production because of the summer heat. Now that it is cooling off outside, should I resume CO$_2$? The hairs of the flowers have not started to change color yet, so I thought I might be able to speed up the process by re-introducing CO$_2$.

BD 69, Richfield, Ohio

YES, IF THE PLANTS have three weeks or more until ripening. The plants' photosynthetic rate will increase immediately.

You can use CO$_2$ during the summer by injecting it into a space using a regulator and tank. Although bottle gas is more expensive than burning natural gas, it is still very economical when compared to the cost of electricity. The ratio of yield-to-cost is very high, so it would be well worth setting up next summer. It would also give the plants tolerance of higher ambient temperatures. They perform best in the low 80's when the air is CO$_2$ enriched.

THE DARK PERIOD

What does the plant do during the night? Is it necessary to maintain good circulation and CO$_2$?

HEMPMAN, San Diego, California

DURING THE DAY, TWO main metabolic processes occur in plants. Photosynthesis is the process that plants use to convert water and CO$_2$ into sugar using light as an energy source. These sugars are then used to fuel metabolism. The plants use oxygen obtained from the air and burn sugars to power the cell. Respiration takes place continually, day and night.

Growth is the result of the plant using sugars to build cellulose and other tissue. Plants build tissue both during light and dark periods, but the growth is limited by the amount of sugar produced during photosynthesis.

C3 green plants such as cannabis only use CO$_2$ when they are photosynthesizing, so they only need to be enriched during the lighted portion of the day and not during the dark cycle. During the dark period, cannabis, like all green plants, uses oxygen. Air circulation should continue to replenish the micro-environment at the leaf surface with fresh oxygen-rich air.

> *For more on the dark period, see chapter 6, section D.*

WOULD OXYGEN ENRICHMENT HELP?

I know that CO_2 enrichment is important and I plan to use it. I'd like to know if "oxygen enrichment" is possible and if it would be useful?

FRANCISCO D., Internet

OXYGEN IS NOT A critical factor because there is plenty of it in the air. During the day, when the plants are photosynthesizing, they release oxygen as a byproduct of sugar production. No additional oxygen is needed above ground.

The roots use oxygen and absorb it directly from the soil or from water that contains dissolved oxygen. The amount of dissolved oxygen water can hold is determined for the most part by its temperature. The cooler the water, the more oxygen it holds. Warm water doesn't hold much oxygen. Anaerobic conditions set the stage for pathogens to attack stressed roots. There are several ways to add oxygen to your water:

- Keep the soil or hydroponic irrigation water at about 72° F. At this temperature, the water has the ability to hold sufficient oxygen. If the water temperature is higher, use a water chiller, available from aquarium fish supply stores. These units keep the water in the reservoir cool even when the surrounding temperature is quite high. This can save plants when the air temperature reaches the 90's. The cool roots, with access to plenty of oxygen, keep the plant healthy and mitigate the damage that hot air would normally cause.

- Use an air pump to keep the water circulating or use a small submersible pump to create a mini waterfall. This turbulence helps the water make contact with air. During this contact the water exchanges any carbon dioxide it is holding for oxygen.

- A loose soil, that provides spaces to hold air as well as water, provides sufficient oxygen exchange for roots. Oxygen can be supplemented using hydrogen peroxide (H_2O_2) at the rate of about 1 part per 500 in the water-nutrient solution. Using 10% H_2O_2, often sold in indoor garden shops, dilute it at the ratio 1 part in 200, or about 6 ounces per gallon. Using pharmacy-grade 3% H_2O_2, it is diluted at the rate 1 part hydrogen peroxide to 5 parts water, or 20 ounces per gallon.

- Hydroponic water can be enriched with hydrogen peroxide at the same rate as irrigation water. H_2O_2 is used to kill pathogens and algae in hydroponic systems at the rate of about 1 part per 200, which is about 6 $^1/_2$ ounces of 10% H_2O_2 or 20 ounces of 3% H_2O_2 per gallon.

Hydrogen peroxide, H_2O_2, is water that is charged with an additional oxygen (O) atom. This atom has a tendency to jump from its unstable bond and combine with some other molecule. That is why hydrogen peroxide can burn skin and clothing. Since it is an unstable molecule, the O may jump off the H_2O_2 and combine with another O atom to form a molecule of 2 O atoms, O_2. The remaining H_2O is a water molecule. The O_2 molecule remains dissolved in the water. It is ready to be picked up by an oxygen-hungry root and destroys pathogens by "burning" them.

Hydrogen peroxide remains effective for about three days. Then more is added.

4 INDOOR ENVIRONMENT: SOIL & HYDRO

A. GENERAL RECOMMENDATIONS
1. GARDEN SET-UP
2. SELECTING A METHOD: SOIL & HYDRO
3. CONTAINER SIZE

B. SOIL
1. PLANTING MIXES
2. FERTILIZERS & NUTRIENTS

C. HYDRO
1. SYSTEMS
2. TYPES OF HYDROPONIC MEDIA
3. NUTRIENTS

D. WATER & PH

RELATED TOPICS
Troubleshooting nutrient problems: chapter 9 Troubleshooting.
Outdoor medium and watering: chapter 5 Outdoors & Greenhouse.
Garden changes over time: chapter 6 Plant Life Cycle.

A. GENERAL
RECOMMENDATIONS

1. GARDEN SET-UP

LOW BUDGET GARDEN

I don't have a lot of money to buy all those special lights and the other equipment. What would you recommend me to do to get a garden growing?

BLUNTMAN, Fairview Heights, Illinois

THERE ARE INEXPENSIVE WAYS to set up a garden. The most important item on the buy list is the light. A 1,000-watt high intensity discharge (HID) light is the best and most inexpensive way to light a garden when both the cost of the light and cost of electricity are factored. HID lamps are so much more efficient than any other form of light production that they pay for themselves in a year or less. Although they are on the expensive side, they are worth it. Used lights and other equipment are sometimes offered for sale inexpensively in the classifieds.

Just installing a good light and simple ventilation system is the first step to a successful garden.

You can set up an inexpensive homemade hydroponic system or grow the plants in containers using a planting medium. Either system can be assembled fairly cheaply. For instance, small water pumps sell for under $20.

Use the dull side of aluminum foil to reflect stray light back to the garden. The ventilation fan should be regulated by a humidistat/thermostat. This keeps the air cool and dry.

The next step would be a CO_2 tank with regulator. No matter which route you take toward a home garden, the two cheapest ways to assure a high quality yield are by growing clones or seed from excellent known varieties or at least excellent stash, and to read or study a book about marijuana cultivation. The mistakes you avoid will repay your investment in information hundreds of times and save you months of frustration.

For info on lights, see chapter 2.
For info on CO_2 and air control, see chapter 3.

HIGH-END GARDEN

How would you set up a high budget garden?

HIGH HEFNER, Internet

THE FACTORS THAT INFLUENCE a plant's growth can roughly be described as light, temperature, water, nutrients and CO_2. Optimizing each of the conditions will produce the best plants. However, the most important factor is the genetic make-up of the plants.

My first concern would be to obtain plants that will produce buds that I know I would like. That of course would entail a virtually round-the-world trip sampling the best. Of course Canada or Amsterdam would be a good start. Other countries that I'd want to sample are India, Nepal, and equatorial and southern Africa.

The garden that these genetically enabled plants would enter would be lit by natural sunlight supplemented by HPS lamps. The HPS lamps would be turned on and off automatically to maintain high light levels during the lit period. Thus the growth period would continue after the sun goes down, or when the light is too dim. During the dark period the garden would be shielded from all light. A greenhouse would be suitable.

If the garden were indoors I would use HPS lamps fitted with air- or water-cooled reflectors. The garden would have an effective input of perhaps 75 watts per square foot during the late stages of flowering. In addition the plants would receive perhaps 30 watts input per square foot of light from fluorescent tubes designed to illuminate reptiles or be used as sunlamps.

The garden's temperature would be maintained at 78° F. There are lots of different ways to keep the room temperature moderate. As a choice I would use a heat exchanger, similar to a window air conditioner. The air remains in the room, but it is cooled. That way it is easy to maintain high CO_2 levels.

> For info on lights, see chapter 2.
> For info on CO_2 and air control, see chapter 3.

A. 2. SELECTING A METHOD: SOIL & HYDRO

SOIL OR SOILLESS FOR THE BEGINNER?

I am a novice grower. Would I be better off using a soil or soilless mix? I was thinking that soil gives you more room for error. Can soil be used in the "sea of green" method?

J.F., Orlando, Florida

I HAVE SEEN NOVICE growers succeed and fail using both soil and hydroponics. However, soil and planting mediums are more forgiving than hydroponics. Planting mediums form weak bonds with excess nutrients. As the plant uses nutrients, the medium releases more. This activity is initiated by microorganisms that find shelter on the surface of the medium.

There are many hydroponic methods and some are easier than others. The easiest systems use a planting medium with granules that "imitate" soil particles, such as perlite, rockwool, inert planting medium and sand. Mediums that include compost, worm castings and peat moss have some buffering action and lock up nutrients until they are needed. The hardest ones to use are NFT and aeroponic systems, which must be kept functioning in perfect order for plants to survive.

Hydroponic growers sometimes encounter nutrient problems. Soil growers often have water and sometimes have nutrient problems. Each type works well when it's done right.

THE MEDIUM

I have been reading ads for different mediums: rocks, lava, bio-dynamic compost and others. What really matters? The medium, the nutrients and sunlight, or just the type of seeds?

R. N., North Carolina

THE PURPOSE OF THE medium is to anchor the roots and hold the nutrients and water so that the plant can use them. Any medium that accomplishes this and also holds suitable quantities of air will do. Most mediums, such as lava, ceramic beads, perlite and other commercial materials work well.

While the nutrients may affect the health of the plant and its growth, they have little to do with its potency. Light also affects the growth of the plant and the bud, as well as its potency to a small extent. However, the main factor affecting potency is the plant's genetics. Both potential yield and potency are determined by the plant's genes.

> *For info on genetics, see chapter 1; chapter 11; chapter 12.*

FROM SOIL TO HYDRO

What is the best way to switch plants that have just germinated in soil into a hydroponic system? How will this affect the plant?

TJ, Camarillo, California

HOLD THE SEEDLING BY the rootball end and dip it in 70° F water to let the soil fall away from the roots. When all the soil is removed, place the seedling in the hydroponic unit. If you are going to place the seedlings in Oasis™ cubes, cut a slit that the roots can fit into. If planting in rockwool, pull the cube partially apart and place the seedling inside, then gently firm the cube parts back together. Be careful not to break the roots when using hydrostone. First put the seedling in place and then gently push the stones around it. With perlite, the bare root seedling can be handled as it would be in soil. After the seedling is in place, immediately irrigate it. Keep the roots well irrigated. Decrease the light intensity so the plant isn't stressed.

If the seedling's roots are kept in an environment with adequate amounts of water and oxygen, they should adjust to the new environment within two days.

A. 3. CONTAINER SIZE

POT SIZE

What size pots should be used to grow full-size indoor plants?

W., Alice, Texas

CONTAINERS THAT CONFINE THE roots inhibit the growth of the plant itself. Containers smaller than 5 gallons (3 gallons hydro) inhibit plant growth above 4 or 5 feet. The plants will grow slower and smaller than those in larger containers. Plants in small containers also require more attention. The amount of water and nutrients available to the roots is limited by the small mass and must be replenished often.

ADEQUATE CONTAINER SIZE

I set up a system and planted it with "White Widow" and now, eight days later, the plants are 6-8 inches tall with multiple leaves growing in 1-gallon milk containers. I already see roots at the bottom of the containers. Will they be an adequate size for the plants?

SISTER SINSE, Seattle, Washington

THE ONLY WAY TO grow these plants without transplanting them is to force them to flower in about a week when they are about 12 inches tall. By the time they are harvested they will be rootbound, but will grow big buds using a balanced bloom fertilizer.

SIZE OF SEA OF GREEN CONTAINERS

I am starting a sea of green garden and wondering what is the optimal pot size? I will be using a 400-watt HPS to flower approximately 20 plants in a closet 2'x 2.4'x 5'.

SHIZIFTY, Toronto, ON, Canada

YOU ARE PLANNING TO grow 20 plants in about 5 square feet, so each plant will have a canopy space of about 6'x 6'. The best containers for you to use would be 6-inch square containers that are about 8 inches tall. This will provide enough space for each plant to grow a single large bud.

> For info on sea of green pruning, see chapter 6, section B.
> For info on sea of green hydro, see "Passive or Active Hydro" in next section, C.1 of this chapter.

SODA-BOTTLE POTS

I have a 10'x 12', 120-square-foot garden. I grow in soil using twenty 20-gallon pails. Can I use 2-liter soda bottles in my garden? Should I do it? How?

POKEY, Chattanooga, Tennessee

THERE ARE BOTH ADVANTAGES and disadvantages to switching from large containers to more of a sea of green system. The large buckets with planting medium are easy to maintain, and only a small number of large plants grow, which is safer since mandatory sentencing guidelines are determined by number of plants regardless of their size.

A sea of green garden using small hydroponic containers with either an ebb-and-flo or drip system requires more maintenance. The plants have to be irrigated more often, and even though watering operations can be performed automatically, the system will require more of your time. Increasing the number of plants to more than 100 also brings in the federal mandatory minimums. If you decrease the size of the buckets to 15-inch diameters, seventy-two plants would fit in the garden and you would slide under the mandatory minimum sentencing guidelines. The plants would fill the canopy much faster than it takes the twenty plants.

For more on the law, see chapter 8.

B. SOIL

REGULAR VS. SPECIALTY POTTING SOIL

Is using a regular potting soil good or bad for the plant? It's too much of a hassle purchasing and measuring fertilizers that I read about in magazines.

DEEP KNEE, Internet

SOME REGULAR POTTING MIXES will support healthy growth of plants for a month or two because they are enriched with nutrients. Other mixes have little nutrient content and must be used with fertilizer from the start.

Nurseries that propagate bedding and annual plants seek fast growth. They use peat moss–based mixes and supply nutrients as water-soluble fertilizers in the irrigation water. In Switzerland I saw nurseries grow marijuana using this technique.

The most important things about a mix are its pH, texture, porosity and water- and air-holding capacity. The mix should have a pH of 5.8-6.5. If it is above or below that, use pH Up or Down in the water to buffer it. The medium should not pack hard when squeezed in a fist. If it clumps, it should fall apart when poked. The material should have large enough particles so that there are spaces for air so the roots can obtain oxygen. It should allow excess water to pass through, but should hold enough to keep the roots moist.

SOILLESS PLANTING MIX

I'm looking for an easy to use soilless mix that is best for someone who hand waters with organic tea fertilizer solutions. What would you recommend? Also, what size

containers would conserve space, but allow clones to grow to 14-16 inches before flowering is initiated?

KING COLA, New Orleans, Louisiana

THERE ARE MANY PREPARED soilless planting mixes that you can use with an organic nutrient–water solution.

Retail nurseries sell several grades of potting mixes including ones with added organic fertilizers. Some also include water-holding crystals. Most of these mixes are made from either peat moss or forest products, meaning compost, bark and other forest products. The mixes are also likely to include sand, perlite, organic fertilizers and compost.

Some of the enriched mixes contain enough nutrients to support the plants in 10- or 12-inch diameter containers for three to five weeks, through second stage vegetative growth, when the plants have developed an extensive root system. However, even plants in enriched mixes grow larger faster when they are given water-soluble fertilizers. Inexpensive mixes are usually just a mixture of peat moss, bark and textural amendments that contain no nutrients. Plants grown in these mixes are fed only through the water–nutrient mixture.

All mixes composed of organic ingredients decompose in the presence of nutrients. Microorganisms feast on the combination of fertilizer food and carbon in the planting mix. At the same time the medium acts as a buffer, first absorbing, then releasing nutrients. This makes planting mixes more forgiving than straight hydroponic mediums such as rockwool or clay pellets.

There are many water-soluble organic fertilizers to choose from. They should be supplied each time the plants are watered.

You did not mention how wide or tall the plants get by ripening. However, the strongest most productive soil-grown plants should have between $1/2$ and 1 gallon of soil for every foot of height the plants are to grow. The broader and more branched the plant, the more soil needed.

For more about vegetative & flowering cycles, see chapter 6.

RE-USING SOIL

Since farmers can build up their soil and since soil in containers can be leached and/or treated, why do so many advisers on growing say to replace potted soil each season? Wouldn't a good program of conditioning help save soil in containers and therefore save money?

PROFESSOR T. H. CUSTER, CHAIRMAN, The Homegrowers of Connecticut

SOIL USED IN CONTAINERS can be reconditioned by leaching it and adding nutrients. The reason that many advisers suggest using new soil is that reconditioning soil is tedious and critical. Too great a buildup of some minerals causes a hard-to-reverse toxic condition. Since the crop is so valuable and soil is relatively inexpensive, the advisers feel the work is not worth the bother.

B. 2. FERTILIZERS & NUTRIENTS

FERTILIZING ADVICE

I am using two different commercial mixes. The first is very rich and is composed of 50% worm castings. The second is an organic mix with bat guano, worm castings kelp meal and other organic additives. How should I fertilize these plants?

WANDER WOMAN, Gays Mills, Wisconsin

BOTH OF THESE MIXES are fortified with fertilizers and amendments that will give the clones a jump start. The plants in the large containers are going to grow for four to six weeks before they are forced to flower. The roots have a lot of rich soil to grow into so they probably have enough nutrients for the vegetative growth stage.

During flowering, add a flowering formula fertilizer high in phosphorus (P). There are many organic and standard fertilizers you can use. Guanos are quite soluble and come in high phosphorus formulas.

If you see one potting mix vastly outperforming the other, check its pH. It may require supplements with an appropriately balanced fertilizer mix.

IDEAL N-P-K

We have tried different variations of N-P-K ratios in nutrient solutions. Is there an ideal N-P-K ratio for vegging and flowering?

GREENGENES, Internet

N-P-K IS THE PERCENTAGE of three key nutrients—nitrogen, phosphorus, and potassium—present in fertilizer. While there is no ideal fertilizer, a general guideline would be around 7-5-5 for vegetative. As the plants enter flowering, the nitrogen can be kept at a similar level, but as flowering progresses, the nitrogen should be lowered. Higher phosphorus supports the plants' formation of flowers, but it is quite acidic, so the pH is balanced with a corresponding increase in potassium. A good flower formula is 3-10-10.

The nutrients should be diluted to 1,200-1,800 parts per million (ppm). A garden's fertilizer needs are individual for several reasons. First, the quality of water, including its mineral content, varies, which changes the fertilizer requirements. Second, different varieties of marijuana may use nutrients at different rates. Third, plants' nutritional needs change with environmental changes to the garden. Light and temperature conditions have a tremendous effect on plant needs. Fourth, marijuana's nutritional needs change through the life cycle. Early and late vegetative, and early, mid and late flowering each have unique nutritional needs.

For more on N-P-K changes between vegetative and flowering phases, see "When to Adjust Fertilizer" in chapter 6, section E.

C. HYDRO

GOING HYDRO

I plan to start growing hydroponically. Which type of system should I use?

ANDREW, Colorado

THE SECRET TO SUCCESS in hydroponic gardening is to keep the system simple. Passive systems don't circulate water so they require the least attention. These include the wick and reservoir systems. Ebb-and-flo and drip systems circulate the water but also work well with only a little learning curve. NFT and aeroponic-based systems are more difficult to master. They have the same reputation as English sports cars—fantastic when they are working.

Beware of systems that don't have redundancies in case of breakdown, such as power failure. For instance, a drip system using perlite or rockwool for medium can hold water for up to a day if water isn't delivered. Hydrostones dry out in 6 hours or less. But if the hydrostone is sitting in an inch of water, it will draw water through capillary action.

Materials for constructing hydro units can be found at indoor garden shops, nurseries, pet shops and houseware and hardware stores.

For info on rinsing hydro systems, see section D in this chapter.

PASSIVE OR ACTIVE HYDRO

I am planning my first home garden. It will be constructed in a 2'x 2'x 5' cabinet, using a "sea of green" approach. I

can't decide whether I should use a reservoir or a drip system. Some sources say an aerated reservoir is good for a simple system, while other sources say the plant roots should not sit in the water. Also, for a flow system, some kits come with submersible pumps, while other authors say never use a submersible pump because the pump will heat the nutrient solution and burn the roots.

GERRY, Columbia, Maryland

EITHER SYSTEM WILL WORK well in the garden. The reservoir system uses horticultural clay pellets or pea-sized volcanic lava in plastic pots. The containers are placed in a tray that contains water–nutrient solution about one quarter of the height of the container. A 10-inch-high container should have a bit more than 2 inches of the rock under water. A 5-inch-tall container should only have about an inch of soaking rock. Most of the medium remains above the water line. The rock stays moist through capillary action, which draws up water. All the clay pebbles in the container stay moist as long as there is water in the reservoir.

WICK SYSTEM

Once the water–nutrient solution is added to the tray, plain water without nutrients should be added to keep the water level and strength of the nutrient solution stable. As water evaporates, the nutrient concentration increases. Adding water lowers it.

Most books say that roots should not be sitting in water. There are two reasons why this is true some of the time. First, the sitting water may not contain dissolved oxygen. Roots use oxygen and become diseased without it. Second, some planting mediums are very dense and absorb so much water that little air is left. The roots suffer from lack of oxygen. In the reservoir system, large air spaces are left between the pieces of both the clay pebbles or lava so there is plenty of air and oxygen easily accessible to the roots above the water level.

The roots that grow into the water look different than those growing above it. They don't have the fine network of root hairs and are thicker and grow well even in water that is oxygen depleted. The other roots seem to supply oxygen to the water roots.

Gardeners who are concerned about the water roots possibly living in an environment without oxygen can easily provide the gas using a small air-stone attached to an air pump. The column of rising bubbles circulates the water. More surface area comes in contact with air and absorbs oxygen while releasing CO_2.

The constant drip system also uses clay pellets or pea-sized lava in containers that are sitting in a tray that drains into a reservoir below. A pump constantly supplies a gentle stream of water through the tubing to each container so that a thin stream of water is always trickling over the stones. This system is simple yet it encourages very vigorous growth.

Blocking the drain hole with tubing that raises the drain to the desired height easily makes a combination constant drip/reservoir system. This way, the plants are getting a constant stream of water and the reservoir provides a space for water roots.

Small submersible pumps use little power and create little heat. They can be used in reservoirs without fear of boiling the roots. Generally speaking, the water temperature should be kept at about 72° F.

The best advice for small gardens is based on the word KISS-Keep It Simple, Stupid. Not referring to you, personally, of course.

For info on the Liz's garden hydro setup, see "Small Garden" in chapter 2, section E.

WICK SYSTEM

Photo by Ed Rosenthal

SETTING UP WICK SYSTEM

I have a 2'x 2', 8-foot-tall shower. I want to make a hydro system for four plants. What should I do for lights, hydro system and care? I don't want to spend a lot of money on this.

STONED, Newburgh, New York

A 250-WATT HIGH PRESSURE sodium (HPS) lamp will provide a bright light for the garden. Line the stall with thin Styrofoam boards, Mylar, white polyethylene or aluminum foil (dull side out). All of these materials are good light reflectors listed in order of their efficiency at reflecting light.

You can buy an inexpensive commercial hydro system from a hydroponic supply company or you can construct your own. The commercial systems are available at indoor garden shops and on the internet. Most of the systems seem to work pretty well. You can construct your own for much less, however.

Wick systems, which are extremely reliable, use a nylon cord or rope to draw water–nutrient solution into the container from a reservoir up to the medium as it is used. The wicks are threaded through the drainage holes in the plant container and hang down into the reservoir. The containers are held above the water level using supports. These systems use planting mixes or horticultural clay pellets on a bed of planting mix as the medium. The planting mix wicks the water–nutrient solution to the clay pellets or lava. A balanced water-soluble fertilizer supplies the nutrients. Water the containers and then fill the reservoir. No electricity, motor or pump is required and there is no pumped water so accidents are less likely. The system can even be used outdoors.

To build a wick system, thread a piece of $3/16$- or $3/8$-inch woven nylon rope across the bottom of the container and out the sides so that each end hangs down about 6 inches Place the container on a block above the 3-inch water line inside a 5-inch-high plastic container. Fill the container with water–nutrient solution to just below the top of the block, making sure that the wicks hang down into the water.

The system is now ready to go. When new water is added to the system, add it from the tops of the containers to rinse off the salts that have built up on the rocks.

> *For more on watering in the wick system, see section D of this chapter.*

WRONG WICK

I built a wick system using felt as described in an article by Max Yields, but the wick made from felt does not work well. Any suggestions?

CONFUSED FIRST TIMER, Lindenhurst, New York

WOVEN NYLON CORD $3/16$-INCH thick for small containers and $3/8$-inch for large ones works very well in drawing water from a reservoir. The nylon does not deteriorate from contact with the water–nutrient solution and can be used for years.

OXYGENATING THE WICK SYSTEM

I'm using a wick system in my hydro-garden and I was wondering if the wick can absorb and deliver a sufficient amount of oxygen to the roots? I oxygenate the water by shaking it first. What else should I do?

PHELL O'GREENTHUMB, Chatanooga, Tennessee

IN A WICK SYSTEM, you don't have to worry about the roots getting enough oxygen. There is enough air exchange in the container for the roots to obtain adequate amounts of oxygen.

Wick systems use woven nylon rope to draw water up to the planting medium. The water is drawn up automatically as needed to maintain a certain moisture level. Most planting mixes maintain a moisture level sufficient for plant roots to draw upon, but have good drain and maintain air spaces between the particles. Since water is drawn up to the medium rather than by flooding, air spaces are maintained continuously and the used air, which contains CO_2, is exchanged for oxygen-rich fresh air.

The wicks are continuously drawing up water, which is held in a thin film around the sides of the nylon threads. This provides a very large surface area in relation to the water depth. As a result the water absorbs oxygen.

You may find that the roots grow through the openings in the containers and follow the wick down to the reservoir, growing a dynamic root system in the water. These water roots are thick with less branching and no root hairs. These roots are adapted for directly soaking up water–nutrient solution.

READER TIP ▶ **HOMEMADE EBB & FLO**

I built my own ebb and flow system very inexpensively. I placed a 5-foot kiddie pool on a 1/2-inch-thick Styrofoam board to protect it from a cold concrete floor. I placed two shipping pallets on top of each other in the pool. And placed another 5-foot kiddie pool on top of them. I drilled

two 1-inch drain holes on the bottom of the pool and three 2-inch diameter holes two inches from the bottom side. I slipped 2-inch tubes into the holes and ran them down to the reservoir. These were my emergency drains. The pool is filled to a 2-inch depth using a 100-gallon-per-hour submersible pump. These are controlled by a seven-day, six-event timer with battery backup.

The pools hold 6-inch plastic pots filled with high-grade planting mix. They are irrigated three times a week, on Tuesday, Thursday and Saturday. It takes the pump a few minutes to fill the tray. Four foot by eight foot heat-reflective emergency camping blankets from a camping store ($2 each) surround the perimeter of the garden and are also placed over the containers to reflect the light back up to the leaves.

LIZ'S HYDRO GARDEN

Photo by Ed Rosenthal

The garden works great and the whole thing was inexpensive to set up except for the 1,000-watt high pressure sodium (HPS) lamp, and light tracker, which I purchased used.

BEE DISCREET, Neeses, South Carolina

THANKS FOR YOUR DESCRIPTION, Bee.

C. 2. TYPES OF HYDROPONIC MEDIA

PERLITE

Can perlite be used by itself in a passive hydroponic system?

JIM DEAN, Internet

NO. PERLITE DOES NOT have capillary action. It does not draw water up from the reservoir, so it cannot be used alone. It can be used as a component of a planting mix containing peat moss, coir or compost, lava rock or horticultural clay pebbles.

LAVA ROCK

I have just harvested my first hydro closet garden and am using marble-sized lava rock for the medium. How many times can I re-use the lava rock?

TRELAWAY, Internet

THE LAVA ROCK CAN be used indefinitely. It should be washed thoroughly after each crop in warm or hot water to remove most roots and precipitated salts. If there is a question of infection, it can be placed in boiling water or sprayed with 3% hydrogen peroxide to kill any pests.

ROCKWOOL FOR WICKS?

Can rockwool be used as a medium for wick systems? Can foam rubber also work?

LEARNING, USA

ROCKWOOL BLOCKS WILL NOT work in a wick system. They do not exhibit capillary action, which draws water into the medium. Good materials for wick systems include lava and clay pellets on a bed of planting mix, commercial planting mixes, and which draw water. These mediums are often mixed with other materials such as sand, perlite or even rockwool fluff to obtain a drier planting mix.

Lava and expanded clay pellets work best if they are mixed with compost or planting mix in a ratio of 5 parts pellets to 1 part mix. The two mediums are moistened and then mixed together. This coats the rock, making the surface moister.

ROCKWOOL EBB & FLO

I grow in 4' x 4' x 3' high rockwool cubes using an ebb-and-flo table. How high should the water flood? How often should I irrigate?

TIMMY K., Fairbanks, Alaska

THE WATER SHOULD FLOOD to a depth of about two inches. Irrigate at least once daily to start. As the plants grow or if the temperature causes a lot of evaporation and transpiration, you will have to increase the number of irrigations.

ROCKWOOL DANGERS

What are the dangers of rockwool? I find that it doesn't bother me to handle it, so I take no safety precautions. Is this smart?

NO NAME PLEASE, Eugene, Oregon

HANDLING ROCKWOOL FIBER PRESENTS danger to the skin and the lungs. When rockwool is handled, the extremely thin pieces of the fiber pierce and lodge in the skin. Symptoms of this are small swellings where the pieces have entered, and itching. The highly alkaline strands are presumed to eventually dissolve in the body's acid environment.

Handling dry rockwool fiber creates a dust of short pieces, some of which are microscopic. Rockwool flocking, which is stuffed into containers is much more likely to lose strands than are the cubes or slabs.

The dust particles are easily breathed in and stick to the small air passages in the lungs, creating small temporary ulcers or sores. Once they are lodged there, the body's acid environment interacts with the alkaline rockwool to dissolve it.

Here are three important tips for handling this material:

1. Cover your entire body when handling rockwool. Wear gloves, long pants and long sleeved shirt, shoes, hat, face mask (a paper bag is okay) goggles and high quality dust respirator. Disposable paper painter's overalls are ideal.

2. Wet the rockwool before handling it, so that it does not create as much dust. Wet fibers are less likely to break, and less likely to become airborne if they do break apart.

3. If possible work with the material outdoors or with good ventilation.

READER TIP **NEW MEDIUM**

I have grown plants in polyester batting like the material used to stuff quilts. It holds lots of air and water, is fibrous yet pliable, and it never rots. I put some cuttings into blocks that were stacked together.

I have also used florists' foam as a wick in a reservoir system. Placed in the bottom of a growing container, it draws water like crazy and the roots penetrate.

R. M., Kansas

THANKS FOR THE SUGGESTIONS.

VERMICULITE

I notice that you used to recommend vermiculite but you don't anymore. Why?

JOHNSON, El Cerrito, California

VERMICULITE IS HAZARDOUS MATERIAL that contains asbestos. It is not worth the risk of using it.

C. 3. NUTRIENTS

NUTRIENT PH FOR ROCKWOOL

What pH should the hydroponic solution be for pre-conditioned rockwool?

PROF. OREGON I, Eugene, Oregon

PRE-CONDITIONING ROCKWOOL BY SOAKING it in a low pH solution is just a temporary solution. Within a few weeks this "mask" wears off and the naturally high (alkaline) pH of the rockwool returns.

To counteract this, the nutrient–water solution is adjusted to a pH of about 6.0-6.1.

For more on pH, see section D in this chapter.

READER TIP ▶ **BAT GUANO TEA FOR HYDRO**

I read an article on using bat guano in a tea-type solution for hydroponic systems. He said that he put the guano into a coffee or tea bag and let it seep for two days and that he had gotten good results. I have a home-built hydroponic system and I tried it. After two days the water was only slightly discolored. I tested it with my TDS meter (total dissolved solids) and it tested at only 350 ppm (parts per million). The tap water tested at 120 ppm.

To concentrate the nutrient I decided to use a percolator type coffee pot. In just a minute it started to brew the "guano java." A dark liquid came out. After it cooled it tested at 1,700 ppm, a much better result. Then I changed the water several times but used the same guano, which resulted in a slightly lower ppm each time. I put the residue in a soil mixture.

POT PROTESTER, Pennsylvania

THANKS FOR THE BREWING tip, Pot. I tried your method and it worked great.

MONITORING NUTRIENTS

I use a hydroponic system. After calibrating my ppm (parts per million) dipstick, I get a reading from the water of 150 ppm of dissolved solids before adding anything. Do I figure

**these numbers in with my total ppm or should I start from
there, with this figure zeroed out?**

KILL NUGS, West Palm Beach, Florida

FIND OUT WHAT THOSE dissolved solids are composed of. Call the
water company and ask them to send you a copy of their tests. Then
check for nitrates, nitrites and calcium as well as other minerals.
When configuring your nutrient mix, these minerals should be
taken into account.

Most hydroponic growers use one of the "brand name" hydroponic fertilizers. None of these fertilizers is perfect for all water
conditions so growers can use several strategies to deal with nutrient problems.

Aside from monitoring the water, growers should look closely at
the plants at least twice a week. The condition of the leaves, old,
middle and new growth gives you an exact reading of the water
conditions. Based on this reading, appropriate adjustments should
be made.

> *To identify specific leaf/plant nutrient problems, see chapter 9,
> section B.*

D. WATER & PH

WHEN TO WATER

What time of day is the best to water budding plants?

MIKE, Austin, Texas

PLANTS GROWING VEGETATIVELY OR being forced to flower should be watered in the morning. This way they have plenty of water to carry on their metabolic processes during the day. The plants transpire water the most during the day to keep cool and for photosynthesis.

> *For more on the plant's growing and care cycle, see chapter 6.*
> *For info on watering adjustments with CO_2, see "CO_2 & Watering"*
> *in chapter 3, section B.3.*

WICK WATERING PRACTICES

Are there any advantages or disadvantages to letting the plants use up the total nutrient–water supply before adding more water to my wick system? I've read that one must keep the nutrient reservoir at a constant level. However, my plants seem to grow better if I let the growing medium ($1/2$ perlite – $1/2$ vermiculite) completely use up the nutrient and dry out every three to four weeks. My concern about this procedure is that if I allow the system to dry out, the roots will grow in their search for water. When I do add the nutrient, my growing medium becomes quite wet.

A FRIEND, Texas

THE WICK SYSTEM WORKS by using a wick, usually with a piece of nylon cord, to draw water from a reservoir to the planting pot using capillary action, similar to a tissue or napkin drawing water. As the

117

moisture in the planting container is used by the plant or evaporated, the wick draws more to the container. A constant level of moisture is maintained. However, there are plenty of air spaces, which
are vital to the roots.

Many plants do best when the medium is given a chance to
dry out, which simulates conditions in the plant's natural environment. However, cannabis seems to be able to thrive without
this cycle.

If the dry-out is watched and does not reach the critical level
where the leaves begin to wilt, there is no harm, except if the
nutrient–water solution becomes too concentrated. Since your
plants grow better using a dry-out cycle, you should continue the
practice. Novice growers will probably find it a better idea to
maintain the suggested water level so that the nutrient–water
solution remains constant. Then the solution can be drained with
no rinse required.

> *The wick system is described and pictured in section C.1. of this chapter.*

THE HYDRO RINSE

> **When I change the nutrients in my hydro unit, I always pH-
> balance the water I use to rinse the growing medium.
> Another successful grower told me that it's not necessary
> as you're only rinsing, not feeding, the plants. Am I wasting
> my time? My unit's pH is usually around 6.5 and our tap
> water is about 8.5.**
>
> J. T., Rock Springs, Wyoming

THE RINSE WATER AT 8.5 pH is highly alkaline. It should be balanced
before it is used.

Most hydroponic books suggest changing the water and rinsing
the unit every two weeks to a month, but it's really not necessary to
be as thorough as the instruction manuals advise. However, some

growers rinse "just to be safe." When the water is drained from a unit, only an insignificant fraction of the nutrients are left in the medium or the unit. This has little effect on the nutrient or pH levels of the new nutrient–water solution. It is wise to rinse and sterilize between crops.

WETTING AGENTS

I use dishwashing soap to break the surface tension in the water. It makes it "wetter" so that it is easily absorbed in soil. I water by hand and use organic soil and nutrients. What do you think of the use of wetting agents and using detergents?

WAY BACK, Eugene, Oregon

SOAP AND DETERGENT CONTAIN a "wetting agent" to break the surface tension of water. Instead of beading on soil, the water is absorbed by the planting medium. Usually wetting agents are used the first time planting mix is watered. After that the planting medium usually accepts water readily.

To keep your project organic, make sure to use an organic wetting agent. Several organic products are made for horticultural use. If you use a wetting agent regularly, one of these would be better to use than detergent.

PROPER PH

What is best pH level for marijuana?

BETTY CHRONIC, Internet

PH IS A MEASURE of the acidity or alkaline quality of the water or soil. The pH scale runs from 1, which is highly acidic, to 14, which is highly alkaline. Seven is neutral. Every tenth of a point is a significant increase in the pH level. If you are using a hydroponic system, the water's pH should be kept between 6.1-6.3, which is mildly acidic. Soil has a little more latitude, but should be kept within 5.9-6.4. When rockwool is used, keep the pH at the lower end of the recommended measure to counteract rockwool's strong alkalinity.

PH & TOXIC SALTS

My tap water is quite alkaline and I have been adjusting it with pH Down which is composed of phosphoric acid. By using it, am I changing the phosphoric acid (P_2O_5) ratio of my fertilizer solution? Could this result in toxic salt buildup and stress in my plants? When I used rainwater, the stress stopped.

FRESHWATER, Milwaukee, Wisconsin

THE P_2O_5 HAS BEEN raising the ppm of salts in the water. This may have thrown the nutrient ratios so out of balance that the plants showed a toxic reaction. This is most likely to happen if the starting water has more than 400 ppm dissolved solids, or if it is very alkaline. Then the water should be purified using reverse osmosis. An alternative is to use bottled water.

For troubleshooting advice related to pH, see chapter 9, sections B, D, G.

5

OUTDOORS & GREENHOUSE

A. PLANTING & TRANSPLANTING OUTDOORS

B. OUTDOOR BASICS
1. GENERAL PRINCIPLES
2. CARE

C. SEASONS & PLANTING SCHEDULE
1. SPRING
2. FALL
3. WINTER

D. SPECIAL CONDITIONS OUTDOORS
1. TROPICAL CLIMATES
2. DESERT CLIMATES

E. OUTDOOR SUPPLEMENTS
1. ADJUSTING THE SOIL
2. COMPLEMENTARY PLANTING

F. GREENHOUSE GROWING

RELATED TOPICS
Outdoor problems: chapter 9 Troubleshooting, section H
    Outdoor Problems.
Outdoor pests: chapter 10 Pests & Disease.
Camouflaging ideas: chapter 8 Stealth & Safety.
Plant development, including sex, dark cycle, and pruning:
    chapter 6 The Plant Life Cycle.
Ripeness, harvesting and yields: chapter 7 Harvest.

MORE ABOUT
UV outdoors: "UV Light," chapter 2 Lighting Equipment,
    section B Converters/Specialized Lights.
Soil, fertilizer and pH: chapter 4, Indoor Environment,
    section B Soil and section D Water & PH.

A. PLANTING & TRANSPLANTING OUTDOORS

PLANT OR TRANSPLANT

Is it best to sprout seeds indoors and transplant them outdoors or just sow them directly in the ground? After they start growing do you just let nature take its course or do you baby them like indoor plants? When is the best time to start the garden?

THE GRIM REEFER, Tennessee

IT ALL DEPENDS. PLANTS that survive germination and the first few weeks of outdoor living will probably grow larger than plants germinated indoors. That first assumption—surviving the first few weeks—is not always easy to ensure. Further, it is much more efficient to plant only female clones, and they are produced indoors.

Indoors or out, marijuana plants need water, nutrients, light, CO_2 and a well-drained medium. As long as those needs are met, the plant will thrive. If you are fortunate, it requires little effort to supply them to the plant. Other growers must go to great lengths to supply the plants with satisfactory conditions.

TRANSPLANTS

I live in New Hampshire and plan on transplanting some two-month-old plants outside. I'm starting the seedlings under fluorescents and giving them 18 hours of light a day. Should I reduce the number of hours of light I give them before transplanting them outside?

THE PLANT TENDER, New Hampshire

DURING THE SECOND MONTH of growing indoors, bring the number of hours of light down to 16 or 17 so that the plants don't start flowering when they are placed outdoors. They receive about 15½ hours of light outside in late June. Indica, indica-hybrid and other early season plants are most likely to bolt. Sativas are not likely to start flowering early.

The plants may have other problems adjusting to the outdoors. They have been growing under low light conditions of fluorescents as compared with sunlight and they are likely to get burned by the sun's intensity and the UV light that the plants are also sensitive to. Let the plants adjust by first placing them in the shade and then giving them brighter light over a week-long period.

WHEN TO START UP NORTH

I am planning to grow in Alaska. My main concern is the long number of hours of daylight in the summer. At the solstice, June 22, there are about 21 hours of light. It decreases at the rate of 6 minutes a day. I was thinking of starting indoors for three weeks under continuous light and then inducing a head start on flowering by changing their light regimen to 12/12 on/off for a week. They would be transplanted outdoors June 1st.

Can I germinate the seeds outdoors around the end of May? I am planning on using an outdoor mix of indica strains.

Z LAST, Leadville, Colorado

I WOULD START THE seeds indoors early enough so they are fast growing young plants when they are placed outdoors in May. After four to six weeks of growing, start shading the plants in June, blocking all but 12 hours of sunlight. Cover them at the same time each day. Choose a time between 6 and 8 PM. Remove the blackout cloth 12 hours later, in the morning between 6 and 8 AM. The plants will immediately start flowering and will be ready for harvest 60 to 80 days after forcing. They will be blooming while the sun is at its most intense and will ripen before the weather changes and human predators become active.

DAYLIGHT SHOCK TO 24-HOUR PLANTS

Should the clones I am going to plant outdoors grow under continuous fluorescent light, or should I root them under 18 hours of light? Will the shift from 24 hours of light to 14 ¹/₂ when I transplant them outside shock the clones of an early variety into flowering? Can I take cuttings directly to the outdoor garden?

DEAMAS, Shelburne County, Nova Scotia

ALL VARIETIES, ESPECIALLY early and mid-season varieties can have problems moving from indoor continuous light situations to the outdoor regimen, which has only 13-16 hours of daylight. There are two explanations for most problems.

The first is that each strain has a critical dark period: the number of hours of darkness required to tip the plant into flowering. For convenience, we place all varieties under 12 hours of uninterrupted darkness to flower them indoors. However, some plants flower given fewer hours of darkness. For instance, many varieties start to flower outdoors in August when the dark period is 8-11 hours. When the length of darkness is longer than a plant's critical dark period, the plant begins to flower. The only way to prevent flowering is to interrupt the dark period with short periods of light. A bright incandescent light shining for a few seconds every couple of hours during the dark period prevents the plants from triggering into flowering.

Second, plants that usually need a short period of darkness to force flowering, such as indica hybrids, sometimes react to a sudden change of regimen from continual light to 9 or 11 hours of darkness by flowering. Even late-ripening sativas may start growing flowers while they continue growing vegetatively, eventually flowering fully.

Clones grown under a regimen of 18 hours of light with a 6-hour dark period are less likely to be shocked into flowering when they are placed outdoors. A plant with a known critical dark period can be grown under a slightly shorter dark period to maintain vegetative growth during rooting. When it is placed outdoors, it will not be shocked by a dramatic change in light regimen. For instance, a plant that flowers under a dark period of 11 hours or more can be grown vegetatively under a period of 9 hours of darkness and 15 hours of light without fear of it flowering prematurely. It will have a seamless transition to outdoor life.

LATE PLANTING

I am growing a plant that ripens indoors in 56 days. I was just given the opportunity to take some plants to an irrigated garden in the country. It's July 20. Is it too late to plant outdoors? How should I do it?

JOKER 1, Austin, Texas

IT ISN'T TOO LATE. The plants will continue to grow vegetatively for a while and then start to flower. Late planting has several advantages over planting earlier. There is more food around for herbivores, so the plants are less likely to be eaten. The plants will not grow very large so they will be harder to detect and easier to care for.

The plants have to be acclimated to the outdoors gradually. The medium should be kept very moist and the leaves can be sprayed with water. The leaves are sensitive to UV light and you are placing them outdoors during the most UV-intense part of the year.

Anti-transpirant sprays help prevent wilting from stress by covering the leaves' stomata. The sprays help plants make the transition to outdoors from indoors. They are temporary and easy to use.

Another possibility, since you have a long season, is to place the clones outdoors in containers during the day, then bring them indoors during the evening to bask under electric lights. When the plants are larger, leave them outdoors to flower. Or better yet, continue to bring them inside each evening to protect them from nature's whims.

STRESS & BUDS

This fall was our first Vermont crop. We harvested nineteen 6 ½ foot beauties that produced little buds and a multitude of shake leaf. Between germination (mid-May) and harvesting (mid-September), they were transplanted three times. Did the transplanting process shock the plants, inhibiting growth, or did we just seed them too late?

WASTED WILLIAM,
Burlington, Vermont

TRANSPLANTING OFTEN INHIBITS GROWTH a little, but it usually does not delay maturation. However, three moves are a little much for the plants and may have overstressed them. The buds lost a little weight from the transplanting. It is also likely that budding was cut short by the short season and cold nights that encourage ripening.

B. OUTDOOR BASICS

1. GENERAL PRINCIPLES

OUTDOOR GROWTH

I grew some plants in 1-gallon containers indoors. I had to leave town for two weeks so I placed the plants outdoors in July until I returned. Their growth rate increased amazingly. Why did they grow so fast?

SNAPPER HEAD, Ft. Lauderdale, Florida

THE PLANTS GREW FASTER outdoors because they were receiving more intense light. Light powers photosynthesis, the process in which green plants convert CO_2 from the air, and water to create sugar. All plant growth is dependent on sugar, both for energy and tissue building. With more sugars being made, the plant grew faster.

If you plan to continue growing them outdoors, you'd better transplant them to larger containers.

WHICH SIDE OF THE MOUNTAIN?

Does it matter which side of the mountain you plant on?

NICK RANGER, Webster Springs, West Virginia

YES. MARIJUANA THRIVES IN full, unobstructed sun. The south facing side of the mountain receives sun nearly all day. The east and west sides receive direct light in the morning and afternoon, respectively. These plants will not grow as vigorously as the plants on the south side. The north side gets no sun and receives the least light.

COVER OF WOODS

Will marijuana grow well under the cover of woods?

JOE W., Tennessee

IT DEPENDS ON HOW much light penetrates the canopy. Light powers photosynthesis so the more light the plants get, the better they will grow. Indoor plants and plants adapted to high latitudes are more likely to tolerate low light conditions than light-hungry equatorials. Indicas usually do better in the shade than sativas.

With three hours of direct light, the plants will produce skimpy buds. At six hours the plants will have thicker, chunky buds.

LIGHTNING & FLOWERING

Can untimely lightning delay flowering in an outdoor crop?

HAPPY FEET, New York City

CHRYSANTHEMUMS REACT TO LIGHT periods in the same way as cannabis—both are short day plants. They flower based on the number of hours of total uninterrupted darkness the plants receive each night. In marijuana this is 9-12 hours each day.

Studies were conducted on mum flowering for nurseries before automatic controls were developed. The controls received 12 hours of uninterrupted darkness each night during early summer using shading. They produced normal flowers. A second group received the same regimen six nights a week, but the shading was left open on the seventh, subjecting the plants to longer periods of light. A third group had the curtains left open on two consecutive nights. These two groups grew flowers that were respectively $6/7$ and $5/7$ as large as the controls. Ripening was slightly delayed.

Marijuana flowers subjected to occasional interruptions of the light cycle grow airy, lanky buds, and may ripen a little later than normal.

However, the brightness of lightning does not reach a threshold to affect flowering. Consider that a bright full moon doesn't affect it.

I haven't seen any papers or reports indicating that lightning affects flowering time, even in areas where it consistently strikes close during flowering season.

B. 2. OUTDOOR CARE

PLANT IN SHADE

My outdoor plant used to be in direct sunlight, but now in the second week of flowering, I had to move it to the shade because of helicopters. The plant now gets only a few hours of direct sunlight. Will this affect the yield, potency or ripening time? Does the plant need 12 hours of direct sunlight?

THEA, California

MARIJUANA DOES BEST IN full sunlight. In the summer there is more than enough light to fuel marijuana's vegetative growth. However, when the buds are forming in autumn, the intensity of light decreases and the sun's rays are more likely to be blocked because of the sun's low angle.

Growing in the shade, the plant will yield less and the buds will be thinner and airier. They will not be as potent as full sun buds either. They will mature a little earlier, if the daily number of hours of light is shortened by the plant's new position.

PRUNING OUTDOORS

I am growing outdoors. When do I prune the plants? Do I take off all the fan leaves? Do I take off branches too? If I take off some branches, would the other colas on the ones that are left grow bigger?

MERCURY, Internet

THERE ARE SEVERAL REASONS why plants are pruned. The most important reason is for stealth. Pruning a plant to keep the size down or to alter its shape helps to disguise it. Pruning can also improve yield. Short or shaded branches draw resources that would otherwise go to more productive plant parts that are in bright light. Removing the unproductive branches will improve the vigor of the plant and increase the yield of the remaining branches.

Plants should be pruned before they turn from vegetative growth to flowering. Pruning early stops the plant from investing resources in non-productive growth.

Fan leaves are the plant's sugar factories. Sugar fuels both plant metabolism and growth. Removing the shade leaves results in less growth and ultimately, smaller buds. Shade leaves should be clipped off or trimmed only when they block light, the energy source, from getting to the growing buds. If only parts of the leaves are shading the buds, they can be trimmed rather than removed.

> For more on pruning, see "Planting, Pruning & Flowering" in section C. 2 of this chapter.

WATER CONSERVATION, GUERRILLA-STYLE

I live in an area where my outdoor bush garden needs to be irrigated throughout the summer. To save water, I placed a garbage bag at the bottom of each hole I dug to add good soil for my plants. I reasoned that the water and nutrients wouldn't simply drain right through the bottom of the holes. I think it will limit root growth to about a foot deep, but the roots' horizontal growth is unlimited. What do you think?

BUDDY, Internet

I THINK THAT IS a good way of holding water in fast draining soils. As you thought, the roots travel the route of the water and nutrients. Dig the hole just a little deeper, about $1^1/2$ feet. Line the wall with the bag so that it creates a basin about 6 inches deep. When the plant roots reach this pool, they grow water roots that are thicker and don't grow root hairs. Adding gravel, twigs or rockwool to the basin increases its water-holding capacity.

GROWING IN THE PINES

> I grew in a clearing in a pine forest this year, but hiked in my own soil because the forest soil was so acidic. I want to expand the patch this year. Is there something I could use to sweeten the soil? How should I do it?
>
> PINE GROWER, Florida

THE ACIDIC SOIL CAN be prepared for planting a spring crop. Test the soil, and then use the amount of dolomitic limestone recommended by your local nurseryman to lift the soil to a pH of 6.2. Mix the limestone in as soon as possible so it has time to react. You can mix in organic fertilizers at the same time. The soil pH will be more suitable and the nutrients will be available to support the growing plant in two or three months.

C. SEASONS & PLANTING SCHEDULE

SEASON & PLANT MORTALITY

Do plants started outdoors in the early spring have a higher mortality rate than those started later?

K.C., Raleigh, North Carolina

YES. PLANTS STARTED IN early spring are more vulnerable to the forces of nature than those started later in the season. Hungry insects and other pests are more likely to attack the greenery if there isn't much else to eat. The vagaries of spring weather also take their toll on young plants. They are drowned and washed away in heavy rain, and often set back by cold weather.

SOUTHERN SPRING PLANTING

I live in Florida where the summer is very harsh so it would be easier to grow in the spring. How tall or old should plants be before they can survive outside?

A.L., Holiday, Florida

PLANTS THAT ARE PLACED outside between early September and early February and are not subject to light from passing cars or streetlights will begin to flower almost immediately because they receive 11 hours or more of uninterrupted darkness. Indica plants, even very small ones, stop growing soon after they switch from vegetative growth to flowering. They grow 25-50% taller than when they were forced. Sativas continue to grow as they flower until they

133

reach a somewhat larger size, often 4 or 5 feet high. Indica/sativa hybrids grow more than indicas and less than sativas.

Plants can be placed outside at any stage. It depends on how tall you want them to be when they are finished.

Plants that ripen early in the winter can be forced into vegetative growth again using incandescent lamps or a powerful flashlight to break up the night cycle. This is done daily in the middle of the night or at least several hours into darkness and/or before dawn. When the plants have regrown vegetatively they can be forced back into flowering by stopping the daily treatment.

Sativas placed outside through early January or indicas placed out by February will finish flowering in early April. After the buds are picked, plants left in the ground will regrow vegetatively and flower once again in the fall.

On March 22, spring begins and night (the dark period) falls below 12 hours. However, most plants will continue to flower for another month, so there is some leeway in the planting schedule.

To force flowering in the spring, the plants should be shaded each evening and the tarp removed 12 hours later. This must continue throughout the flowering period.

C. 2. FALL

TEMPERATURE & FLOWERING

Does temperature affect the flowering time of outdoor plants? Fall can come early here and nighttime temperatures in the 30's are not uncommon by the end of September. Since flowering doesn't start until mid or late August, we don't usually harvest until the middle of October. Does exposure to low temperature hasten bud maturity and accelerate resin gland production, or does the cold merely slow growth and damage plants and buds?

ANONYMOUS, Wisconsin Rapids, Wisconsin

MARIJUANA IS CONSIDERED A short day plant, which means that it flowers when it receives a long period of uninterrupted darkness daily. Factors that are used by other plants to determine when they flower, such as moisture or temperature, do not affect marijuana flower initiation.

Flower growth and development is affected by both of these factors, however. Low temperatures slow growth, and dry conditions hasten maturity but result in smaller buds. The lower intensity of sunlight and low temperature in autumn slow bud growth because photosynthesis slows as intensity diminishes, and the low temperature slows respiration. At low temperatures the plants are more susceptible to fungal infections, too. Earlier maturity would result in a better crop.

There are three ways that plant maturity can be speeded up. The first and easiest is to find an earlier maturing variety. A short season variety will naturally mature earlier than a later variety. This is by far, the best long-range plan to harvest earlier.

The plants can be forced to flower by increasing the dark period to 12 hours a day. This can be done using a lightproof tarp or cover. If the plants are covered early each evening starting in late July, and the cover is removed each morning, the plants will initiate flowering a few weeks earlier and will ripen in September. By late August, when the plants would ordinarily just be starting to flower, they no longer need to be covered because the longer dark period of late summer would trigger flowering

Aside from a fully ripened bud, there are other advantages to early flowering. Since the plants are blooming during mid-summer, when the light is much more intense than it is in fall, the buds will be considerably larger and tighter. The higher UV-B content of the light (the part that causes tanning) results in higher THC levels. There are fewer human predators looking for bud at this time and the molds of fall, prevalent as the weather cools, are not present.

The third is to pollinate the flowers and harvest just a week later, as the plants are forming seed pods, but before there has been much seed formation. Growers want to harvest before a killing freeze. If this ordinarily occurs September 30 and the plants are three weeks or a month from maturity on September 15, the flowers could be painted with previously collected and stored pollen.

Once the flowers are fertilized, the plants immediately stop producing new flowers and spend their energy on seed production. The pistils dry and recede into the calyx as the fertilized ovary begins to develop into a seed. At this point, before the seed develops a hard shell, the buds are harvested. The glands will be well developed and the buds will look firm and lush.

ED'S TIP ▸ SCHEDULING OUTDOOR PLANTING

Indoor plants placed outdoors between mid-August and September quickly begin to flower because of the long nights. On September 22, the night length is 12 hours, and it grows longer each night. This encourages fast ripening. Fast maturing indoor varieties will ripen outdoors six to eight weeks after transplanting.

Budding cannabis does best in areas that stay above 45° F in the evening and remain sunny in mid autumn. Dense buds growing in cool, foggy or wet areas are susceptible to mold. Tomatoes are a good indicator plant. If they still grow and produce ripe fruit in mid-autumn, then fast-maturing marijuana plants will also mature.

PLANTING, PRUNING & FLOWERING

I live in the central valley of California and normally plant in May. The average summer temperatures are between 85° and 100° F. My plants are 15-foot monsters by October, when nighttime temperatures drop by 50% and flower clusters begin to swell. The commercial marijuana growers around me in the foothills of the Sierras harvest in September when their climate gets cooler earlier, but my plants grow another 4 feet.

My questions are: should I plant later, perhaps in June

or July? How tall should my plants be before I prune? Can early pruning alter the gender of the plant? Is there more flower production on a tall plant than on a severely pruned 6-foot wide plant? Would pruning techniques be the same with indicas as with sativa? They both seem to flower at the same time, around October.

DENNIS, Central Valley, California

THOSE ARE SOME GOOD questions. By planting later in the season you can limit the size of the plants. If the plants grow to 15 feet when they're planted in May, they may grow only half that tall if planted four to six weeks later. This may eliminate the need to prune and entails less risk because the plants are in the ground for a shorter period of time.

The primary purpose of pruning is to keep the plants from being detected by their height. Growers' situations vary, and different varieties of marijuana have different growing habits, so it is hard to generalize about pruning. Trimming the top of the plants will cause the two branches below to elongate and also the plant will bush out. If the plant is still growing too tall, it can be pruned again. One way to encourage bushing is to prune when the plant is $1^1/_2$ feet tall, and again when about 3 feet tall.

If it can be avoided, plants should not be pruned after vegetative growth slows–that will lower the yield. Plants can also be trained to lie low. New growth can be tied down using string attached to the ground or to weights. I saw one plant that was trained into a ground hugger 9 feet in diameter but was only 3 feet tall. Grown plants can be pulled down so that their main stem is nearly parallel to the ground. Sometimes the plants' roots will tear if this procedure is followed. On hot sunny days this may be really traumatic to the plant since it cannot be well watered several hours before and then again immediately after forcing the stem down. The best time to do this is after the sun's energy has begun to wane, or even better, on a cloudy day. A mixable spray, Wilt-Pruf®, available at many nurseries, coats the leaves' stomata so the plant transpires less. This helps prevent wilting. Once the plant has adjusted to its new position, the branches will start to grow vertically.

The gender of marijuana is rarely altered by stress. However, some male flowers may appear as a result of severe stress of heavy pruning. There have been no controlled experiments to see if pruned marijuana yields more. From casual observations I would say that yields remain about the same, though heavily pruned plants usually have less yield.

LATE PLANTING DOWN SOUTH

I live in north Texas. I am planning to plant some seeds in containers indoors around July 15 to plant in the ground in the middle of August. If I keep them in containers I could control the flowering cycle by shading them daily. Or I could just put them in some fertile soil out in the pasture with tomato cages for support. I don't have any neighbors. Is it worth trying?

STACEE, Winnsboro, Texas

IF THE SEEDS ARE planted July 15, the plants will have only a month to germinate and grow before being transplanted. Once they are moved from indoors under 18 or more hours of light to the outdoors in Texas, which offers 14 hours or less, the plants will immediately start to flower. One problem the plants face is the intense sun and heat that evaporates water quickly. The roots must be kept moist and cool so the plants don't wither in the sun.

Make sure the containers are light colored so they reflect the sun's rays. Black or dark green containers get hot and boil the roots. Burlap wound around the containers is one way of keeping them cool. When you water, wet the burlap. This cools the container as the water evaporates.

If you are planning on growing large plants they should be started two to three months before transplanting and the containers should hold 15-30 gallons of planting mix. Smaller plants can be grown in 5-gallon buckets.

LATE PLANTING UP NORTH

It is late July and I was just given two clones of pure indicas, some Jack Herers and a four-way cross of 60- to 80-day indoor plants. Is it too late to plant them outdoors?

JACK, South Shore, New Jersey

NO. IF THE CLONES are planted now, in late July they will continue to grow vegetatively for two weeks to a month depending on the variety and the light regimen they experienced while rooting.

The pure indicas are the first to flower. They may start changing from vegetative soon after planting and ripen in late September. The plants will not grow much before they start flowering. They will have moderate branching and heavy buds distributed throughout the plant. During flowering, they grow another 25%.

> Make sure outdoor containers are light colored so they reflect the sun's rays. Black or dark green containers get hot and boil the roots.

The JH's are a three-way cross between Haze, Northern Lights and Skunk #1. If they are second generation they will vary quite a bit, but all the variations originate from good genetics. First generation JH's flower in the third week in August and finish in early October. After flowering begins, they stretch out another 40-60% and produce a heavy yield from the main top branches. The lower branches produce much smaller buds.

The earlier flowering indoor plants will trigger into flowering within about a week and will be ready in early to mid October. The later maturing plants will take longer to start flowering, two to three weeks, and they will take longer to mature, so they probably won't ripen before cold weather and weak sun become problems. If they were forced now using blackout cloth, they would mature in early October.

The main problem that plants face when they are transplanted in mid-summer is their sensitivity to the harsh sunlight. The plants should be "hardened up" by exposing them first to shade for longer periods each day and then to partial shade and finally to full sun over a week to 10-day period. The best time to plant is late afternoon, after the day's most intense light. A shade cloth or lace cloth can be used to help the plants adjust to the sun's intensity. The plants also need adequate amounts of water so the soil must be kept moist.

A spray-on anti-transpirant, sold in nurseries, helps the plants withstand the shock of flowering. These substances temporarily clog the stomata so less water is transpired, preventing wilting.

EXTREMELY LATE PLANTING

I commute between Philadelphia and Birmingham once a month spending one week in each city. I also get out to nearly abandoned areas where I could plant with absolutely no hassles. My friends all have lots of clones so I could start right now. Is it too late to plant these babies August 15-20 in Philly and the 22-29 in Birmingham? What varieties should I use?

STEREO STEVE, Memphis, Tennessee

IT IS NOT TOO late to plant in either location. One problem that you will have in both locations is adjusting the plants to the intense August sun. This is a critical move and should be done very carefully. First, the plants should be sprayed with an anti-transpirant designed to eliminate transplant shock. (Anti-transpirants clog a plant's stomata so the plant does not transpire as much water.)

If the plants are to remain in containers, they should be transplanted to large ones and placed outdoors in the shade for a few days. Transplant at the end of the day. Loosen the soil around the young plants and water so that the medium is thoroughly moistened. After the plants have adjusted to the new environment, they should be fed with a bloom-type water-soluble fertilizer. Make sure to use a light-colored container. It reflects light rather than absorbs it as heat. The container can be wrapped in cloth, painted or placed in a basket. I like baskets best for outdoor plants, because the basket deals with the sunlight, not the container. There's an air space between basket and container, too. The hot are rises, leaving the container cool.

In Pennsylvania the main concern is getting the buds to ripen before the cold weather comes. Realistically, the plants should be harvested there between October 1 and October 15 depending on micro-climatic conditions.

The plants must start flowering and then ripen in about two months. I would suggest early indica varieties or mostly indica hybrids. These plants will not get very big because they will go into flowering soon after they adjust to their new lighting. They will not fill out much vegetatively while they flower. For this reason the plants can be spaced on 2-foot centers.

In Alabama, you will harvest by November 15. This extra time and more intense sun gives you greater leeway in choosing varieties. Indicas, and indica/sativa hybrids will start to flower almost as soon as they are placed in the ground. They will grow another 25-50% taller and wider. They will mature 60 days after planting. Commercial varieties that will perform include skunks, Northern Lights x Haze, sativa/indica hybrids and sativas. These plants mature later in the season and continue to grow as they mature. They should be spaced about 3 feet apart.

C. 3. WINTER

THC & FROST

What happens to THC when the plant is harvested after the first frost?

NAME WITHHELD, Oneonta, New York

THC IS NOT AFFECTED by frost. However, the plant's tissue can be damaged. Generally, temperatures below 45° F (9° C) affect the plant. Leaves suffer some damage and need to repair themselves before growth or ripening resumes. This may take a few days of good weather. When cold weather continues for several days, the damage is compounded, weakening the plant and lowering its ability to repair itself.

In order to get back on the path towards maturity, the temperature must rise into the 60's and the plants have to get sunshine to provide energy for photosynthesis.

When temperatures slip down to 40° F (4° C), leaves, flowers and other plant parts suffer a bit. It takes a few days for a plant to recover from this damage, and it is unlikely to do so under normal fall conditions because cool weather is usually associated with cloudy skies. This limits the energy available to the plant so bud maturation and THC production is curtailed. Eliminating THC production saves the plant energy, especially when the substance is not needed as much to protect from insects and UV light.

Under these conditions the THC already produced by the plant is not destroyed by frost, but there is no new production.

Unless there is a real possibility of warm weather in the near future, harvest the plants.

PROTECTED PLANT

D. SPECIAL CONDITIONS OUTDOORS

FLORIDA SAND

> I grow in straight worm castings in Tampa, Florida. What's
> the best kind of drainage during the monsoon rains? Does
> the rain have anything to do with the yellowing of my
> leaves? Should I use organic or chemical fertilizers?
>
> BRIAN, Tampa, Florida

WET, WARM SOIL QUICKLY digests organic matter because the micro-
life works faster at high temperatures. Expect compost and manure
to decompose over the season. As they are digested, microorganisms release some of the nutrients. However, as they become water
soluble, they may be washed away in a heavy rain.

Yellowing bottom leaves are an indication of nitrogen deficiency. To remedy this you will have to feed the garden with water-soluble fertilizers high in nitrogen.

Next season you can prevent this by mixing time-release fertilizers in the soil. Use less fertilizer than recommended in the instructions because in hot, moist soil the fertilizer releases its ingredients
faster than stated on the package.

> *For more on yellowing leaves, see chapter 9, section B.2.*

HAWAIIAN GROWING

> I live in Hawaii, where the weather is ideal for plants
> around the year. The island has strange seasons. There is

one long season, beginning in April and going through
September or longer, and then a continuous short season
through the end of March. When should I plant and what
varieties should I use?

DA KINE, Maui, Hawaii

THERE ARE LOTS OF possibilities. During the short season you can
grow sativas, sativa/indica crosses, and indicas. Sativas such as
Colombian and Thai come from latitudes close to the equator and
are adapted to small or no variation in day length. However, they
respond to dark periods of more than 12 hours. The plants flower as
they grow. As the days get shorter and they reach a height of 3-4
feet, more of their energy goes into flowering. Sativas from higher
latitudes such as Mexico and Jamaica also flower as they grow but
mature earlier.

Sativa/indica hybrids vary in their response to darkness. Plants
in the mid-range, for instance, indica/sativa F1 hybrids, receive half
their genes from each parent. They continue to flower as long as the
dark period remains longer than 11 hours per day. After April 1-15
these plants will stop flowering and start growing vegetatively
again. They may pop some flowers once in a while, but will not
flower again until the early fall. Once their flowers ripen they can be
coaxed back into vegetative growth by breaking the dark cycle
nightly using an incandescent light from a bright flashlight. It has
to be shined on all the plant branches several hours into darkness.
Once the plant reaches the right size it can be flowered again as
long as the dark period remains 12 hours or longer.

Indicas originated in Afghanistan and the neighboring countries in the Himalayas. This area, like most of the hash producing
regions, is at the 30th parallel. These plants begin to flower when
the dark period is about 10 hours, late July in Afghanistan. As soon
as they are outdoors during the short season, they will begin to
flower and will stop growing. The buds may be a little on the small
side as the plant ripens quickly under these long night conditions.
Some Hawaiian growers use a light system to get the plants to the
right size and then place them outdoors to ripen.

During long season, it is still possible to get some buds. Hawaii is at about the 15th parallel. Even during the peak of summer, June 22, Hawaii receives 10 hours or more of darkness. Indicas planted outdoors just before the peak will get a chance at growing before the long nights force them to flower. The will ripen in late August or early September.

During the long season most sativas grow vegetatively. They won't begin to flower until late September and will ripen eight to ten weeks later. Some sativas have the potential to grow into very big plants. Hawaii provides a good environment for plants to reach large size. Northern-adapted sativas will begin to flower in mid-July and will ripen by the beginning of September because of the short daylight hours in Hawaii even in mid-summer.

Mid-range sativa/indica hybrids start to flower in late August through late September and ripen six to eight weeks later, in October and November.

All of these varieties can be planted in late summer so that their size and exposure to peril is limited

Many of the indoor varieties, especially the fast ripening ones are mostly indica that have been adapted to the lower light levels of indoor cultivation. These plants will grow bud even when partially shaded from the tropical sun.

RAINFOREST GROWING

I am trying to produce some resinous plants on the edge of the rainforest. The rain stunts resin production. What can I do?

HARRY BOY, Princeville, Hawaii

THE MAIN REASON THAT THC levels are lower in the rainforest is the lower amount of UV light that the plants receive. Make sure that the plants get unobstructed rather than filtered light during midday, when UV levels are highest. Another problem is the rain knocking off the glands from the plant. If the plants can be protected with a cover during rainstorms, the glands will be able to accumulate.

TEXAS HEAT

I live in central Texas, where it gets very hot during the summer. If I were to plant on the east side of some steep cliffs would this help protect my plants from the heat? They would still be getting all of the morning sun but it would get dark a little earlier. Would this also make them flower any earlier?

CARMEN, Waco, Texas

THE PLANTS WILL BE protected from the sun's harshest rays and the area will stay cooler if it is shaded all afternoon. The plants will not be as big as they would get if they had full sun all day and adequate moisture. They will probably ripen a week or two earlier than if they had been growing in full sun because the shaded area will darken 20 minutes earlier.

GROWING IN HEAT

I live in the southwestern Arizona desert, where it is not uncommon for the sun to reach 115-120° F.

I have grown plants for two years and when I first started growing, I would keep them outside in full sunlight and the sun killed my pot plants by June. The only way I found to keep my plants from dying was to keep them shaded from the East so they received direct sunlight only from 2-7 PM.

Is there any way to protect plants from the terrible dehydrating sun?

K. A., Yuma, Arizona

CLEAR SKIES AND DRY, hot climates need not be stressful to marijuana. The plants in your garden probably died because they could not obtain enough water or because they had shallow roots, which fried in the hot upper portion of the soil.

If the plants are well watered so that the water penetrates deeply into the medium, the roots will follow it down. The deeper soil layers are not subject to the radical temperature changes found in the upper layers.

During the summer, the soil must never be allowed to dry out. The roots draw water that is transpired by the leaves. Should the water source dry up, the leaves start to lose the water from their cells. They lose their turgidity and they wilt. As the drying continues, the cells die. Even a slight wilt due to water stress hurts the plants. If the plants are not watered, they die in a matter of hours.

During the hottest part of the day, although the plant has enough water, sometimes its leaves droop a little. This is a normal reaction. It may be a protective measure that the plant uses. When the sun is too intense for the leaf, it changes its angle in relation to the sun by wilting a little so that it receives less light.

Plants grown in partial shade under these conditions do well, as you experienced. The soil is not as likely to go through radical temperature changes, and the plants receive enough light to grow well and yield. Even indirect light may provide enough intensity in some unclouded areas to grow plants that have a decent yield.

There are some commercial products available that may be of interest to gardeners cultivating in sunny, hot, dry climates.

Anti-transpirants are sprayed on the leaves to slow water loss during stressful periods. The directions recommend it for transplanting and during stressful climatic conditions such as hot, dry winds. These products are available at many nurseries.

Water-holders are made from starch or polymers. They look like corn flakes and are lightweight when dry. They are mixed into the soil. When they come into contact with water they puff up to hundreds of times their weight in water. One tablespoon of flakes holds 6-8 ounces of water. As the soil dries, the particles release their moisture. The soil stays moist longer and less water is lost.

E. OUTDOOR SUPPLEMENTS

1. ADJUSTING THE SOIL

BALANCING THE SOIL

The soil in my area has a very high alkaline content. How do I adjust the soil?

K.L., El Centro, California

ALKALINE SOILS ARE ADJUSTED using sulfur, which is acidic. They can also be neutralized using acidic organic materials such as coffee grounds, manure, cottonseed meal, pine needles and citrus rind.

First measure the pH and then ask a local nurseryman for recommendations to adjust it.

> For info on pH, see chapter 4, section D.
> For more on soil, see chapter 4, section B.

ORGANIC FERTILIZERS

Is it a good idea to work organic fertilizers into the ground in the fall and let them decompose over the winter for planting in the spring?

JOHN S., Illinois

YES. WORKING ORGANIC FERTILIZERS into the soil in the fall will improve the fertility and quality of the soil. A compost pile of organic debris can be powered using a high nitrogen fertilizer such as coffee grounds, manure, cottonseed meal or fish emulsion fertilizer. The nitrogen is used by bacteria and is converted into organic matter as the pile shrinks into a rich compost.

MANURE STOCKPILE

If I dug a big hole this fall and filled it full of manure, would it be good enough to grow a plant in next year?

JOE W., Tennessee

OVER THE WINTER THE manure will compost and will support a plant's nutritional need. However, the compost may be too acidic for marijuana unless lime is added. Mix 5 parts fresh or dried leaves and other vegetative debris with 1 part manure to speed up the process. The mix is limed after it has composted.

URINE

Is human urine good for plants?

FRANK J., Newport, New Jersey

URINE CONTAINS LARGE AMOUNTS of nitrogen and is used by plants to support growth. The composition of urine varies according to diet, but a typical rating is 0.5-0.003-0.003 N-P-K (5,000-30-30 ppm). It is quite concentrated as fertilizer. Dilute it at the ratio of 5 parts water and 1 part urine. It also contains many trace elements, hormones and enzymes. The nitrogen is available immediately in the form of urea or uric acid.

Urine, unlike feces, is generally considered free of pathogens and is safe to use without processing. Obviously, use it on outdoor plants only.

GROWING IN CORN

There are cornfields near my house. Is growing marijuana in a cornfield a good idea?

CHRIS, Palatine, Illinois

THERE ARE SEVERAL THINGS to consider when making a decision about cultivating: horticultural suitability and stealth.

Corn and hemp both grow well in nutrient-rich, well-drained soils under full sun. Most cornfields are fertilized with chemical fertilizers, which most hydroponic gardeners use, too. There is enough space between the rows of corn so the plants have a chance to grow well. Some fields are treated with herbicides that kill plants including cannabis.

Will the plants be detected? Even if they're hidden at ground level, they may stand out from the air. It is really incredible how clearly every little thing can be seen from 1,000 feet in a small plane or a balloon. It is probable that cannabis can be seen from the air. Then the question comes up, is it a weed or planted? Concealment and camouflage are a state of mind. If no one is nosey or suspicious, the plants can be out in the open. However, prying neighbors can trace pebbles in the cornfield.

How safe are you? Will someone say, that hippie living next to the field has buds hanging on a line across his kitchen and the trail leads from his house to the patch in the middle of the corn? Do you have a way in and out? Are people looking? Does the law fly the fields? Can you do the time?

F. GREENHOUSE GROWING

OFF-SEASON GREENHOUSE

I was thinking about constructing a greenhouse to produce plants off-season, primarily in the spring. Would this work? How can I heat it during cool spells?

REAL, Eureka, California

SPRING CROPS ARE OFTEN easier to produce than other season's harvests. Insects usually aren't much of a problem and cops and robbers are not on the prowl. During the early spring the light intensity is a little low, but it gets stronger as the plants flower.

Design the greenhouse with blackout curtains, which are used to regulate the number of hours of light the plants receive. White/black polyethylene plastic is an excellent material for this. The white side reflects the light, keeping the greenhouse cool, and the black side prevents light from penetrating.

The greenhouse will be heated through the greenhouse effect during the day, but at night it will lose heat unless it's insulated. You could put black painted barrels filled with water along the north wall. They warm up from sunlight during the day and release heat at night. They

> Blackout curtains can be used in greenhouses to regulate the number of hours of light the plants receive.

are entirely passive and require no power. A propane or LP-fired heater on a thermostat would also keep the greenhouse cozy. It's best if the temperature doesn't dip below 50° F.

During the day the sun warms the greenhouse, so it will need to be ventilated to keep the temperature in the low 80's. This will occur daily in late spring. Movable sides or a movable roof that can be opened during the day create appropriate ventilation.

GREENHOUSE YIELDS

I am considering growing in a greenhouse in Arizona. What do you think the yield would be compared to indoor growing?

ANONYMOUS, Phoenix, Arizona

IN ARIZONA, WHERE IT is sunny most of the time, growing in a greenhouse would be a good way of harnessing sunlight rather than using artificial light. Sunlight is more intense than electric light, and produces incredible growth.

The greenhouse should have blackout curtains so that plants can be forced to flower at any time. The light is going to create a lot of heat so the structure will require adequate ventilation and cooling. In the dry heat of Arizona, a misting system or greenhouse cooling/humidifying fan will supplement the ventilation system and moveable sides or roof.

LOW-LIGHT GREENHOUSE

What can we do about the low light levels we have here in Holland?

HANS W., Amsterdam, The Netherlands

THE LIGHT CAN BE supplemented using artificial lighting or innovative designs. During low-light days, sunlight can be supplemented with metal halide or high pressure sodium lamps applied during the brightest part of the days so that the combination of lights creates a high intensity. Usually no more than 5 hours of supplemental light is needed daily. Light sensors can be used to regulate lighting. Plant growth and yield will be increased significantly using an automated system.

To increase the natural light entering the greenhouse, the north wall should be covered with reflective material. A reflector above the north wall of the greenhouse can be used to deflect light back into it.

Low-light greenhouses often suffer from cool soil, and this slows plant growth. If soil heaters were used to keep the temperature in the low 70's, or the plants are kept above the ground in containers or a hydroponics system, the growth rate would increase.

A CO_2 system designed to get the gas right to the plant canopy would increase the growth rate, especially during bright days. It could turn on only when the light reaches a high intensity.

GREENHOUSE FLOWER FORCING

I was in the greenhouse business for almost 20 years. During that time I grew thousands of mums (chrysanthemum plants). What I would like to know is – can I force pot plants like I did my mum plants? I would like to plant pot plants in 4-foot-wide beds that are 50 feet long. My plan is to plant April 15th, pinch two weeks later, and use block cloth two weeks after that. (The cloth would block light from 5 PM until 8 AM). I plan on pulling males as soon as possible to give the females more space.

B. J., North Carolina

THE THEORY IS GOOD, but your technique might need to be adjusted. Space the plants closer and avoid pinching, which sets the plants back a week or so. Each plant will produce a little less, but have bigger bud. Overall, production for the space is increased.

From April 15 to May 15, use periodic lighting (5 minutes every hour – incandescents are okay) to break up the dark period. This prevents premature flowering or sexual deviation caused by long night periods during germination.

Let the plants go for 6 weeks to 2 months until forcing flowering, and keep shading throughout the flowering period. Even with careful investigation, expect some seeding from stray males. Perhaps next year the garden can be all-female clone starts, which are a lot less trouble than a mixed sex garden.

TOXIC GREENHOUSE

I had the soil in my greenhouse tested (in Holland), and the service reported that it contained unacceptably high levels of dissolved salts and also lots of sulfur. How did this stuff get there, and what can I do about it?

ANONYMOUS, Amsterdam, The Netherlands

THE WATER TABLE IS regulated in Holland using pumps and dams and is usually kept at about a half-meter (18 inches) below ground level. Any fertilizers added to the soil tend to stay right where they are rather than draining as they would with a lower groundwater level. As the fertilizer is added for crop after crop, the salt level builds up. Another factor affecting the soil is dairy herds. The soil often suffers from manure contamination. Such high levels of manure are dropped in the fields that nitrogen and other salts build up to high levels. The cows are also fed salt, and this is evacuated in the urine, which increases the sodium chloride levels in the soil.

The sulfur was contained in the fertilizers and may also result from its repeated use as a fungicide. Commercial growers in your area sometimes have the soil leached. First, large holes are dug in the ground and then the soil is flooded with uncontaminated water. The water fills the holes and is pumped out. The dissolved salts are removed with the water. This is a costly process. Instead, you could try growing in units above the ground level. Either standard containers or hydroponic units work well.

TOO TALL FOR GREENHOUSE

I planted some seeds in my greenhouse in late June. It's now late August, the plants are beginning to flower and they are hitting the ceiling of the structure. My questions are:
 1. **Will the plants cease vertical growth as they flower?**
 2. **Will they have time to finish up or are they starting to flower too late?**

DANIEL, Moline, Illinois

THE PLANTS CONTINUE TO grow as they flower, about two feet. Rather than clipping the budding parts from the plant, try bending the branches so that they run horizontally rather than vertically. This is done most easily by using a strong vertical stake in the ground with several horizontal slats which form crosses. The plants' stem and branches are tied to the stake.

Another idea is to bend the entire plant down and then tie it to a tent stake secured in the ground. Stems can be bent at 90° F and then held up by a stake so that they don't break at the pinched spot.

The plants should be finished flowering in about six weeks, by mid-October. They should have no problem finishing up in a greenhouse at that time.

LIGHTING A SHED

I am planning to grow in a shed and was going to place some lamps in it. I plan to replace the roof with green translucent fiberglass material to give the garden more light. Will this benefit me or will I lose light through the roof?

BRUCE, Tampa, Florida

GREEN FIBERGLASS IS THE exact wrong material to use since it filters out the light spectrums most useful to the plants, red and blue. Plants do not use green light, they reflect it. Instead, replace it with white translucent fiberglass panels that allow red and blue spectrums to pass through. During the spring and summer, no additional lights will be needed. To maximize the light, make sure to cover all interior surfaces with reflective material or paint the interior white.

To regulate the flowering cycle, blackout curtains are used to force the plants to flower during long days. To keep plants growing vegetatively during short days, hang a string of incandescent lights figured at about 10 watts per square foot or one 100-watt bulb every square yard above the plants. These lights are turned on using a timer for a few minutes every few hours during the dark period. The few minutes of light prevents flowering.

GROWING IN AN UNINSULATED SHED

I'm growing in a shack using both hydroponics and some containers with soil. The shed has no insulation and gets cold when the lights are out. Temperatures outside get into the 30's in October and 20's in November. Can I use heating cables to keep the soil or water warm? What is the coldest temperature a plant can handle effectively?

PA-POP, Hershey, Pennsylvania

THE COLDEST TEMPERATURES THAT maturing plants can handle without tissue damage is in the mid-40's. However they will survive a dive into the 30's and take a few days to get their vigor back.

Why don't you insulate the shed? You could also then turn the lights on at night rather than during the day. That way the shed will be heated by the sun during the day and the lights at night.

Heating the roots is another good way to keep the plants healthy in cold weather. Using heat cables, heating mats and water heaters, you can keep the temperature at about 80° F. The upper part of the plants will withstand temperatures 5-10 degrees lower than they ordinarily would.

6

THE PLANT LIFE CYCLE: VEGETATIVE TO FLOWERING STAGE

A. SEXING: MALES & FEMALES

B. PRUNING

C. WHEN TO FORCE

D. LIGHTING CYCLES

1. VEGETATIVE
2. FORCING FLOWERS
3. LIGHT POLLUTION/DARK PERIOD

E. CHANGING CONDITIONS: VEGETATIVE TO FLOWERING

F. CYCLE PROBLEMS

RELATED TOPICS
Hermaphroditism: chapter 11 Genetics & Breeding,
    section B Hermaphrodites.
When to take clones: chapter 1 Seeds & Clones, section B.1
    Cloning Methods; chapter 7 Harvest, section C
    Revegetation & Mothers.
Lighting: chapter 2 Lighting Equipment.

MORE ABOUT
Pruning: chapter 7 Harvest, section C Revegetation &
   Mothers; chapter 5 Outdoors & Greenhouse.
Cycle Problems: chapter 9 Troubleshooting; chapter 10
   Pests & Disease.
Sexing seeds/seedlings: chapter 1 Seeds & Clones, section
   A.1 Seeds & Genetics.

A. SEXING: MALES & FEMALES

WHAT ABOUT SEX

What determines the sex of a plant? Is sex determined by the genes contained in the seed or by environmental factors, such as heat, light or stress in which the plant is grown?
DOWN UNDER DOPERS, New Farm, QLD, Australia

MARIJUANA IS UNIQUE AMONG annuals in having male and female characteristics on separate plants. Its other sexual characteristics are unusual, too. For the most part, its sex is determined by x and y chromosomes. However, there is also an autosomal response, which has an effect.

In addition to sexual information found on the x- and y- chromosomes, the other chromosomes, called autosomes, also affect sexual response. Some of the DNA in these autosomes gets turned on only under certain circumstances. Stress could be one of those events.

Marijuana's sex can be altered using chemicals. Treatment with ethylene, a plant hormone, results in a higher percentage of female plants. Gibberellin, another plant hormone, induces male flowers on female plants. These chemicals mimic natural plant chemicals used to express gender change.

My theory is that most marijuana plants are genetically male or female. However, certain stress conditions such as long dark regimens at germination, irregular lighting regimens during flowering, drought or nutrient stress, turns on DNA in the autosomes and induces maleness. Studies show that under stress conditions a higher proportion of males and hermaphrodites are produced in a given population. Some female marijuana plants are naturally hermaphrodites. Their autosomes are turned on all the time so they produce reproductive organs of both sexes.

For a more detailed explanation of this phenomenon see "Fiber

161

Hemp in the Ukraine, 1991", by Hennick, de Meijer and van der Werf, in the book *Hemp Today*, 1994 (Quick American Archives).

> *For more on genetics, see chapter 11.*

DETERMINING SEX

How can I determine the sex of my plants before they are full grown?

BUD HUR, McKeesport, Pennsylvania

SOMETIMES PLANTS GROW A single flower at the node, the juncture of leaf and stem, weeks before the plant starts to flower. This flower indicates the plant's sex. It is easiest to view with a small photographer's loupe or magnifying glass.

Marijuana flowers when it receives a regimen of 12 hours of uninterrupted darkness each day. The age or development of the plant does not matter, so any plant, whether seedling or well developed will flower if it is subject to this pattern.

> *For more on sexing, see chapter 1, section A.*

EARLY SEXING

My small greenhouse garden is mostly sunlit, but the light is supplemented with a 1,000-watt HPS lamp. I plan to grow plants to about 3 feet and then to force them to flower in the spring. Should I turn back the light to sex the plants? I'm afraid that putting the plants into flowering and then back into vegetative will slow them down and perhaps mess them up sexually. How can I sex the plants without putting everything into flowering?

BACON, Albuquerque, New Mexico

SEXING WHOLE PLANTS EARLY sets their growth back several weeks and can mess up their sexual expression. An effective way of determining sex is to use a proxy. Take a couple of cuttings from each of the young plants once they develop side branches.

Tag each clone and the plant from which it came from. Prepare the cuttings for cloning. Place the tray of clones under a light regimen of 16 hours of uninterrupted darkness and 8 hours of light daily. The clone material will indicate sex in 7-10 days. Each clone will have the same sex as its clone mother.

ED'S TIP ▸ **SEXING**

The question growers most often ask me is "How can I tell a male plant from a female plant?"

Male and female marijuana plants look different as they prepare to flower. The male, which is often the more vigorous plant during the vegetative stage, begins to elongate and starts to grow a flower spike that will tower over the females. Left undisturbed, the sacs on the spike will open and drop the pollen over the females. The plant looks thinner and less vigorous as the flower sacs mature. The flower buds look like little sacs hanging off the flower spikes. As the male buds mature, they open into little five-petaled flowers.

As the female plant prepares for flowering, the stem gets stockier and the spaces between the leaves (internodes) shorten, giving the plant more strength to hold the heavy flowers and seeds that are soon to develop. The female flowers have no petals, just two hairs (pistils) that stand out and try to capture any pollen floating in the air.

Both the pistils and the young male buds can be seen before flowering if the plants are looked at carefully. It's easier to identify the sex using a magnifying glass or photographer's loupe. Individual early flowers sometimes grow in the joint between the leaf and stem near the top of the plant. Once a plant is determined to be male, remove it

from the garden. Even a single male plant can pollinate a crop. Be vigilant in your search for stray males. Fertilized female flowers will soon produce seed.

FEMALE   MALE

Photos by Ed Rosenthal

MALE/FEMALE SMELLS

I was smelling a friend's vegetative plants by running my hands over the leaves and then smelling them. The plants we knew to be female smelled much more skunky than the males. The males just smelled green.

Is this a good way to test unknown plants? It seems logical to me since females produce more resin than males, they should smell stronger.

FEELING UP DA BUD, Alaska

THIS IS AN EXCELLENT observation and deserves investigation. However, breeders often look for a fragrant male to cross with their females, as they are considered the best candidates to produce potent females.

Your method would preserve most females and the most potent, or at least resinous, males. It would eliminate dud females and most males. This is a very good approach to pre-sexing.

Readers should be interested in trying this technique. Without destroying anything, the smelly plants can be marked. When they flower, you can see how accurate you were.

MALE FLOWER ALERT

I noticed some very small bright yellow flower petals in the middle of buds that are eleven weeks into the flowering stage. When I squeezed one some fine powder was left on my finger. Are these male flowers? They are on about 90% of the buds.

ZZ, Internet

YOUR SUSPICIONS ARE CORRECT. Those five-petaled, cream-colored flowers are males. The plants are very ripe and ready to be picked. Some varieties develop male flowers just as they ripen. It can be considered a ripeness notice telling you that it's time to harvest. This is not cause for alarm, just an indicator that the buds are at the last stage of ripeness.

MALE PLANTS

READER TIP
TEMPERATURE & MALE FLOWERS

I have been studying my plants' flowering for a while now and have found out some interesting information about flowering. When the temperature in my garden falls below 55° F (13° C), the male flowers do not open. As soon as the temperature increases, the flowers open.

Also, I have been able to preserve pollen for later fertilization by placing it in glassine bags in a glass container and freezing it. I have stored it for up to 3 months with no seeming loss of fertility or genetic problems.

THE DOO-DAH MAN, Rotterdam, Holland

SAFETY IN DISTANCE

What is the minimum distance that you can place a lone male plant from your female plants without causing pollination?

NAME WITHHELD, Seligman, Missouri

CANNABIS IS A WIND-FERTILIZED plant. The pollen floats in the air and a very small percentage of it comes in contact with the females. Prodigious quantities of pollen are produced to ensure adequate pollination.

Indoors, male plants will fertilize females kept in the same room with them. Outdoors, pollen can travel for miles. However, it becomes so dispersed that at distances greater than 500 feet, only an occasional seed will result. The pollination rate depends on airflows. Female plants upwind of a nearby male may not be pollinated.

UNWANTED MALES

> When you tell us to remove the male plants from the females, do you actually mean to throw them away or to move them to a different room? Don't they have any potency of their own?
>
> VEE, Illinois

MALE PLANTS DO HAVE some potency, but the disadvantages of keeping them around usually outweigh their potential value, except for seed production.

Male plants produce much less smoking material per unit of space than females. The smoke is not very valuable–it is more like leaf and is usually not as potent as the female.

A single flowering male can destroy an entire sinsemilla garden. The flowers sometimes seem to appear overnight, so the plants must be carefully watched. The only use for males is to pollinate female plants for seed.

MOSTLY HERMAPHRODITES

> I am growing a garden indoors. I am using clones from my outdoor plants, which had no hermaphroditism but the majority of my plants are hermaphrodites. What should I do?
>
> Almost every female has at least a few small bulbs, which will become male flowers. I have removed them. Will they appear again? The seeds are from southern Italy. I used a 15-10-15 fertilizer in vegetative and now I use a 5-20-30. The plants are growing in a dark humus-compost.
>
> LJUBO, Croatia

THE VARIETY YOU ARE growing is apparently not adapted to indoor conditions and the plants' hermaphroditism is a sign of stress.

Getting a crop of sinsemilla from hermaphroditic plants is difficult, but it can be done. Each plant should be inspected daily for male flowers, which should be removed before they open. Marijuana is wind pollinated and even the slightest draft carrying the pollen of a single male flower can ruin a good portion of the crop.

The few plants that did not produce male flowers should be used as clone mothers for the indoor crop. Even though the plants are flowering, cuttings can be taken. They should be placed under constant light and they will revert to vegetative growth.

Seeds from these plants are from plants that express themselves only as females outdoors. There are no males. Thus these seeds would produce female non-hermaphroditic plants outdoors.

SLIGHTLY POLLINATED

What happens when a young flower gets slightly pollinated? Will it continue to flower or will the developing seeds take most of the plant's energy?

RICHARD, Shreveport, Louisiana

SLIGHTLY POLLINATED COLAS (clusters of buds) usually continue to grow and produce new stigmas. If only a few pistils were touched, then the seeds will form; otherwise, the rest will be just like sinsemilla. These are the proverbial buds with just two or three seeds.

If only a single bud was pollinated, the rest of the buds would continue growing as sinsemilla.

When many of the pistils are pollinated, much of the plant's energy goes into producing seed and the flowers suffer for it. New flower production slows and may stop. If the flowers were just starting to develop and were pollinated, flower production will slow for 15-20 days while the seeds are being produced. However, flower production may pick up again as the seeds mature and the plant uses less energy producing them.

B. PRUNING

SHOULD PLANTS BE PRUNED?

Should I trim or prune the plants?

N<small>O NAME</small>, Place Unknown

W<small>HEN MARIJUANA PLANTS ARE</small> given a chance to grow indoors before they flower, they produce many branches. Each of them will eventually produce a bud. However, the plant's resources are stretched. By trimming the plant and eliminating some of the growing points, the plant puts its energy into fewer branches. The result is fewer, but much larger, high quality buds and more grade-A smoke.

Any fan leaves casting shadows on growing buds should also be removed so the buds can get light energy to grow.

HOW MUCH TO PRUNE

Can you tell me about pruning branches and shade leaves on indoor plants?

B<small>UDD</small>, Internet

T<small>HE BEST PRODUCTION COMES</small> from well-pruned plants whose energy is concentrated in fewer branches, or leads. Branching is more pronounced in some varieties than others. Side branches start at the leaf node, develop a bit and then produce their own side branches.

If the plants have started branching, cut back weak side branches a week or two before forcing flowering. The remaining branches shouldn't interfere with each other. Shade leaves that shield new growth from the light should also be removed. Looking down at the canopy, the first few inches of buds should have just small leaves so that the lower portion of the canopy, under the first 5 inches, gets light.

▶ **PRUNING**

When marijuana plants are given a chance to grow indoors before they flower, they produce many branches. Each of them eventually produces a bud. However, this stretches the plant's resources. Trimming the plant to eliminate the weaker growing points forces the energy into fewer branches. The result is fewer, but much larger, high quality buds and more grade-A smoke.

Any fan leaves casting shadows on growing buds should also be removed so the buds can get light energy to grow.

PRUNING FOR A SINGLE STEM

How can I make my plant grow straight up like a rod?
CURIOSITY GROWER,
Modesto, California

THE SIDE BRANCHES grow from the joint between the leaf and the stem. Remove them with a blade, scissors or by twisting between thumb and forefinger. Without the side branches, the plant puts all of its energy into the main branch.

BETTER YIELD WITH BUSHIER PLANTS?

Does cutting the plant back to make it bushier increase the yield?

AMATEUR GROWER, West Palm Beach, Florida

IT DEPENDS ON TWO things: the variety of plant and the amount of time before the plants go into flowering. Unpruned sativa plants such as Mexicans and Colombians grow symmetrically into a conical Christmas-tree shape. The lowest pairs of branches are the longest ones, stretching out so that the leaves reach light. The next sets of branches face the bottom branches at a 90-degree angle, and are slightly shorter, maximizing the amount of light the leaves receive. This pattern follows up the stem. The interesting thing about this pattern is that each of the mature branches contains approximately the same length of leaf and bud. Looking down at one of these plants, one observes that the plant captures every bit of sunshine, letting no light touch the ground.

Some indicas grow only short side branches from the main stem while others have a bushier profile. The short side-branched plants don't bush when pruned, but grow several asymmetrical top branches. Indica plants that grow into a rounded bush capture all the light in their perimeter.

> Trimming the plant to eliminate the weaker growing points forces the energy into fewer branches, which results in fewer but much larger, high quality buds.

Marijuana varieties react in different ways to pruning. Most sativas and sativa/indica hybrids branch out when their main stem is cut. If the top branches are pruned several times, the plants become bushy. The pruned plants produce many more growing tips than the unpruned, and each of these tips produces a bud. However, the buds grow smaller and may be lower quality because the plant is spreading its resources.

Indoors, plants should be pruned. Lower buds that receive little light remain small and produce grade-B bud. They can be pruned during the first two weeks of flowering. This opens up the bottom of the plants to air circulation and directs more resources to the top buds. Plants that encroach upon a neighbor's canopy may be trimmed to keep them from getting unruly.

The length of time before the plants begin flowering affects their response to pruning. Conically shaped plants can be trained to bush out by trimming the top of the plant at the fourth or fifth set of leaves. Two main stems then grow with a bit of side branching. Clipping the main stems after they grow another four sets of leaves encourages bushiness. One last pruning gives the plant a completely rounded look. The growth that this requires, twelve to fifteen sets of leaves, takes from $1^{1}/_{2}$- 3 months. If the last pruning is performed too late in the season, the plants will not have time to grow vigorous new growing tips. This will result in smaller buds and reduced harvest. Pruning should end several weeks before the plants receive critical length of dark period that triggers flowering.

Indoor varieties that have the genetics to grow big buds can be trimmed to a few branches that grow larger, tighter, higher quality buds. Sometimes the buds get so heavy that the branches must be supported using stakes, netting or support string hung from above.

TRAINING CANNABIS

Can you train cannabis to grow like a vine? How do I do it?
FELLOW POT SMOKER, Los Angeles, California

MARIJUANA IS NOT A vine, but it can be trained to look like one. It is done by tying the branches to fence or wire as they grow. Indoors, tying taller plants to horticultural plastic fencing keeps them two-dimensional. This conserves space and makes sure that shorter plants' light is not blocked. It also changes their shape so that they are not conspicuous as cannabis.

Once a branch is tied down, the new growth changes direction and starts growing up, against gravity. Branches will grow from many of the nodes of the tied down branch.

C. WHEN TO FORCE

WHEN TO CHANGE THE LIGHT

How many days do I leave my light on 24 hours? When do I cut back to 18/6 and finally 12/12 for budding?

BUD BROTHER, Bismarck, North Dakota

THE CANNABIS PLANTS IN your garden are all short day plants. They flower when the number of hours of uninterrupted darkness they receive reaches a critical number, usually 8-12 hours, which indicates the coming of autumn outdoors. When the plants don't receive a critical number of hours of uninterrupted darkness, they continue to grow vegetatively.

Plants can be forced to flower at any size. Rather than using a time schedule to determine when to cut back the light, their size might be the determining factor. Indoor varieties vary in how much they grow after forcing—they may increase another $1/3$ to $2/3$ in height from their height at forcing.

There is no reason to have an intermediate 18/6 regime. This slows growth because a 25% reduction in does nothing to promote flowering. When the plants are the right size for forcing, cut the light back to 12 hours, so the plants receive 12 hours of uninterrupted darkness each day.

WHEN TO FLOWER

I have been growing my seedlings in a wick system set-up for almost a month and a half now. There are three female plants that are over a foot tall with a large amount of leafy growth. When is it time to start flowering them? If I were to start the flowering regimen now would it hurt my mature flowers in any way later on?

TICALCAO, Santa Cruz, California

IT DEPENDS ON WHAT size you want the ripened plant to be and the variety that you are growing. Once the light regimen is switched from vegetative (18 to 24 hours of light daily) to flowering (12 hours of uninterrupted darkness daily) the plant's growth changes to flowering. After the light regimen is changed, varieties with mostly indica characteristics grow another 25-50% before they stop vegetative growth.

Most varieties offered by seed companies are hybrids with many indica characteristics. They are suitable to grow as medium-sized plants, growing 2-3 feet tall with a canopy of about a 1-3 square feet. Some of these varieties can be used in sea of green set-ups. The plants are forced to flower at a height of 12 inches and are 15-24 inches tall at ripening. Each plant claims a canopy of 1/4 square foot (6" x 6") to 1 square foot (12" x 12").

Sativa plants tend to continue growing vegetatively for a while. Some pure sativa varieties continue to grow to a certain size, usually 3 to 5 feet, even when forced to flower at 12 inches. Many sativas are insensitive to 12/12 light regimens because they come from equatorial zones. Light at the equator, which passes through Colombia, the Congo and Borneo, is near 12 hours all year round. The plants use other indicators of flowering time. These may include other environmental factors, but the plant's size and possibly its age are factors that determine flowering. Flowering can extend for four months or more. The first flowers appear as the plant is still growing vegetatively and the plant puts more energy into reproduction as time passes.

Sativas from the 20th parallel have some light sensitivity but continue to grow even while they are flowering. Land-races from Vietnam, Thailand, Jamaica and southern Mexico fit into this category.

Commercial sativa/indica hybrids are sensitive to light and generally ripen mid to late in the season. Indoors, they are easiest to grow by giving them some room to spread out, at least 2 square feet (18" x 18") of canopy per plant. They also require at least 4 feet of vertical space. They don't do well in sea of green set-ups.

Hybrid sativas and indicas can be forced to flower at any size. The quality of the buds is not time dependent, nor is it a factor of the size of the plant. Buds maturing on two clones from the same plant, one newly rooted and the other a large plant growing vegetatively for three months will produce equal quality buds.

Ultimately, the decision is yours. Figure out how big you want the plant to be when it's ripe. The smaller the plant is when it is forced to flower, the smaller the plant will be at ripening. There are several factors to take into account when making this decision. Federal sentencing is based on plant count. A tiny seedling or a mature sativa giant are both counted as one plant. This is a very important consideration.

Sea of green offers faster crops because each plant has to grow just a little bit for the canopy to be filled. The plants are ready to be forced soon after they are transferred into the garden. With fewer plants it takes more time for the plants to grow to fill the canopy.

> For more on wick system setups, see chapter 4, section C.1.

SIZE AT FLOWERING

In my flowering cupboard, 18" x 4' lit by a 250-watt Son T Plus HPS lamp (6 square feet @ 41 watts psf), I notice that the upper profile of the plants (3-4 plants max) bud off. I flower my plants at 14 inches. They mature out at 2 1/2- 3 feet. I have wasted area of leaf and stalk.

Should I force them to flower earlier, at 9 inches? Will

yields be as good on a 9-inch plant as a 14-inch one?

The plants have little side-shoots bearing leaves and small flowers. I am reluctant to remove these leaves and side branches. Even though they are shaded, they remain green. Would stripping these branches result in bigger buds? My instinct is to let the plant have all the leaves it can get.

CATHY XXX, Bristol, England

NINE-INCH PLANTS ARE likely to grow fewer side-shoots than your 14-inch plants. These plants will not yield as much per plant, but they can be spaced very close together, from four to nine plants psf. As a result, the yield will increase per square foot.

Removing the lower branches spurs growth of the upper canopy by shooting resources to the top growth. If they are left on the plant during the entire flowering period, the shaded lower buds will not be fully developed at harvest. If they are left to finish after the harvest, they will grow somewhat larger and mature. However, the additional harvest isn't worth the wait.

D. LIGHTING CYCLES

1. VEGETATIVE

VEGETATIVE LIGHT CYCLE

What is the best light cycle during the vegetative stage, 18/6 or 24/0, and which one will help the ladies go into their flowering cycle with less stress?

LAMP LIGHTER, New Brunswick, Connecticut

MARIJUANA PLANTS PHOTOSYNTHESIZE AS long as they receive light as well as water, air, nutrients and suitable temperature. Photosynthesis is the process in which plants use the energy from light (primarily in the blue and red spectrums) to combine carbon dioxide (CO_2) from the air and water (H_2O) to make sugar while releasing oxygen to the air.

Plants use sugars continuously to fuel metabolic processes (living) as well as for tissue building. The plant combines nitrogen (N) with sugar to make amino acids, the building blocks of proteins. They are the substance of plant tissue. When the light is off, the plant's metabolic processes, respiration and growth continue.

The marijuana plant can photosynthesize continuously, so it produces the most energy and growth when the light is on continuously. Continuous light does not stress the plant, which reacts to it somewhat mechanistically. Plants can suffer from the heat emitted by lamps, but will not undergo stress due to continuous lighting.

Plants under an 18-6 light-dark regimen are producing sugar only three quarters of the time. They are thus growing at only 75% of their potential. Leaving the light on continuously will result in bigger plants faster, which leads to higher yields.

CONTINUOUS LIGHT OKAY?

> In your column you suggested continuous light during vegetative cycle. I learned in biology that a plant needs a light and a dark period. The plant produces energy during the light cycle but uses it during the dark period. Lab experiments have shown that plants grow slower under continuous light.
>
> CAMDEN TOWN JACK, London, England

DURING THE LIGHT PERIOD, plants photosynthesize, but they also continue all other phases of metabolism including respiration and growth. Observations of comparable gardens on 18-hour light cycles and continuous lighting show that marijuana plants do not need a dark period. The plants grow about a third faster on continuous light as compared with 18/6.

INTERMITTENT DARKNESS

> Is it all right to turn the lights off for 30 minutes during the 18-hour light period in the vegetative stage? I want to let the room cool off a bit. Will it make the plants flower?
>
> C WEED, Internet

THE LIGHT CAN BE turned off intermittently when necessary to cool the garden. This will not affect the plants except that photosynthesis stops when it is dark. Plants measure uninterrupted darkness to determine flowering time. The short periods of darkness do not reach the critical level of 8-12 hours that triggers flowering.

D. 2. FORCING FLOWERS

HOW TO FORCE FLOWERING

I want to force a crop. What are the steps to get quick results? Should the drop between 18 hours of light and 12 hours of light be gradual or immediate?

J. M., Pearl River, New York

MARIJUANA IS A SHORT-DAY plant and flowers when it receives 10-12 hours of uninterrupted darkness each 24-hour period. Once the plants start to grow flowers, change the fertilizer to a flowering formula high in phosphorus (P).

When subjected to an uninterrupted dark period of 8-12 hours daily, marijuana switches its growth from vegetative to reproductive and begins to flower. There is no reason to make this switch gradually. The plants respond rather mechanistically to the light regimen.

Outdoors during the summer, when the day length is longer nearer the poles than the equator, the same strain flowers much earlier in Florida than in Vancouver. It begins to flower when a critical dark period is reached. For most varieties this is between 8 and 12 hours of uninterrupted darkness daily.

You can find out a plant's critical light level by observing plants outdoors to see when they start flowering. Check the length of the darkness period when you observe the first flowers. Count back to the darkness period two weeks earlier. To figure the critical period indoors, start at 9 hours of darkness and increase the dark period by 15 minutes each week. Figure the critical period as 15-30 minutes shorter than the dark period length when you see the first flowers. Suppose a plant's critical dark period is 10 hours. This means that it will flower under 14 hours of light. This is 2 hours longer than the 12-hour light period, which is generally recommended. The two hours of extra light each day is a 16% increase in light to the plant. This is critical because light equals growth.

A shorter dark period may lengthen the flowering period a bit.

179

To get the buds to ripen quickly, the dark period can be lengthened to 12 or even 14 hours.

FLOWERING LIGHT CYCLE

> After the plants begin to flower should I leave them on 12/12 of light until harvest? I've read that once the flowers begin to form, the light period is not as important. It seems to me that any light over the 12-hour period would put the plants back into the vegetative state.
>
> MEPERIDINE, Evansville, Indiana

BOTH STATEMENTS ARE TRUE. Once flowering is induced, most marijuana varieties can be forced back into vegetative state by placing them under a short dark regimen.

Although an occasional lapse of the light regimen or imprecise on/off times will not stop the plant from flowering, it will affect the quality of the flowers. They may be small, loose or lanky depending on how severely the regimen has been violated.

> *For info on how to place flowering plants back into vegetative growth (regeneration), see chapter 7, section C.*

CALCULATING FLOWERING TIME

> When do we start calculating flowering time? Do we start when the light cycle is reduced to 12 hours or once we see the first signs of flowering?
>
> QUEBECER, Montreal, QC, Canada

FLOWERING TIME IS CALCULATED as beginning when the lights are turned down to force flowering.

SPLIT THE DARK?

I know that marijuana needs 12 hours of darkness a day to flower. Does it require a 12/12 regimen or can I use two 6/6 light regimens in a 24-hour period?

WRONG NAME, Tampa, Florida

TO BE TRIGGERED INTO flowering marijuana needs a long period of uninterrupted darkness. Giving the plant two shorter periods will not force the plant to flower.

TOO MUCH DARK

I started my plants on a 24-hour cycle. After a month, I switched it to 10 hours on, 14 hours off. The buds are small. How can I make them bigger?

HELP WANTED, Bobtown, Massachusetts

THE BUDS ON YOUR plants would have grown larger if they had been given a light regimen of 12 on, 12 off.

The reason that the buds are small is the lighting cycle. Marijuana flowers when the uninterrupted dark period reaches 12 hours each evening. With more hours of darkness, the buds ripen more quickly, but their growth time is shortened and they reach maturity without growing to full size.

FASTER LIGHT REGIMEN

I have thirty wonderful and very healthy girls ranging from 14-30 inches. We are now beginning to flower and I wondered if there is a significant difference in yield if I go two weeks at 12/12 and then drop down to 10/14 in order to hasten ripening? I've been told that there is a difference but not much.

C. PAQUETTE, Vancouver, BC, Canada

PLANTS USE LIGHT TO fuel growth. If they receive less light they will grow less. Changing the light cycle to 10/14 from 12/12 reduces the amount of light the plants receive by $1/6$ or 16%. Cutting the light cycle during this time results in less total growth because the plant produces less material used for tissue building.

Another result of cutting the light cycle is to hasten the ripening of the plant. By reducing the light during the growth part of flowering, the growth period is reduced. However it is not a good trade-off. Not only is the total time under light reduced, so is the percentage of time with light. The yield of the low light cycle bud will be more than proportionately lower than the high light bud.

During the last 10 days of flowering the bud has little growth. Instead it transforms as the stigmas dry, the ovary swells and the glands fill with THC. Reducing the light period at this time does hasten ripening without reducing yield by giving the plant a clear signal that the time has come.

There are reasons why it may be more important to speed up ripening than to maximize production. Under these circumstances a 10/14 light/dark cycle could be better.

For more on ripening techniques, see chapter 7, section A.2.

SHORT CYCLE

I recently read about a light cycle for flowering of 6 hours on and 12 off, an 18-hour day. I can see how it would speed up the cycle.

PANTHER, Internet

A PLANT GROWS IN direct ratio to the amount of light it receives if all other factors are adequate. A plant growing under a regimen of 6 hours of light each 18 receives illumination only 24 hours of each 72 hours, rather than 36 hours each 72 on a 12 on/12 off regimen. The result is that the plants receive only $2/3$ of the amount of light. With less light the plants will grow less tissue, in this case smaller buds.

The 18-hour regimen may complete the cycle 25% faster than the 24-hour regimen. If this system works, the plant will ripen in $3/4$ of the time of the 24-hour system, but will yield only about $2/3$ of the bud because it receives only $2/3$ of the light energy than on the 12/12 regimen.

12 VS. 8

I have plants ready to bud. If I cut the lights back to 8 hours of light, how long will it take the plants to ripen?

SPORT, Vinton, Ohio

USUALLY GROWERS USING LIGHTS force their plants to flower under 12 hours of darkness each cycle. Most domesticated indoor varieties ripen 8-10 weeks after forcing. However, if the dark period is increased, the flowers will ripen in a shorter period of time at the expense of growth.

Plants given 16 hours of darkness a day, and 8 rather than 12 hours of light will ripen 20-30% faster than plants under a regimen of 12/12. Expect yields of only 50-60% of normal. The reason for this is simple: plants exposed to less light produce less growth.

18-HOUR BLUES

I am growing some Jack Flash plants which were doing well under 24-hour lighting until someone told me that 24 hours was too much and I had to use an 18/6 regimen. I changed the lighting. A week after, most of the plants were showing sex and had slowed their growth. I want them to stay in the vegetative stage, so they can grow more. If I stay on 18/6, will the plants go back to vegetative stage?

Will there be any problem when I flower them on a 12/12 regime? How can I get them back to vegetative stage?

CACTUSMAN, France

To GET THE PLANTS back to full vegetative growth stage, return to continuous lighting. The plants will revert to full vegetative growth. At 18 hours of light, the plants are near their critical point of triggering flowering. It will take a slightly longer dark period to trigger them fully, below that level they continue to grow vegetatively as they produce flowers. They will continue in this ambiguous state until they adjust to the new regimen, then vegetative growth will continue.

Once the cycle is changed to a regimen with 12 hours of darkness each night the plants will switch to flowering with no problems. This particular variety would probably flower well under 14 hours of light. It would take longer to ripen, but the yield would be substantially larger.

FLOWER ONE BRANCH?

If one branch of a marijuana plant were covered by an opaque bag 12 hours a day and the rest of the plant was given continuous light, what would happen?

SAGAMOUR, North Carolina

IF A BAG COVERED a single branch on a plant, only that branch would flower. This technique might prove useful in determining sex of plants early, without removing material from the garden.

If a bag, dark colored on the outside, is used, the enclosed vegetation is likely to die from overheating (the greenhouse effect). Instead, the outer surface should be white or very light-colored in order to reflect the light. An inner cover should be opaque. Uncoated paper allows moisture to escape, while plastic holds it in. Excess moisture produces molds.

SHAFT OF LIGHT

I am growing in my closet. There is about a ¼-inch space between the doors and the wall through which a tiny bit of light can get in. Can this affect the dark period during flowering?

NAMESHY, Staten Island, New York

POSSIBLY. IT DEPENDS HOW much light is getting in. Even a small amount of light can cause light pollution during flowering. It would be best to close the crack to prevent problems. Duct tape or a black polyethylene curtain hanging along the door's edge or along the doorjamb is a simple solution. This material should cover the entire area of the crack to prevent accidents and later disappointments.

Light pollution is insidious. It may not stop the plant from flowering, but will affect the quality of the bud by giving the plant mixed signals. Buds affected by light pollution grow in thin strips or clusters along the stem. They never become dense.

FLASH OF LIGHT

I grow in a closet. If I turn on the light in the room during the dark period when the closet door is open, will it affect flowering? If I keep the closet door open won't the plants produce too much oxygen?

MYSTIC MAN, Kesetovo, Slovenia

EVEN MOMENTARY LIGHT POLLUTION during the dark period interrupts the flowering cycle. Even one incident affects bud growth. The plants are especially sensitive halfway through flowering during the middle of the dark cycle. If light pollution occurs regularly, the result will be loose, runny buds that do not mature well.

The plants produce oxygen only during the light period. Light powers photosynthesis, in which water and CO_2 are combined to produce sugar, releasing oxygen. During this portion of the daily cycle the door can be kept open.

During the dark period, the plants cease photosynthesis but use the sugars they produced to continue metabolic processes. Sugars are used both as fuel and for building tissue. This process releases CO_2. A closed door during this period results in a CO_2 build-up. The plants use this when the lights go on and the plants begin photosynthesizing.

One way to look in the grow room when the lights are off is to use a green light. Plants are insensitive to green light so it can safely be used in a dark room. Both green incandescent and fluorescent tubes can be used.

DARK NOT WORKING

What do you do when you cut the light back to eight hours and the plants still do not flower?

PAUL M., Dallas, Texas

CHECK FOR INTERRUPTIONS IN the darkness cycle. If the darkness is interrupted by light for even a moment, the plants' transition to flowering is delayed.

DARK PERIOD AT HARVEST

What do you think about giving plants 24-48 hours of darkness just prior to harvest? People claim this increases THC or makes the plants more "frosty."

CHUCK, Maryland

IN THE 1970s, Dr. Carleton Turner, at the University of Mississippi found that there was a variation in the amount of THC in a sample depending upon the time that the plant was taken. The most potent point was just before dawn after nighttime darkness. Then in 2000, Dr. Paul Mahlberg of Indiana University showed that THC was produced extracellularly, on the inside of the glandular membrane, which would allow for its daily recycling.

The idea of using a dark period to increase THC before harvest warrants some investigation. An extended dark period right before harvest probably increases THC content.

This research indicated that the best time to harvest outdoor plants is right before dawn.

VISITING THE DARK

How can I visit my plants during the dark period?

THE FUNK MASTER, Address Unknown

PLANTS ARE NOT SENSITIVE to green light. A flashlight with a green filter, or an incandescent or fluorescent green light can be used when entering the grow room. This light will not interfere with the lighting regime.

E. CHANGING CONDITIONS: VEGETATIVE TO FLOWERING

AGE & QUALITY

Does the age of a plant before it buds affect its quality in any way?

ANON, Franklin Furnace, Ohio

THE AGE OF THE plant does not the potency of the plant if it is forced to flower early. Potency is based on the plant's heredity.

For info on genetics, see chapter 1, section A; chapter 11; chapter 12.

HEIGHT & QUALITY

Does overall plant height determine bud quality?

R.G., Tampa, Florida

NO. MOSTLY THE PLANT's genes and the maturity of the bud determine quality. The age and height of the plant at the time of flowering do not affect the bud's chemistry or potency.

For info on genetics, see chapter 1, section A; chapter 11; chapter 12.

WHEN TO ADJUST FERTILIZER

When should I change the fertilizer to the flowering formula—when I turn the lights back or when flowers first appear?

SCAM, North Cairns, QLD, Australia

THE METHOD OF GROWING determines when the fertilizer should be changed. Outdoors in soil, the fertilizer is switched when the plants are in transition from vegetative growth to flowering. The dates differ by variety, since each has its own critical dark period that triggers flowering.

Indoors, the time to change formulas depends on method of cultivation. Plants in systems where there is a high level of residual nutrients in the planting medium such as soil and soilless mixes, should be switched to the flowering formula at the same time as the lights are changed. They retain high levels of nitrogen (N), which the plants use in the early part of flowering. The switch to a high phosphorus (P) or high P and potassium (K) formula will result in the use of the residual N so that little will be left at the end of flowering, when the plants require more P.

With hydroponic systems in which there is no nutrient build-up in the media, the plants should receive N during early flowering. This is used for tissue building, that is, to grow flowers. Flowering formulas sometimes contain little nitrogen. Look at the list of nutrients on the label. If the flowering formula doesn't contain at least $1/3$ the N as P, mix it with the vegetative growth fertilizer during the first two thirds of flowering. If there is no N available, the plant transports it from lower leaves to new growth. As a result the lower leaves turn yellow and die. Only in late flowering should the N level be lowered further.

For more on N-P-K, see chapter 4, section B.2.
For info on yellowing leaves, see chapter 9, section B.2.

WATER DURING DARK PERIOD?

I have a rockwool slab system and a horticultural clay system. Both are on drip. I water the pebbles hourly and the rockwool twice a day. Is it necessary to water my plants in sleep time? Do they feed only when the lights are on?

OZZIE, ELIZABETH VALE, South Australia

AN IRRIGATION ONCE DURING the dark period provides fresh water for the roots to draw upon. The plants use this water to fuel growth. At the same time, it rinses excess nutrients from the planting medium.

Plants do not shut down at night. Although photosynthesis stops because there is no energy to power it, plants continue other metabolic processes including tissue building and respiration. This is the life process that powers cells with sugar as fuel. During the light period, plants produce more sugar than they use for metabolism during both the dark and light periods. To build tissue, plants combine nitrogen with sugar to form amino acids, the building blocks of protein.

For more on watering, see chapter 4, section D.

BIRTH CONTROL PILL FOR MONSTER BUDS?

A friend of mine swears that if you mix a birth control pill with a gallon of water and use it to water the plant once before the plant begins to flower and again two weeks after it begins, the plant will grow monstrous buds. He says it has something to do with estrogen. Is this weed fact or fiction?

UNCLE JESSE, Rock Hill, South Carolina

IT IS COMMON KNOWLEDGE among ornamental gardeners that birth control pills act like a tonic on some plants. I have interviewed several prizewinning flower growers who have told me that birth control pills increased the number and size of the flowers on their plants. Many years ago I interviewed a farmer who used birth control pills on his tomatoes and claimed increased yields.

Using birth control pills on ornamental plants does not pose risk. However, if you think of marijuana as a food plant, then there is a more of a risk. I don't think that I'd want to ingest a food plant treated with estrogen or progesterone.

ASPIRIN & FLOWERING

I experimented this past season (my fourth) with three female plants by giving them a solution of two aspirins per one gallon of water. Six feet from these plants were two other female plants growing to which I did not give aspirin. The plants were treated only once, at the third week of flowering. The two treated plants turned hermaphroditic and thousands of pollen sacs grew. The two untreated plants remained all female.

The hermaphrodite's buds were big, with pollen sacs interspersed with female flowers. Much to my surprise, the seeded hermaphrodites were far better than Colombian, almost as good as sinsemilla.

K. B., Jamaica, New York.

INTERRUPTING FLOWERING WITH VEGETATIVE

What is your opinion on putting plants into a 3-day vegetative stage during flowering? I have heard that it increases potency and yield.

PanTher, Internet

INTERRUPTING THE FLOWERING REGIMEN for a few days with continuous light about halfway through the flowering cycle, giving the plants at least 18 hours of light daily, induces the plant to begin to switch back to vegetative growth.

The theory behind this is that after reverting back to flowering, the plants will have a burst of new flower growth. There is a trade-off for the additional growth. The vegetative lighting regimen sets flowering back three days, then it takes the plant several days to revert back to flowering. As a result, ripening and the harvest are delayed at least a week. If the variety usually takes eight weeks to ripen, but takes nine using this lighting regimen, an increase in time of 12%, then to break even the harvest has to be 12% larger. I don't think that this technique increases yield by that much. Far worse, it causes bud deformities such as lanky growth and looseness.

F. CYCLE PROBLEMS

FLOWERS DURING VEGETATIVE

I have two plants in a Phototron™ outfitted with six fluo-rescent lamps imported from Italy. They are an Afghani hydro and a lush, plump sativa. Their internode spacing is very close, what all closet gardeners hope and dream of. The plants have been growing female flowers for about ten days and have immature white hairs sticking out of the nodes. Is it possible for plants to grow flowers before the 12/12 photoperiod? They have been on 24/0 the whole time and will be forced with 12/12 next week.

IOWA FARMER, Cedar Falls, Iowa

PLANTS GROWING UNDER LAMPS supplying a light strong in the red spectrum often grow a few flowers on upper nodes during vegeta-tive growth. These flowers are indicative of plant sex. They have lit-tle if any effect on vegetative plant growth.

Warm-white fluorescent tubes and HPS lamps emit light spec-trums high in red light that encourage pre-flowering during early growth. The faster and more prolific the pre-flowers, the earlier the plant matures.

> *For info about how the lighting cycle may produce flowers during the vegetative period, see section D in this chapter.*

UNWANTED BUD GROWTH

I bypass the vegetative phase and go from clone to flower-ing to keep the plants small and manageable. The buds are burly, but keep growing skinny shoots from the tops of the colas. How can I stop these shoots from growing? Does it

have something to do with the lack of blue light in HPS
lamps?

DEWEY, Santa Clara, California

THIS IS CAUSED BY high heat radiating from the lamp, not the light
spectrum or size of the plant. The solution is to use an air or water-
cooled light so the plant isn't subject to the punishing heat.

In the short term, prune those shoots off the plants on a regular
basis to prevent the plant from expending energy on new growth at
the expense of the ripening bud.

> *For more on heat & lights, see chapter 3, section A.*
> *For more on pruning, see section B, this chapter.*

TIMER PROBLEMS

My plants are between 6-8 inches tall, but the timer for my
lights became unplugged and they received 20 hours of
darkness. Now they appear to be budding. Is this a problem? What should I do?

STRETCH NUTS, Internet

EVEN THOUGH YOUR PLANTS received one long period of darkness
they will continue to grow vegetatively as long as they are maintained under a continuous light. They will revert back to vegetative
growth within a few days.

7 HARVEST

A. TIME TO HARVEST?
1. RIPENING BASICS
2. TECHNIQUES FOR RIPENING
3. REAL GARDEN SCENARIOS

B. RIPENING & HARVEST PROBLEMS

C. REVEGETATION & MOTHERS

D. YIELDS

E. DRYING & CURING
1. STAGE ONE: DRYING
2. STAGE TWO: CURING

F. MANICURING & STORAGE

G. USES FOR LEAVES

RELATED TOPICS

Maturation changes: chapter 6 Plant Life Cycle, section E
Changing Conditions.
Differences in varieties that may relate to ripening time:
chapter 12 Varieties.

MORE ABOUT
Uses of leaf: chapter 13 Cannabis & Health, section A.3
    Cannabis Processing & Health.
Flowering and ripeness: chapter 6 Plant Life Cycle, section C
    When to Force and D.2 Lighting.
Methods for perpetuating a garden: chapter 11 Breeding.

A. TIME TO HARVEST?

1. RIPENING BASICS

RIPENING TIME

How long does it take for the plants to actually start getting buds on them?

SONOMA 58,
Knoxville, Tennessee

AFTER FLOWER FORCING, the first signs of change are the slowing, and then the cessation of vegetative growth. This takes place within 5-10 days. The plant may still grow, but growth begins to look different because it is reproductive, not vegetative. Within two weeks the first flowers appear. If the plant is more than three months old, the first inflorescences may appear a few days earlier. Marijuana is forced by reducing the number of hours of light per day to 12 hours, so the plants receive 12 hours of uninterrupted darkness each day.

Pistils start to appear at the node where the leaf joins the stem. They also grow all along the tops of the plant. The buds usually ripen 6-10 weeks after forcing flowering.

Sativa plants may continue to grow vegetatively for some time even as they flower.

RIPENING CROP FAST

**What is the best way to ripen a crop? I am growing indoors
and the plants are taking a long time to mature.**

BATTYBOY, Internet

PLANTS ARE GENETICALLY PROGRAMMED to take a certain time to
mature. Maturation time usually ranges from 45 to 70 days after
forcing flowering (providing the plants receive 12 hours of uninterrupted darkness each day). There is nothing you can do to change
an individual plant's traits. However, you can shorten the maturation time by altering the environment. Increasing the length of the
dark period hastens maturation. The yield suffers, though. For
instance, a plant that takes 10 weeks to mature under a regimen of
12 hours of darkness daily takes about 8 weeks if grown under 14
hours of darkness. This is a time savings of 20%. However, the yield
will be reduced to 75% or less under the shorter dark period. The
total yield over time is also reduced.

One way to hasten the ripening of slow maturing varieties is to
increase the dark period from 12 hours to 14 hours about two weeks
before the anticipated harvest time. This signals the plants to ripen
up, cuts a few days from the cycle and helps the plants ripen more
completely without affecting yield very much.

Excess nitrogen delays maturation so make sure the plants are
not being supplied with it during the later stages of flowering.

WHEN TO HARVEST INDOORS

When is the indoor plant ready to harvest?

CSR, Dieppe, NB, Canada

THERE ARE SEVERAL INDICATORS of the optimum time to harvest. First, growth virtually stops. The older stigmas have dried and have started receding into the ovary, which is enlarging a bit. The glands, viewed through a photographer's loupe, are topped with mushroom-shaped glands with tops that appear stretched from the liquid inside. Even if there are a few clusters of new stigmas near a hot light, the buds are ripe.

DEFINING SENESCENCE

What does senescence mean?

J.B GOODE, Baseline, Colorado

SENESCENCE IS DEFINED AS, "the complex deteriorative processes that terminate the natural functional life of an organ or organism." In other words, the plants have completed their life cycle, and are dying.

A. 2. TECHNIQUES FOR RIPENING

MARIJUANA MYTHS, MARIJUANA FANTASIES

Do any of these techniques produce a final shot of oil to the plant's glands?

- Boiling roots immediately after harvest.
- Snapping limbs at maturity and allowing the plant to stay partially attached two days before harvesting.

■ Extreme drought the final week.
■ Erratic light cycles the last week of flowering.

RBBD, Petaluma, California

THC IS PRODUCED AT the gland outside the leaf cell rather than in the sap or any other part of the plant so it is highly unlikely that boiling the roots immediately after harvest has any effect on the plant.

By snapping the stem at maturity and only allowing a partial flow of water and nutrients to the upper parts, the plant goes into a partial wilt. Supposedly this increases THC production. I don't think it's true. The wilt and the light cause a gradual degradation of the THC into less potent cannabinoids.

Soil that is dry, but not to the point of the plant wilting, may increase THC production in the final days before flowering. Extreme drought during the final week limits the energy and amount of photosynthesis taking place. The plants don't have as much energy for the final spurt of glandular production. Erratic light cycles during the last week of flowering would not increase THC production.

One way to assure the highest THC levels is to harvest immediately after turning on the lights. Letting the plants sit in darkness for 24 hours before harvesting increases THC percentage slightly.

> *For more on THC, see "Advice on Storage" in section F, this chapter; chapter 13, section A.1.*

PICKING BUD

How do I prepare the plant for picking? When are the plants ready? What time of day should I pick?

GREENTIME, Santa Cruz, California

THE BUDS ARE READY for picking when most of the stigmas have dried and turned color and the ovaries behind the stigmas have swelled into false seed pods. At the same time, the bulbous tops of the glands extending from the tissue have swelled so much that they look like tiny balloons ready to burst.

THC has several properties. It physically protects the growing and maturing seed from insects and herbivores and its effects deter other animals. In addition, THC seems to protect the plant from the sun's damaging UV rays. During the daylight hours, THC is degraded somewhat. During the evening, the THC is replenished. The best time to pick is at the end of the plant's dark period.

> *For info on THC, see "Advice on Storage" in section F, this chapter; chapter 13, section A.1.*

A. 3. REAL GARDEN SCENARIOS

HARVESTING HOMEGROWN MEXICAN

> **I am growing a high-grade commercial Mexican indoors. I have placed the plants into harvest and they have been flowering for about 70 days. There are lots of stigmas. How do I tell when my buds are ripe?**
>
> NOVICE BUDDER, Yuma, Arizona

INDICAS AND INDICA/SATIVA hybrids have a very definite ripening in which the two stigmas recede into the ovary from which they grew. This ovary swells as the glands covering it fill with THC.

Unlike indicas, Mexican sativas require 85 days to ripen under 12 hours of darkness. Even then, their ripening is a little different than indicas. The stigmas brown and dry, but recede only partially into the ovaries, which enlarge just a little. Traditionally, the Mexican harvest occurred in November and December. The plants flowered for 12 weeks.

To hasten ripening, increase the dark period to 14 hours daily, rather than 12. Keep the medium drier than usual. This is hard to do in some hydroponic systems, but in others, the number of irrigations daily can be manipulated. Make sure to use a low nitrogen fertilizer.

For more on indicas versus sativas, see chapter 12.

WHEN TO HARVEST

I've got one totally skunky plant growing in a spare bedroom and it's been budding for four weeks. The buds are covered with glands and most of the hairs have turned orange. The only white hairs remaining are near the top of each bud. Is this the time to harvest?
WAITING IN HUMBOLDT, Eureka, California

THE PLANTS WILL RIPEN in about 30 days. The stigmas have started drying, but the ovaries behind them have not swelled providing more room for glands to balloon. Eventually the stigmas will recede into the enlarged organ and the trichomes will glisten under direct light. Under magnification, the cap membrane sitting atop the trichome stem will stretch as it fills with cannabinoids. The gland heads will sparkle as the light catches the clear viscous liquid inside. A few glands will have the slightest tint of amber. When the plants fit this description, they are ready for harvest.

OUTDOOR HARVEST

> I have a few plants outside, I wanted to go pick them today but it is raining now and it is supposed to rain for a couple of days. I saw the plants five days ago, and some of the leaves were turning yellow. The buds are big and look ready. Should I harvest? Can you tell me a couple of tips?
>
> DANSSA, Ontario, Canada

TIP ONE: HARVEST THE plants immediately. This is a no-brainer—the buds are ready and hanging out in the rain, deteriorating. Cut them down before they lose more potency or get moldy.

Tip Two: Trim the buds from the chaff immediately. Place the buds in a hot dry space with good air circulation and plenty of light until all the rain and other water evaporates. This prevents molds from attacking the plants. Once the water has evaporated, cool the room and turn off the lights for a slower cure/dry.

TIME TO PICK OUTDOOR PLANTS?

> This year my Afghani-Durbans were almost ready by September 1. Then new flower clusters appeared. I waited another two weeks for them to mature, but more appeared. Finally, on September 19, I clipped them. My friend's Thai had even more late flowers. Should I have waited to pick them?
>
> PAUL, Address withheld

ONCE FLOWERS MATURE, THE THC starts to deteriorate because of the heat and light in the plants' environment. However, plants with new bud development should be allowed to continue growing as long as environmental conditions, rip-offs or the law don't threaten them. Perhaps if pressures are too great to ignore, some small buds and the vegetative growth could be left on the plant—harvest only the buds. The plant may produce second growth.

B. RIPENING & HARVEST PROBLEMS

BUDS NOT RIPENING OUTDOORS

I planted in 10-gallon pots using Pro-Mix® soil. I watered every day. Each week I watered using 20-20-20 water–nutrient mix. I stopped feeding them September 1, but kept watering them. I had lots of buds. Growers who used the same seeds harvested big ripe buds with yellow leaves and lots of red hairs. Now it's October 15. My plants were still very green and were not ready. Were my plants too healthy? Did I overfeed the plants?

SPINMAN, Internet

EXCESS NITROGEN (N) DELAYS RIPENING. Fertilizing the plants weekly created a build-up of N that was not used by the plant. Even though you stopped fertilizing the plants September 1, there was plenty of water soluble N in the planting medium. This was a cue to the plants to continue growing because there were plenty of nutrients to support the growth. Planting media with low levels of N promote flowering. The plants transfer N from the large fan leaves to the points of new growth, the bud. Because N is being transferred, the fan leaves turn yellow before they die while the buds swell and ripen. Your plants stayed green because they continued to pick up N from the soil.

A better fertilizer regimen would have been to use your current fertilizer until the middle of July. Use no fertilizer for a couple of weeks and then use a bloom mix such as 2-10-10 or 1-9-5 for three weeks. The high phosphorus (P) levels promote large flowers and the potassium (K) balances the high acidity of the P. After three feedings, there will be enough residual nutrients in the medium to support growth. The soil should have been kept a bit dryer the last three weeks. This also promotes ripening.

> *For more on fertilizers during flowering, see chapter 6, section E.*
> *For more on outdoor fertilization needs, see chapter 5, section E.*
> *For more on general nutrient needs in soil, see chapter 4, section B.*

HARD TO RIPEN INDOORS

I have a plant that is taking a long time to ripen. It has been under 12/12 light/darkness for 11 weeks. What is the best way to get the plant to ripen?

BOBO, Internet

INCREASE THE UNINTERRUPTED DARK period to 14 hours and lower the temperature about 5 degrees F, (3 degrees C).

The plant is an equatorial variety. There is very little variance in light period near the equator. The plants receive about 12 hours of darkness daily all year in their native environment, so they use other cues as well as light regime to determine flowering and ripening time. They seem to respond to increasing dryness and cooler temperatures as well. Some varieties produce flowers as they grow, but never develop flower heads under indoor conditions.

The high-latitude ruderalis varieties, which start producing flowers early, never develop big buds. The flowers never ripen. Instead, the stigmas die but the ovaries never develop.

> *For more on flowering light regimens, see chapter 6, section D.*

RIPENING DIFFICULTIES

I am using four 20-watt cool-white bulbs (24 inches) in my little, 2-square-foot garden. I may also use side lighting. I will switch to warm-white bulbs to flower and use a 12-hour light\dark regimen. The last time I grew I waited a long time, but maybe not long enough. The plants never

seemed to really ripen with amber glands. Tell me, how can
I get them to ripen real nice?

ZEV, Internet

THERE ARE SEVERAL POSSIBLE reasons why the plants you were
growing did not ripen properly.

The variety may require more light than you were supplying,
causing the buds to form incompletely. They grow thin, lanky and
loose up the stalk.

The plants may have received an irregular light cycle. In order
to flower plants indoors, it is necessary to maintain a regular cycle
of 12 hours of uninterrupted darkness and 12 hours of light (that
may be interrupted). If the light cycle was jiggled rather than kept
on a strictly regular basis, the buds received mixed signals that
could interfere with proper ripening.

The variety could also be very late in developing, or one that
never truly ripens. These plants are occasionally encountered, especially in sativa varieties.

> *For more on sativas, see chapter 12.*
> *For more on the dark period, see chapter 6, section D.3.*

SMALL BUDS I

My buds are growing but they are small. Is there anything I
can do to help them grow larger?

GANJA MAN, Internet

THERE ARE SEVERAL POSSIBLE reasons why the flowers are small:

- The genetics are for a small-budded variety. No matter how
  ideal the conditions, a plant programmed genetically to produce small buds won't grow large ones.

- The plant isn't getting enough nutrients. Plants that don't receive enough nutrients don't grow to potential because the minerals are used for tissue building.

- The plant isn't getting enough light. Light fuels growth. Green plants use photosynthesis to turn CO_2 and water into sugar using light as the source of energy. The more light (greater intensity) the plant receives, the faster and bigger it will grow.

- The plants are growing in a low CO_2 environment slowing photosynthesis.

- The roots are constricted by too small a container.

For more on genetics, see chapter 11.
For more on nutrients, see chapter 4; chapter 6, section E.
For more on lighting, see chapter 2; chapter 6, section D.
For more on container size, see chapter 4, section A.3.

SMALL BUDS II

I have been flowering a 25-inch-tall hash plant for two months in a 2'x 6'x 8' closet. The plant has dark green buds on each branch but I am using a method I read about in which all the fan leaves are trimmed in vegetative growth, creating branches where the fan leaves had been. The problem is that I have 24 buds on the plant. The largest is only a gram dried. I'm using 200 watts of fluorescents surrounded by a space blanket, which really reflects the light like mad. The buds are all covered with white crystals, but they are not getting any bigger.

I grow in a mix of Styrofoam and potting soil and water with a soluble medium-nitrogen, high-phosphorus fertilizer and I use Miracle Gro plant spikes. What can I do to make these buds grow bigger?

PEPE LA PEU, Nova Scotia, Canada

THERE IS NOT MUCH you can do to increase the bud size of your hash plant since it is almost ripe and is past its flower growth stage. The glands are filling with THC as the buds ripen.

There are several things that can be done to produce bigger buds in the future. Prune the plant so that it puts more energy into a few branches, or leads, and not into many small ones. The size of the container may also be a limiting factor. Plants with more room for their roots grow bigger buds.

As you describe your plant, it is a bush, and has been pruned to encourage branching. All of the branches have flowers at their tips. Indoors, with light at a premium, the plants cannot support growth of many large flowers. Instead, the plant should be pruned so that each bud occupies a 6'x 6' space of the canopy. It's often convenient to trim a plant to three to six branches at the same time it is forced to flower. A second pruning may be required several weeks into flowering.

After pruning, all the water and nutrients from the roots goes to the remaining areas, spurring their growth. The plant's energy will be focused on reproductive growth: flowers. This will result in several large buds of higher quality than the many small buds of lower quality.

You didn't mention the size of the container in which the plant is growing. Rootbound containers constrict the roots and slow plant growth. Rootbound plants growing in soil should be repotted to a larger container. Rootbound plants benefit from transplanting through the first few weeks of flowering.

For more on pruning, see chapter 6, section B.
For more on container size, see chapter 4, section A.3.

POLLINATION PANIC

A few flowers were pollinated when they first appeared about two weeks ago. Now the stigmas on even the unfertilized flowers are beginning to turn. They have only been flowering for about four weeks. Is this normal? Should we

harvest now or wait to see if a new growth spurt will occur?

CONFUSED CALIFORNIAN, Riverside, California

IF ONLY A SMALL amount of pollination took place, the buds usually resume growth. Buds with heavier pollination are likely to be abortive shadows of their potential.

> *For more on males and pollination, see chapter 6, section A; chapter 11.*

RAINY HARVEST

Will rain make buds less potent?

BONGMASTER, Lakeside, California

Will shaking plants after a rain prevent mold? Is there any way to prevent mold?

MOLDY MARIJUANA MAN, Charleston, West Virginia

BUDS THAT ARE SUBJECTED to rain face two problems. The first is that rain and wind knock glands off the plant surface. Sometimes they knock off just the gland heads, which contain most of the THC. This happens more when the buds are nearing maturity. Rain and wind also knock debris onto the surfaces where they are caught by the sticky glands.

The second problem is that rain and high moisture promote molds and fungus. Drops of rain get into the tight buds and the moisture remains there. This provides ideal conditions for mold growth— a dark, moist, acidic space with plenty of fresh vegetation for food.

There are a few ways to prevent mold from attacking buds. Mold prefers an acidic environment and does not do well in alkaline situations. The pH can be changed on the buds from acidic to alkaline by spraying with water adjusted to about pH 8 using either pH Up or potassium bicarbonate. These products prevent mold until rain washes them away.

Alkaline water is the preferred method for dealing with mold in nearly ripe buds. It leaves no toxic residue and does not harm the plant. Of course the buds should also be very gently shaken to remove water.

> For more on molds, see chapter 10, section B.3.

HARVESTING A FALLEN PLANT

Our outdoor plant recently fell because of the weight of the large colas during a heavy rainstorm. The colas are ready for harvest and covered with the remnants of dried mud. How do we remove the mud without damaging the resin glands?

DIRTY DURHAM BUZZ, Internet

THE FIRST STEP IS to cut the plants up into 1-2 foot long (about 30-60 cm long) branches. Then separate the muddy branches from the rest. Dry the clean buds of rainwater by keeping them in a warm, dry, breezy space. Once the water has dried, the buds are ready for curing.

Contaminated buds can be dipped in cool water. If the mud falls away with a gentle swishing in water, the buds can be used. Buds that remain dirty are unacceptable for smoking, but can be used to make bubble hash.

C. REVEGETATION & MOTHERS

LONG-LIVED POT

I'm wondering if you could settle a dispute for me. A friend of mine insists that marijuana plants can live indoors for five years or more. I disagree. Isn't pot an annual plant, casting off seeds and dying back at the end of the growing season? Up here it's too severe to tell, but even in the tropics the plants die back after flowering, don't they? Also, my friend says that a plant that dies off in the fall grows back the following spring from the roots.

DAN, THE SINSE MAN, Valparaiso, Indiana

FEMALE MARIJUANA PLANTS FLOWER in response to long uninterrupted nights (8-12 hours, depending on variety). If the plant is kept in a room with the light on constantly, or intermittently, it will not flower. One correspondent had a plant in her kitchen that was three years old and had never flowered.

Usually, marijuana dies after flowering, but this may be due to the climate. Indoor plants can be revived after flowering by manipulating the light cycle. The plants will respond by growing new vegetation. In Nepal, some plants grow for several years and flower several times before dying.

REGENERATION 101

How does regeneration work? Do the plants have to be a certain size?

EL TORO, Seattle, Washington

MARIJUANA PLANTS RESPOND IN a predictable manner to changes

211

in the lighting regimen. Given about 12 hours of uninterrupted darkness each day, the plants change from vegetative growth to flowering. Inversely, plants that have been under the flowering regimen of 12 hours of uninterrupted darkness can be forced back into vegetative cycle using continuous lighting.

> Marijuana plants respond in a predictable manner to changes in the lighting regimen.

Regeneration is easy to do. When pruning the mature buds off the plant, allow some leaves to remain on the stems and turn the lights to continuous operation. In 5-10 days, the plant will start producing new vegetative growth. Then the plant is pruned back to three or four branches to prevent it from growing lots of branches with small buds. Pruning reduces the number of budding sites, but increases the size of the buds on the remaining branches.

Two weeks to a month after forcing vegetative growth, the plant will have grown quite a bit and can be forced to flower again by increasing the dark period to 12 hours daily.

For more on changing the light cycle, see chapter 6, section D.

HARVESTING CORRECTLY FOR REGENERATION

I plan on rejuvenating a plant. If there is a nice cola, say 25 inches long, can it be snipped off or do I have to pick the buds off?

THE PIPER, Address unknown

THE ENTIRE COLA EXCEPT the inner end can be cut. For an individual branch to survive, some leaves must remain on it after harvest. Branches that are stripped clean of vegetation dry up. After the colas and buds have been removed, place the plant under continuous light.

HAIRCUTS OR MOTHERS

I am using the sea of green method. Can I take the next batch of clones off of these plants before going to a 12-hour cycle or should I set some aside to act as mothers? I am worried that if I take clones from my clones, they will not develop properly. I would prefer not to use separate mother plants if possible.

SUN DOG, Internet

YOU CAN USE EITHER mothers or cuts from the current crop to make clones. Each has its advantages. With cuttings from the current crop, no separate garden needs to be set up to hold the mothers, so space is conserved. The disadvantage is that clones must sometimes be taken at an inappropriate time. For instance, if you are growing only one crop at a time, it may take 70 days for a full cycle, but only two or three weeks to make a clone. It's hard to hold the clone for 90 days without affecting subsequent growth. With mother plants, you can take the clones timed to when they are needed. However, if you are growing several crops so there is a harvest every month or even more often, then taking cuttings from the garden before flower forcing could be a productive method of propagation. In a flowering room constantly in operation where plants are harvested as they ripen, cuttings from maturing plants might work very well.

Having a separate mother garden is a more reliable method of preserving genetics. The mother plant serves as a constant source of cuttings whenever they are needed. They are much easier to keep track of and they are less likely to be affected by genetic drift.

For more on cloning, see chapter 1, section B.1.

FLOWERING MAMAS

I have my parent stock growing on an 18 on/6 off cycle. Now some of these plants are starting to flower. This has me perplexed because I've never read anything about it.

Can I still clone from these plants? Can I get these plants back into vegetative cycle or should I just move them into the flowering room? How can I prevent this in the future?

STRANGER IN PARADISE, Reading, Pennsylvania

THE PLANTS ARE RESPONDING to the 6-hours-off part of the cycle. As plants get older, they become more sensitive to the dark period and respond somewhat to shorter dark periods.

To stop the plants from flowering, increase the light cycle to continuous light or break the dark period into two shorter periods of 3 hours with several hours of light between them.

The cuttings from the slightly flowering plants can be used. Place them in vegetative under continuous light as they are rooting. Once they root, they will respond as if they were new plants.

For more on lighting and flowering, see chapter 6, section D.

MOTHERS' POTENCY

Do mother plants lose potency after a few generations or after stress? How long is a mother plant productive?

BIG BUD MAMA, Internet

THE POTENTIAL OF A plant is determined by its genetics. Unlike seeds, clones are virtually exact genetic duplicates of the plants from which they are taken. Although there is a slight genetic drift over many generations, this phenomenon occurs very slowly. Stress will affect the growth of the plant, but will not change its genetic make-up.

A mother plant is less likely to show genetic drift than clones from clones, and can be kept in vegetative growth stage for several years. The main stem becomes thick and gnarly but the branches remain vigorous.

> *For more on genetic drift, see chapter 1, section B.2; chapter 9, section F.*

CLONES FROM A REGENERATE

Can a flowered plant be forced back into vegetative growth and then used to produce viable clones?

RAINMAKER, Internet

YES. REGENERATION IS A great way of preserving the genetics of a plant. Once the plant is forced back into the vegetative cycle it can be used as a clone mother or to re-flower once again.

> *For info on cloning, see chapter 1, section B.1.*

D. YIELDS

YIELD EXPECTATIONS

What kind of yield can I expect per square foot from my garden lit by a 400-watt HPS lamp? How about a 1,000-watt lamp? The garden area is 10' x 10'.

NEWBIE JEFF, Unknown

GARDENS CAN USE FROM 25-60 watts of HPS light per square foot (psf). A 400-watt lamp can illuminate a garden as large as 4' x 4' (16 square feet) or as small as 2' x 3' (6 square feet). A 1,000-watt lamp can illuminate an area from 16-40 square feet. That would be an area of 4' x 4' to 6' x 6'.

Total yield is based on the amount of light the plants receive rather than the area of the garden. Other factors determining yield include the variety and cultivation techniques. A garden in a larger area lit by the same wattage lamps as a small garden has about the same yield. The material grown in the small area will be more compact and dense than the buds grown in the larger space. Figure on yields of 1/4 to 3/4 gram per watt. A 400-watt lamp will yield of 3.5-10 ounces. A 1,000-watt lamp will produce a harvest of 8-24 ounces.

> *For more on light amounts and garden set-ups, see chapter 2, sections D and E.*

OUTDOOR YIELDS

What kind of yields should be expected from an outdoor garden? I've read that eight good-sized plants could yield over 4 pounds of grass. Is this just the manicured buds or is it the total yield of the plants, including fan leaves?

HIGH IN THE MOUNTAINS, Walhalla, South Carolina

FIGURE THAT FOR EACH square foot of canopy, the plant will produce between $3/8$ and 1 ounce of bud. A bird's eye view of a well-developed cannabis plant might look like a circle entirely covered with vegetation. There is only one layer of vegetation, no matter how tall the plant. The reason is that the branch above prevents light from reaching the branch below. Plant height is not an indicator of yield, but the area the canopy occupies is. To figure the potential yield from a plant, take the diameter of the canopy at the bottom of the plant. Then use the formula Area=πr^2. Lets do it for 2-foot, 3-foot and 5-foot diameter plants:

For 2 ft. diameter plant: $3.14 \times 1^2 = 3.14$ ft.^{2}

3.14 ft.^{2} x $3/8$ oz. = 1.17 oz.

3.14 ft.^{2} x 1 oz. = 3.14 oz.

For 3 ft. diameter plant: $3.14 \times 1.5^2 = 7$ ft.^{2}

7 ft.^{2} x $3/8$ oz. = 2.62 oz.

7 ft.^{2} x 1 oz. = 7 oz.

For 5 ft. diameter plant: $3.14 \times 2.5^2 = 19.62$ ft.^{2}

19.62 ft.^{2} x $3/8$ oz. = 7.36 oz.

19.62 ft.^{2} x 1 oz. = 19.62 oz.

NOTE: $\pi = 3.14$, r=radius (one-half of the diameter)

E. DRYING & CURING

1. STAGE ONE: DRYING

DRYING TACTICS

I live in a very small space and have nowhere to dry my bud except in the grow room. Does it harm the bud to dry it in a lit area?

THE BASEMENT BOTANIST, Kalamazoo, Michigan

HIGH TEMPERATURE, LIGHT AND the presence of oxygen degrade THC, the active ingredient in marijuana.

For the tastiest smoke, the bud should be cured first in a room with moderate moisture, cool temperature (60-70° F) and a steady breeze. This keeps the leaves alive. They use some of the starches and sugars in their life processes, mellowing the smoke. After a few days, the environment should change to a dry 85° F to evaporate the water. The breezy space should be dimly lit to prevent the THC from deteriorating.

You could keep the bud in the bathroom for a few days. Keep the air moving with a fan. Put a temporary covering over the window, and then close the door. First keep the space cool then use a dehumidifier to heat it as it removes water.

Once the buds are dry, they should be vacuum packed or placed in a vacuum bag injected with carbon dioxide (CO_2). Other people prefer mason jars. If the jar is placed in the freezer, the THC will barely deteriorate.

> For more on THC, see "Advice on Storage" in section F, this chapter; chapter 13, section A.1.

ng, I ha
switchab
er H.P.S.
e the la
e sides
ays.I th
. gal. o
se.Thcn
s maybe

R.

First

toperiod ?

photoperiod is 12/1
a?What is the
he equator (Sri Lanl
ka.

These are Bud of the Month®, Plant of the Month® and Garden of the Month® winners.

DRYING THE HARVEST

What is the correct way of drying plant clippings?

COURTNEY, Las Vegas, Nevada

IN LAS VEGAS, WHERE it is very dry, the buds and clippings dry out quickly if left out on a warm autumn day. When this happens they do not get a chance to "cure" and mellow as they are drying.

The trimmings should be cured first in a cool, moderately moist dark space. This gives the grass a chance to mellow a bit before drying. Then the trimmings can either be placed on trays or in a bowl and placed in a warm dark space.

Once the grass is dry, it should be placed in the freezer in glass or metal containers.

READY TO SMOKE?

How long does it take for the THC on a cured dried bud to become psychoactive? Can I smoke it as soon as it's dried?

JAY, Aston, Pennsylvania

ONCE THE BUD HAS dried to the point that it sustains a burn, the THC is psychoactive. Some people find that a bud aged two or three weeks has a better, mellower flavor.

BEST DRYING CONDITIONS

What is the best way to dry buds, both small and large quantities? Where should I dry them. What's the proper temperature and humidity? How do I cure the buds to make it smoke smooth, with a nice taste and good aroma?

HIDING OUT IN THE USA, Brooklyn, New York

TO CREATE A SMOOTH enjoyable smoke, marijuana should be dried slowly so the cells have a chance to convert the stored starches to sugars. Ideal conditions would be 3-5 days in a dark space with moderate humidity, temperature in the high 60's and constant air movement. Then the temperature is raised to the 80's and the humidity is lowered to dry the buds faster. This stage of drying should end when the buds are still pliable, but will not smoke unless they are constantly relit. To prevent them from losing any aroma, lower the temperature again and age them for another week or so, until they are slightly brittle and will sustain a light.

These conditions can be created in a small box using a fan and small heater with thermostat, in a closet or room.

I observed a greenhouse harvest in Holland. The plants were cut and transported in long flower boxes to a manicuring factory where the sun and secondary leaves were trimmed. Then the plants were hung tightly in a room being serviced with a rented room dryer. The dryer heated the room to 90° F as it removed gallons of water per hour from the air. The buds were dry in about 36 hours. I thought they were harsh, but other people never mentioned it.

Small quantities of bud can be dried in a microwave. Don't dry them entirely, but just until they are very pliable, almost wet. Then let them air dry for several hours. For immediate use, dry them until they sustain a burn. They will be quite harsh.

A few buds can be dried in a short period by placing them in a brown paper bag. To extend the drying, close the bag part of the time.

I do have reservations about using food dehydrators, which blow warm air through trays. Some models blow air hotter than the evaporation temperature of some of the odor molecules. Dehydrators with thermal controls should be set at low, so the air temperature remains lower than 90° F.

MICROWAVE DRYING

Does drying marijuana in a microwave have any effect on the potency of the weed?

KEN M., Northern New Jersey

IT DOESN'T SEEM TO. However, weed dried completely in a micro-wave has a harsh taste and all of the chlorophyll is left. Instead, try drying the plants halfway in a microwave and then letting them dry naturally. They will have a better taste. Some growers dry the plants for a while naturally and then finish drying them in the microwave. Don't use a microwave on buds with seeds that you want to remain viable. The microwave kills them.

E. 2. STAGE TWO: CURING

HOW TO CURE

After clipping the fan leaves, I hang the harvested plants upside down until the buds are almost completely dry to the touch. The stem is dry too, but won't snap if bent.

I hang the plants to dry in a warm room with plenty of air circulation. It is dimly lit and has high humidity. Drying takes about five days. Then I trim the bud and put it in plastic bags for a day. It regains its moisture. Then I dry it completely.

I'm sure my buds are choice, but after all this, the buds smell like grass clippings. What am I doing wrong?

BABY G., Palatine, Illinois

IN A COOL ROOM buds dry slowly because the air can hold a small amount of moisture. This gives the cells time to convert starches back to sugars, and creates a smoother smoke. The coolness pre-serves odor molecules, which evaporate at higher temperatures.

Drying the plants in a room with high humidity and tempera-ture is sort of self-defeating. The odor molecules evaporate in the high temperature but the moisture has no place to go because the air is already saturated. With lower humidity, the plants would dry quickly and little odor would be lost.

Ideally, plants should be dried in a cool room (low 70's) for five days. Then the temperature should be raised (high 70's) and the humidity kept low for the dry. A dehumidifier or room dryer may be needed.

Whole plants are hard to handle and generally inconvenient to deal with. It might be better to cut them into 12-inch to 18-inch sections and place them on drying racks or hang them using clothespins or stem crotches.

Placing the plants in plastic bags, where they sweated probably destroyed some odor molecules as a result of anaerobic bacteria that thrive in low oxygen environments.

STICKY SPRAY

Is there a type of spray that stores sell that could make my weed moister and sticky?

JOHN, Reading, Pennsylvania

NOT THAT I KNOW of. The moistness comes from a slow cure before drying and the stickiness is the result of a plentitude of mature glands. It certainly would be a lot easier getting it from an aerosol rather than having to grow it.

ED'S TIP ▸ PREPARING THE SMOKE: DRYING & MANICURING

There are many techniques for manicuring and drying plants. Some people like to manicure while the plants are still wet so fewer THC containing glands fall off. However, manicuring wet plants takes much longer than dry ones.

Whether the plant is manicured wet or dry, cut it into individual branches. Remove the large fan leaves from the branch. Then remove the secondary large leaves followed by smaller leaves that hide the buds. Then cut the bud from the branch. Inspect the bud for mold. Any infected parts should be discarded.

Some people remove the leaves by hand, pulling down

on the leaf stem so that it snaps off the plant. Most people use small scissors with a sharp point to clip the leaves where they join the plant. Scissors with springs on them, which open automatically, are very popular.

To dry properly, the buds or branches should be placed in a cool, dark area with air circulation so the vegetation dries slowly. This converts some of the starches to sugars resulting in a smoother smoke. When the buds have lost most of their water but are still very pliable, raise the temperature to the mid-80's so the buds lose the rest of their moisture.

If it is a large harvest or the air where the buds are to dry has high humidity, some of the moisture should be removed or the buds will not dry properly. This is accomplished using a dehumidifier, which dries the air and raises its temperature.

For info on mold and smoking, see chapter 14, section C.

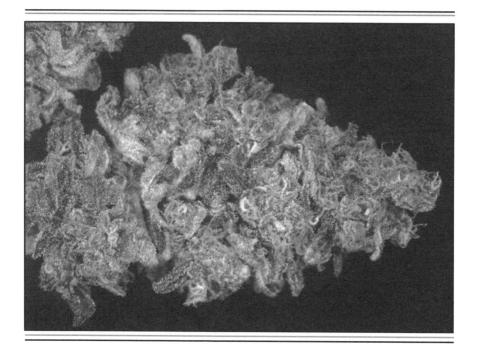

F. MANICURING
& STORAGE

HOW MUCH TO MANICURE

I have read lots of stuff about harvesting and curing buds but little about the manicuring process. Do you try to remove as many leaves as possible? It seems a shame to take off all those sugar leaves covered in stalked glands.

B. BUD, Portland, Oregon

MANICURING IS NOT A complicated art. The idea is to remove the material that is less potent while preserving the parts covered with resin glands. First, the fan leaves and secondary leaves should be removed. This should expose the flowers and tiny leaves surrounding them as well as some single-fingered leaves that are sticking out from the bud.

Check to see if the inner parts of these leaves, close to the flowers, are gland covered. If they are, just trim away the outer portion of the leaf. If not, spread the bud by gently bending it and then cut the leaf off.

Some general ideas about manicuring:

- Fewer glands fall off the bud when it is manicured still wet than when it is dry. However, many people find it faster and easier to manicure dry plants. Rather than using scissors as on wet plants, they can take off the dry outer leaves quickly with their fingers.

- Manicuring over a 100-line-per-inch mesh silk or stainless steel screen separates fallen glands from other debris. Glands drop through the mesh, leaving vegetation above. These glands are called kief; they are the raw ingredient for hashish, and make an excellent extra high potency smoking material because they are so concentrated.

224

■ There is no one particular pair of scissors that is comfortable for everyone. Try out different models until you find something that feels right to you. Uncomfortable scissors may create muscle fatigue and worse.

ADVICE ON STORAGE

I had a much larger harvest than I expected. How should I store my stash, both short and long term?

FAT FARMER, Internet

THC IS THE ACTIVE ingredient in marijuana. It is found on the glands attached to the surface of the leaves, stems and flowers of the female plant. THC is produced on the surface of the gland membrane, outside of the cell. (The glands can be seen fairly clearly when they are viewed under a photographer's loupe.) When it is in the living plant, a water molecule is attached which makes it less active than in the dry form. After thorough drying, the THC in the marijuana is in its most psychoactive form.

THC deteriorates when it is exposed to light, oxygen and heat. The worst idea for storing would be to put dried marijuana in a big open bowl in the sun. Putting marijuana in a zipper bag and putting it in a pocket may be a close second or may actually be worse. The THC deteriorates fairly quickly because of the body heat and the abrasion from rubbing. In addition, the polyethylene bags carry an electrical charge that attracts the glands. By the time the stash is finished the bag may be cloudy with glands that were lost to you.

A wood, hard plastic or metal container is the best way to store a marijuana stash that is carried around. The container should not be in a shirt or pants pocket. The further from your body heat, the better. A purse or knapsack would be good places as far as maintaining quality is concerned. Of course, the first concern is safety and security.

Long-term, the best way to store marijuana is in a large sealed container in a freezer. In a scientific study it was found that marijuana kept in a freezer for a year showed practically no signs of deterioration. Refrigerators also retard deterioration, but not quite as effectively. The reason refrigerators and freezers work: it's cold and dark so chemical reactions slow down. Filling the container with an inert gas would be a redundancy. Storing the buds in a vacuum-sealed bag in the cold and dark would also keep the buds fresh.

> *For more on THC, see chapter 13, section A.1.*
> *For info on molds, see chapter 14, section C.*

READER TIP ▸ STORAGE IMPROVEMENT

Regarding your tips for long-term storage of marijuana, I have been storing marijuana for extended periods for several years. Your directions for refrigerating or freezing were very good, as this has preserved my best stash for periods of up to three years.

I found that the best storage container is a tightly sealed mason jar with a tight rubber seal for storing jellies and things. Not only does this last better than plastic containers, but the glass does not leave any aroma or taste on what is inside.

Some mildly flavored herbs, especially sativas, absorb odor and taste from plastic containers. The glass cleans much easier when it's time to reuse it.

W.S., Baltimore, Maryland

THANKS, W.S.

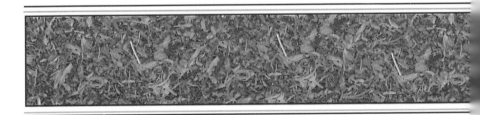

G. USES FOR LEAVES

LOTS OF LEAVES

> I find myself with a large amount of male leaves. I was wondering what kind of screen, metal or silk you would use?
>
> H.O., Allentown, Pennsylvania

USUALLY FEMALE GLANDS ARE screened over a mesh that is woven at 100 or 110 lines per inch. I think the male glands are somewhat smaller than the female's. I would try screening the leaves over a 110-line-per-inch mesh. Don't expect a high yield.

With steel mesh you can be more precise regarding your screenings. However, many people prefer silk.

ED'S TIP ▸ LEAF RECYCLING

There are many different ways to process leaf. The first step to transform leaf from garbage into harvest is to separate the glands from the vegetative material using mesh screen or cold water. These loose glands are called kief. If this material is pressed, it becomes hash. Kief, hash, or whole leaf can be used to cook, make tinctures or make capsules. Some people use leaf as a topical medicinal in the form of a poultice. Another book, *Ask Ed: Marijuana Gold—Trash to Stash* covers these methods in detail. It is available through the publisher's website, www.quicktrading.com, or at most bookstores.

USING LEAVES FOR MULCH?

This year I had my biggest harvest to date: over 151 pounds of primo purple hair bud from ten of my own Colombo-Oaxacan hybrids. But I also collected 7 pounds of leaf and buds from male plants (which I cut down when the buds were about to open), 3 pounds of fallen leaf, 7 pounds of upper and lower leaf, and 3 pounds of bud leaf. What should I do with this stuff? My friends say it's better to use it as mulch.

SINSEMILLA DAN, Little Rock, Arkansas

MULCHING UNPROCESSED LEAF IS a waste of good highs. The leaf is high in nutrients, but the THC it contains will be broken down by next growing season and will not be picked up by the new plants. First process the leaf by screening, making water hash or tinctures. After the cannabinoids are removed, it is ready to be used in the garden as mulch or for compost.

STEALTH & SAFETY

A. STEALTH
1. ODOR CONTROL
2. DETECTION TECHNOLOGY

B. LEGAL RIGHTS
1. PREVENTING LEGAL PROBLEMS
2. BUSTS & RAIDS
3. ACTIVISM

A. STEALTH

1. ODOR CONTROL

SMELLY PROBLEM

I am growing in a 10' x 12' room. I am using a Zestron ion fountain and a HEPA-style air filter, which circulates the air eight times an hour. My 480 cfm (cubic feet per minute) fan is wired to a thermostat-humidistat and is vented through air vents in the roof.

Photo by Pepper Design

My house is tightly situated between two other homes, and there is heavy foot traffic across the street. Will the air filter and the ion fountain be effective in keeping the skunk aroma under wraps during the budding stage?

BIG DADDY, Tacoma, Washington

ODOR IS CREATED IN the grow room, but the problem begins when the smell migrates to other areas. This may seem obvious, but your system is designed to minimize the odor in the grow room and does not solve the problems outside that space.

Ion generators are inexpensive, use very little electricity, and are very effective. They work by loading the air with extra electrons. Most odor particles are solids, which are electrically charged because they are missing an electron. When the ions and the electron-deprived particles meet, the electron migrates to the particle. The particle is neutralized; it loses its odor and precipitates out of the air.

When ion generators are used in the grow room, they eliminate most of the odors but not the ones that leave the room. The

231

generators also make the grass itself less odoriferous. The solution is to use the generators in the areas surrounding the grow room including any outflow vents and doorway areas.

Ozone generators create ozone, O_3. Usually gasses, including oxygen, float around as two-atom molecules (O_2). Ozone is a three-atom molecule and it isn't stable. One oxygen molecule is ready to jump and combine with another atom. Since most odor molecules are missing an electron, they easily combine with the oxygen and lose their odor. Both ion and ozone generators can be placed inside vent tubing or in a plenum so they are cleaned before they exit.

Electrostatic filters are placed in vents to filter the air using electrical charges. There are both electrically charged and passive precipitators. These devices strip the air of its odor while it is streaming through venting or tubing.

Carbon filters use carbon's ability to filter molecules including odors. They can be placed in vents to clean the passing air.

The HEPA filter eliminates bacteria and fungal spores as well as some odors that are airborne so it should be kept in the grow space. Perhaps it could be employed as the first step in venting air from the garden space.

I recommend cleaning the air using an electrostatic filter, carbon filter and ozone generator. I like redundancy.

ION GENERATORS

Is the activated carbon filter (acf) in my new air cleaner/negative ion generator effective or would I be just as well off with a simple negative ion generator? Will the acf absorb CO_2, slowing ripening? Does it absorb odor?

My 5'x 5'x 7' chamber is very clean. Does the dust that collects on the acf qualify as hash? Do negative ion generators placed in proximity to plants diminish potency?

NEW FRONTIERSMAN, Portland, Oregon

As you noticed, the acf is effectively screening dust from the air. Obviously the combination of a negative ion generator and air cleaner is more effective than an air cleaner or ionizer alone. Activated charcoal absorbs minuscule amounts of CO_2 and does not affect plant growth.

Odor is caused by solid particles floating in the air. They are airborne because they are missing an electron and are positively charged. The negative ion generator emits electrons that attract positively charged bits of dust, odor molecules, bacteria, fungi and other dust floating in the air. Once their charge is neutralized, they precipitate, meaning they fall to surfaces. Odor disappears and is replaced by grimy dust on surfaces.

While the grime may contain some odor molecules, it does not contain any appreciable amount of THC and also contains a lot of undesirable dust, grease, microorganisms and pollutants.

Negative ions affect odor molecules outside the glands so that the grow room loses most of its odor. It is possible that the ions also penetrate the glands and deactivate some odor molecules. This is consistent with growers' observations that buds lose some of their odor, but not their potency in grow rooms with negative ion generators. The plants retain their odor when the ionizers are placed outside the grow room. Buds grown with a negative ion generator may seem odorless until they are broken apart—then the perfume floats out.

NEGATIVE ION GENERATORS

Please list the advantages and disadvantages of negative ion generators.

S.H., Des Plaines, Illinois

NEGATIVE ION GENERATORS FLOOD the air with negative ions, or molecules with a negative electrical charge. Negative ions transfer their negative charge to positively charged solid particles, neutralizing them. Without electrical charge, they drop out of the air. Odors and dust as well as mold spores, bacteria and other pollutants are removed from the air and deposited near the ion fountain. Plants grow faster and humans have reduced tensions and increased attentiveness in a negative ion–filled environment.

Negative ion generators are noise-free and use minute amounts of electricity. When using negative ion generators without collector plates, place newspaper around the machine. It will collect a lot of the pollutants and it can be discarded when it gets filthy.

LOUD BALLASTS

I have a 1,000-watt MH lamp. The ballast creates a loud buzzing hum. Are all ballasts noisy? Or is something wrong? Do you have any suggestions on how to reduce or eliminate the noise?

BUZZ W, St. Louis, Missouri

SOME BRANDS OF BALLASTS are noisier than others. However, individual ballasts from the same brands also vary in noise level. Perhaps the box is noisy because a loose connection is causing vibration. Have a technician from an indoor garden shop check it and tighten everything up. This may eliminate some of the noise. To minimize the sound, place the ballast on a surface that does not vibrate. Foam pads under the ballast help to absorb some of the vibrations and lower noise intensity.

A. 2. DETECTION TECHNOLOGY

DETECTING SEEDS

Can dogs smell marijuana seeds?

TWEETY-BIRD, Midland, Michigan

MARIJUANA SEEDS ARE ODORLESS and contain neither THC nor aromatics. However, some of these substances may stick to the seeds so there might be a slight odor. The seeds can be washed and dried just to make sure there is no residue on them. Well-wrapped seeds are undetectable to canine smell-checkers.

DRUG TESTS & FRESH MARIJUANA

Can smelling growing marijuana cause a person to fail a drug test? I am not referring to second-hand smoke, but the odor of the growing plant.

FAMILYMAN, Lebanon, Ohio

THE ODORS FROM GROWING marijuana are not cannabinoids. They are mono- and di-terpenes and flavinoids similar in chemistry to many other plant odors. When you smell them, you are not coming in contact with THC or similar compounds, so it has no effect on drug tests.

Second-hand marijuana smoke does contain THC and a very sensitive test will pick it up. Tests are usually calibrated to have a higher threshold of detection and avoid the confusion regarding sidestream contact.

For more on drug tests, see section B.1, this chapter.

B. LEGAL RIGHTS

1. PREVENTING LEGAL PROBLEMS

SEED LEGALITY

What are the US laws concerning importing cannabis seed?

CURIOUS, Internet

ALL CANNABIS SEED CAPABLE of germination is illegal according to US law. Only sterile seed, incapable of germination, can legally be possessed.

Smuggling is a separate crime from possession and the federal government can take a very dim view of the small percentage of smugglers who get caught. The individual states also have possession laws that outlaw seed possession.

LEGAL STATUS OF CULTIVATION

Where is it legal to cultivate marijuana?

DAVID, Hackensack, New Jersey

IT IS ILLEGAL TO cultivate marijuana anywhere in the US because federal laws treat it as the felony of manufacturing drugs. In addition, every state has anti-cultivation laws that treat marijuana as a felony. Some states have medical laws that allow patients or their caregivers to grow, but it's still against federal law. A grow can be prosecuted by the feds, the state or both under the concept of "separate sovereigns." However these forces often work together, especially when forfeiture is involved.

There are no countries or areas in countries where it is legal to grow. Small-scale cultivation is tolerated in Holland and other European countries, Vancouver and some other areas in Canada.

236

STATE LAWS

How can I find out about laws for growing in the state I live in?

TANK, Internet

THE **NORML** WEBSITE HAS the most comprehensive and updated information on the laws by state for the US. A list of state-by-state penalties is on the NORML web site: www.norml.org. The Marijuana Policy Project also features legal and political updates in a state-by-state format, as well as a state-by-state description of medical marijuana laws. The Marijuana Policy Project website is www.mpp.org.

THE ARGUMENT FOR LEGALIZATION

I am doing a research paper on the legalization of marijuana and I was wondering if you could give me a few tips or words of wisdom on what I should look out for.

GRACE, Internet

IF THE PURPOSE OF law is to protect the society from harm, then no law should be more harmful to society than the behavior it attempts to regulate. By any yardstick the marijuana laws are more harmful than the use of marijuana. Here are two glaring examples.

According to the Drug Awareness Warning Network (DAWN) nobody died from the use of marijuana last year, or any year since the statistics have been gathered. However enforcing marijuana prohibition cost over fifty lives a year in the US, mostly civilians. Certainly that cost alone is enough to warrant an end to prohibition.

There are about 750,000 marijuana arrests a year. Each arrest affects the parents, children, spouse, employer and friends of the arrestee. Perhaps 5 million new people are affected each year by a marijuana arrest. Certainly an arrest is more harmful to a person and his or her community, as well as to society, than that person's use of pot.

Don't get caught in the conundrum of differentiating between the user and provider of marijuana. If it is okay to use the substance, then it should be lawful to provide it to willing buyers. Differentiating between provider and consumer for something that is deemed lawful to use still denotes disapproval and inevitably leads to corruption. Commerce should be transparent, not hidden.

For words of wisdom, I defer to Bob Dylan who stated in Subterranean Homesick Blues, "Don't follow leaders, watch the parking meters." I take this to mean: Just because some prominent person says it or wrote it, doesn't mean it's true; second, don't stand out from the norm in a way that brings official types around. If you are subverting the law, keep your car in good working order and mow your lawn—don't let a minor detail lead to a major bust.

ED'S TIP ▸ STUDYING FOR DRUG TESTING

The only relatively sure way to pass a drug test is to have abstained from the use of any drugs for which you might be tested. But if you've ever used, how long is long enough to pass the test?

Of the drugs typically tested for, marijuana has the longest detection time after use, which can be up to six weeks when subjected to a urine test. There are too many factors involved to know how long marijuana's metabolites can be detected; it varies from person to person. The following affect detection time:

- the person's metabolism
- the frequency of marijuana use
- the length of time one has been a marijuana smoker
- the potency of the marijuana
- the individual's tolerance to marijuana
- the person's intake of fluids

The basic rule of thumb for detection—a person who uses infrequently and has a fast metabolism will have a shorter detection time than a person who uses frequently, has used over a long period of time, or has a slow metabolism. The detection time generally ranges from 3 days to 45 days after use.

BEATING THE ODDS

I've been a semi-regular smoker for years. Now I'm trying to get a job, and so many places require a pre-employment screening test. I disagree with these tests, but refusing to take them is financial suicide. Will I test positive if I haven't smoked for the last three weeks? Do the products out there work to fool the tests? Or are there other ways? Please help.

PISSING FOR DOLLARS, Denver, Colorado

MANY PRODUCTS OUT THERE can help you pass a test.

The most common method used to clean up before a drug test is to try to flush out metabolites from the body by drinking specialized products, or just drinking a lot of fluids. This has a sound basis in science. Products such as Test Pure, Clear Choice and Urine Luck contain chelating agents that may lower metabolites if ingested anywhere from 12 hours to 4 days before the test. Home remedies such as activated charcoal, vinegar, goldenseal and vitamin C may work as detoxifiers but have no proven influence on cleaning out marijuana metabolites when used short-term.

Besides specially designed products, a common strategy is to do what you've done, quit smoking, and then increase fluid intake to dilute the metabolites already in your system.

Products that you add to adulterate the sample, or clean samples for purchase to use in place of your own, are both riskier. Getting caught adding stuff to the sample or trying to switch it out can create more problems than not passing a test.

Even if you've abstained and tried to flush your system, there is always the possibility of testing positive. Although it can be very difficult to contest results, never freely admit to use in the past or present and they'll never know for sure.

SMALL-TOWN BLUES

I live in a small town where everybody knows everybody. Whenever I go to buy plant food or growing supplies, I'm asked what I'm growing and I can't really say. What plant is most like the marijuana plant?

STUMPED, St. Joseph, Missouri

PEOPLE USUALLY SAY THEY are growing corn or tomatoes. However, these are fruiting plants, not flowering plants like marijuana, so their needs are significantly different. You want to promote flowers. You could tell them that you are growing a flower garden of annuals such as marigolds, zinnias, snapdragons, petunias and pansies. They will set you up with fertilizers that promote healthy plant growth and flowering.

Perhaps there are other solutions. You could drive to a mall or larger town, where you can go to a self-service store and buy things anonymously. Another idea is to find the closest indoor garden shop. They might be able to help you with your needs.

INCRIMINATING PHOTOS

I have lots of pictures of inside and outside plants that I grew. Is it possible to get busted because of those pictures?

CONCERNED ROB, Ogdensburg, New York

IT IS NOT ILLEGAL to possess photos of plants. However, after a bust, the prosecutor might use the photos as evidence of a crime or of a continuing crime. If a person showed the photos to another, and explained that he had grown the plants depicted, that would be enough to at least start an investigation.

The photos should be stored in a place that is not likely to be connected to a garden. That way, they cannot be seized and used as evidence.

RED-HANDED WITH "DITCH WEED"

The other day I got into trouble for possessing ditch weed. I was under the impression that ditch weed was not pot, just a cousin. What is ditch weed?

NITRO, Crawfordville, Indiana

DITCH WEED IS DESCENDED from the industrial hemp that was grown all over the Midwest during the nineteenth and early twentieth centuries. Although farmers stopped planting hemp, it naturalized and evolved. It has been so successful that it is considered a noxious weed in some areas.

This feral hemp has very low THC content and usually will give you a headache before it gets you high. However, it contains cannabinoids such as THC's precursor, CBD.

Hemp can be bred with marijuana and these plants are considered the same specie. Both plants are artifacts of cannabis' interaction with humans. Hemp and marijuana plants were developed for different purposes using selective breeding. I would say the plants are sisters, rather than cousins. Unfortunately, both are considered "marijuana" by the law.

Although you didn't think of it as marijuana, the law does. Get yourself a lawyer who specializes in marijuana or drug cases or at least criminal law. Make sure the attorney is on your side before hiring the person.

RIGHTS AT TRAFFIC STOP

When you are pulled over for speeding and the police officer asks if he may search the car for drugs do you have to let him search or can you refuse?

NTVMIR, Banning, California

THE COP WOULD NOT be asking for your permission if s/he didn't need it. If the cop asks you why you refuse permission just say that you are doing it to help preserve the Constitution and the Bill of Rights—you know—use it or lose it. Change the subject—then say something like: "I'm sure you respect that answer officer, because I know you believe in the Constitution, too." Then politely ask, "Now that I have been warned or given a ticket can I go?"

TERMS OF ENTRAPMENT

> The other day my friend and I were riding in his car. He had smoked in it earlier so it smelled of smoke. A cop car was sitting on my friend's street. The cop pulled us over for running a stop sign. He never said anything about smelling anything. He walked back to his car and wrote a careless driving ticket. Then he told my friend about how to go about paying it.
>
> Out of nowhere he asked if he could search the car. My friend said no. Then he said that if we had anything in the car, we should go ahead and give it to him and proceeded to tell us that he was going to get the K-9 unit over there if we didn't give him stuff or let him search the car. After a couple of minutes of hassling about searching the car he radioed to some more cops. My friend handed one of the cops a roach and they patted me down and found about a $1/2$ ounce in my underwear and then automatically arrested me. I would just like to know under what terms are they allowed to search the car and better yet search me considering I hadn't even been smoking.
>
> GATH, Internet

I SPOKE WITH BILL PANZER, a noted California attorney who practices in state as well as federal courts. His opinion is that once the cop gave your friend the ticket, his investigation of reckless driving was completed. He had no further reason to detain you. At the point when your friend told him that he couldn't search the car, you were free to go. His arguing about it and threatening to detain you for a canine search was illegal. Your friend who handed the cop the roach was coerced into it when the second cop arrived. The fruits of this illegal, coercive search should not be allowed as evidence.

The cop had no right to search you because you were not driving and were not under investigation.

JUDICIOUS ADVICE

I was recently found guilty of cultivation of marijuana. Four potential jurors were dismissed when they voiced their opinion regarding the marijuana laws. I would have been found innocent had they saved their opinions for the jury room. This would be a great help to the cause.

Don't shirk jury duty. If we all stand together, we will stop our persecution.

JOHN, Morgan Hill, California

JURORS ARE SUPPOSED TO tell judges if they have a bias or prejudice. Few who are prejudiced in favor of police or in favor of conviction ever mention their prejudices. They do it in the jury room by their votes. Maybe if more pro-pot people stayed silent before being chosen, there would be fewer convictions and ultimately, fewer persecutions.

Further, remember that's it's not a crime to argue the merits of the case and whether the prosecution was appropriate. Even if the rest of the jury wants to convict, a single holdout hangs the jury.

BUSTED IN TEXAS

I am a college student in Texas. My house was raided. The pig's response for them coming in without a search warrant was that they were responding to a 911 call, which is absurd. It seems someone ratted me out for growing one plant. If the law somehow convicts me of the charges

brought against me, conspiracy to cultivate, am I looking at a felony or a misdemeanor?

BUSTED BUT NOT BEATEN, San Marcos, Texas

CULTIVATION AND CONSPIRACY TO cultivate are felonies. If you are convicted you would become a felon. You will lose eligibility for federal college loans.

The warrantless search was bogus and a good criminal attorney knowledgeable in drug law in Texas may be able to get the case thrown out on motions. Further, the 911 call should be investigated to find its source. Even if you have only a public defender, you can fight this unjust case. To find out more about this, check out free information on my website, www.quicktrading.com, regarding marijuana law. It contains detailed instructions on how to win a marijuana case.

B. 3. ACTIVISM

CONSIDERING CONTRIBUTING

I am a business owner in Raleigh, North Carolina. I earn a substantial amount of money and believe 100% in supporting the cause. I am willing to do what it takes to awaken our political officials to the stupidity of the prohibition of marijuana.

I am somewhat apprehensive about making donations to the best places such as Cannabis Action Network, Marijuana Policy Project or Green-Aid as I am afraid that those contributions may lead back to my company and jeopardize my professional license. I have made donations to the Libertarian Party but would rather be more direct.

How can I work behind the scenes in an inconspicuous way to further decriminalization?

THE VIPER, North Carolina

WITH SUPPORT LIKE YOURS marijuana will be legalized in another 500 years. You need to put your money directly to the issue.

It is not crazy to be paranoid in this country, but quite another to completely compromise yourself out of fear. If you are fearful about writing a check from your account, you could send the organizations postal money orders. The purchase of these checks is anonymous.

Nobody gives you your freedom. You have to fight for it. If, for whatever reasons, you are unwilling or unable to get active in securing your civil liberties, the least you can do is to support others while they do battle for us all. You are not doing them a favor when you give them financial support. They are doing you a favor fighting for everyone's rights.

READER TIP ▸ CONTEMPLATING CRAZY PAST OMISSIONS

I can't believe the crazy excuses I've heard and read for not speaking out about the marijuana laws. The most common are: I might lose my job, friends or end up in jail. Are these people crazy?

Every time you possess, buy or grow pot you are more at risk than if you write a letter to your governor or Congressman or join a legalization group.

I'm a prime example. I wouldn't speak out or write a letter. Now I'm doing two years in prison for possession. Every day I wonder, "If I had spoken out and donated a few dollars to the movement and written some letters, would I be right here now or would I be at my local grocery store buying some munchies?" One more person might make all the difference.

You are definitely crazy if you give any excuse. Maybe even stupid.

PRIME EXAMPLE, GREEN ROOM CLUB,
Springfield State Prison, Springfield, South Dakota

THANKS FOR YOUR REMARKS. I hope more people get involved. After all, "These laws are doomed."

DARE TO FIGHT DARE

My 12-year-old daughter's school recently initiated a DARE program at the insistence of the new police chief. She was very upset after the first program and asked me to excuse her from future sessions. She said there was a movie that depicted dysfunctional families and heroic cops and that she and some of her friends were asked to inform on classmates. She told me that she never expected that her classmates even thought about drugs. Three other children were also excused by their parents.

Now after a trial period, the chief wants to make this a

permanent program. I think that it's destructive and is a family value issue better dealt with at home. Are there any studies on this program? How can I get help against this police state brainwashing?

MOTHER OF TWO, Indiana

THERE HAVE BEEN A number of studies on the DARE program. They all show that the program is ineffective at best and often has negative results.

DARE programs are a boondoggle for cops, who serve "classroom duty" rather than protecting the public. The online Shaffer Library of Drug Policy is a good source for evaluative studies on the DARE program. The URL is www.druglibrary.org, and the studies on DARE appear in the subsection "Kids and Drugs." One of the most comprehensive papers posted here is "A Different Look at DARE" (www.drcnet.org/DARE/). Another good source for the newest available studies on DARE and drug education is the Drug Policy Alliance: www.drugpolicy.org.

There is absolutely no reason why parents should allow a program that denigrates the role of the family in favor of the police. Parents can remove DARE from school programs. When funding for DARE came up for renewal in Oakland, California, concerned parents, armed with facts and supporting studies, were able to prove that the program was a waste of money or worse. The police chief was unprepared for the debate, and had only platitudes and anecdotal evidence for the panel. The Council refused to fund a new DARE package.

One area the parents did not investigate is how much the police department collected from private industry sponsors for the program. In many cities, the police use DARE as a source of non-budgetary funding and have complete discretion over use of the money. Another DARE opponent said that showing parents material from the curriculum invariably turns them against the program.

DARE BACKER

Your letter entitled, "Dare to Fight DARE" got my wife and me wondering about what was being said to our middle school children. After several months of inquiry, resulting in direct, honest answers, we've come to the conclusion that DARE is a relatively good thing. I know I never thought I would say that, but it does deter some kids from using speed, cocaine and heroin.

Our kids have never been asked to turn anyone in, nor have they been asked personal family questions.

FATHER OF THREE, Phoenix, Arizona

VIRTUALLY EVERY INDEPENDENT STUDY of DARE shows that kids who are exposed to DARE are no less likely to experiment with drugs than kids who are given no drug education classes.

Other problems with DARE result from its being taught by cops, who have no expertise about drugs from a sociological, psychological or biological perspective. The main expertise that police have regarding drugs is how to recognize them and how to arrest people for them.

The harm reduction paradigm is being adopted all over the world. You know that kids are going to experiment, so give them knowledge and steer them from the most harmful substances. A program that condemns all drug use convinces few.

In addition, cops are very expensive teachers. It costs $70,000-$100,000 a year to pay a cop's expenses and training. Professionally trained drug experts could teach a well-designed curriculum for the same price that we now pay for a cop's soft duty and superficial classes. Take that cop out of the school and put him/her back on the beat where s/he belongs.

You are the victim of the DARE propaganda campaign. DARE stinks.

TROUBLESHOOTING

A. SEEDLING/STARTING PROBLEMS

B. LEAF PROBLEMS
1. BROWNING/SPOTTING/CURLING
2. YELLOWING LEAVES

C. BRANCH PROBLEMS

D. PLANT PROBLEMS

E. BUD PROBLEMS

F. PROBLEMS OVER GENERATIONS

G. HYDRO PROBLEMS

H. OUTDOOR PROBLEMS

RELATED TOPICS

Bugs & other pests: chapter 10 Pests & Disease, section A Pests.

Viruses, molds, powdery mildew: chapter 10 Pests & Disease, section B Viruses, Fungi & Molds.

Hermaphrodites: chapter 11 Genetics & Breeding, section B Hermaphrodites.

Vegetative/flowering problems: chapter 6 Plant Life Cycle, section F Cycle Problems.

Heat problems: chapter 3 Ventilation & CO_2, section A.2 Heat.

Ripening problems: chapter 7 Harvest, section B Ripening & Harvest Problems.

MORE ABOUT

Nutrients: chapter 4 Indoor Environment, section B Soil; chapter 6 Plant Life Cycle, section E Changing Conditions.

Problems over generations: chapter 1 Seeds & Clones, section B.2 Clones & Potency; chapter 11 Genetics & Breeding, section D Generations & Stability.

A. SEEDLING/
STARTING PROBLEMS

SPINDLY SEEDLINGS

I started some seeds.
They are starting to get
long and spindly. How
do I prevent this or is
this normal? Why are
they doing this?

RON, Wasilla, Alaska

THE PLANTS ARE SUFFERING
from lack of light and are
stretching in an attempt to
get more of it. This is not normal. A healthy seedling has a short
and stocky stem. The seedlings can be saved. Stake them up using
skewers and twist ties. Increase the amount of light the plants are
getting.

Seeds can be started under an HPS lamp or under fluorescents.
When the seeds are started under an HPS lamp, they grow very
short and stocky. They go into their second stage, the growth of the
first true leaves, followed by rapid growth. Seeds can also be germinated under fluorescent lights. For each square foot of space the
seedlings require a bare minimum of 20 watts of fluorescents per
square foot. Compact screw-in fluorescents may be the answer for
small areas. Once the seedlings have germinated they should be
placed under stronger light.

For more on seedling care, see chapter 1.

B. LEAF PROBLEMS

1. BROWNING/SPOTTING/CURLING

BROWN SPOTS ON LEAVES

I'm growing eight plants in three parts potting soil to one part perlite in 4-inch pots.

The plants are 5 weeks old and are about 10 inches tall. Some of the plants developed light brown spots on the tips and centers of the fourth set of leaves. These soon spread to other sets. The affected leaves become limp and droop but don't fall off. What's wrong?

K.J., Lawrenceville, New Jersey

THE PLANTS ARE SUFFERING from a calcium (Ca) deficiency. The perlite contains no calcium and the amount in the potting mix is insufficient to supply the plants. Rather than a soil, the mix you bought is probably composed of forest byproducts, sphagnum moss, lime and other materials. Limestone is composed of calcium, but the mineral is now chemically bound. This was caused by acids in the mix.

The plants and soil should be watered with a dilute limestone solution. Hydrated lime is the most soluble of the agricultural limes. One reader told me that he used plaster of Paris, which is made mostly from lime, to be the most soluble. Add about a tablespoon per gallon and water the pots to saturation. New growth will be healthy.

In the future, add about a tablespoon of dolomitic limestone per cubic foot of mix when preparing the soil. In addition to calcium, dolomitic limestone contains magnesium (Mg), which is also needed by the plants. Like calcium, magnesium is often missing from fertilizers, even "complete hydroponic" mixes.

TAN PINPOINTS ON LEAVES

I had some problems in the last two weeks of flowering. Many of the fan leaves had little tan or brown pinpoints on the upper sides and also some yellow patches. What gives?

BUDMAN OF ALCATRAZ, San Rafael, California

YOUR GARDEN IS INFESTED with mites. They can be found on the leaf underside. The pinpoint dot is dead tissue where one stuck the plant with its straw-like mouth and sucked on plant juices. To get a good look at the pests, use a magnifying glass or photographer's loupe. You'll see they are eight-legged, like spiders. They may be colored yellow, red, brown and black, but the most common one is the two-spotted mite. It has two black spots on its back.

Mites are a serious problem and should be eliminated from the garden before the infection spreads.

For info on mites, see chapter 10, section A.8.

LEAF CURLING & BROWN TIPS

I use six 40-watt tubes in a 2' x 4' shelf. I use a soil mix with a pH of 6.8 and use half-strength fertilizer every time I water.

I ran into problems with my last crop. The clones and seeds started fine but when they were 10-12 inches high after 4-6 weeks they started getting upward leaf curl and browning of the leaf tips, which then start drying and crumbling. Some remain green but also get this upward curl and crumble. The condition starts right below the new growth and spreads to the rest of the plant. What's happening?

PERPLEXED, Ohio

THE PLANTS ARE DYING from over-fertilization. The nutrients in the soil mix are so concentrated that they are drawing water from the plant, leaving the leaves curled and dry.

To solve the problem, flood the soil to rinse it of excess nutrients. Flood the container with water so that a gallon drains out for every 2 gallons of container space. For instance, 3 gallons should drain from a 6-gallon container. Start fertilizing only when there is an indication that the plants need additional nutrients. In the future, supply the plants with only half the fertilizer they are currently receiving.

For more on fertilizing, see chapter 4, section B.
For changing fertilizer at flowering, see chapter 6, section E.

BLOTCHY LEAVES

I grow Jack Flash and Original Misty in Canna® coco mats (coir in plastic bags) using a run-to-waste dripper system. I follow the instructions on the Canna® coco fertilizer and everything seems fine up until the third or fourth week of flowering. Then the lower fan leaves start to go blotchy all over while the top leaves become very dark green. The splotchy appearance spreads up the leaves eventually reaching the newer ones. By harvest time there is little green leaf remaining.

I feed the plants three times a day and flush with fresh water once a week. The pH is kept between 5.2-5.8. I also use a b.cuzz booster designed for coco. I have tried adding Epsom salts but it made no difference.

DAZDON, Internet

THE PLANTS ARE SUFFERING from potassium deficiency as well as other possible deficiencies including nitrogen and phosphorus. The reason is that the salts in the fertilizer are insoluble and unavailable to the roots in the highly acid, low pH water.

Adjust the water's pH from 5.2-5.8 as it is now, to about 6.2. The minerals in the fertilizer will become soluble and available to the roots. New growth on the plant will not be affected by the deficiencies, but the damage to the old growth will remain.

One way to get needed nutrients to the deficient tissue quickly is to make a foliar spray using a liquid kelp extract and dilute fertilizer solution. The spray will provide micro-nutrients and plant stimulants, too.

SIDEWAYS FAN LEAVES

I grow four plants—two hydroponically and the other two in an organic planting medium. They are illuminated using a 250-watt metal halide lamp. About halfway through the light cycle each day the fan leaves turn sideways. Then toward the end of the day they straighten up again. Why do they do this?

I.S., Pacifica, California

THE PLANTS ARE TURNING the leaves sideways as a reaction to stress. By turning sideways they minimize the amount of light they receive, so they require less water and nutrients and absorb less heat. Perhaps the containers are too small. As a result the root systems cannot supply the leaves with enough water. Repot the plants.

B. 2. YELLOWING LEAVES

YELLOWING LEAVES

My plants are about two months old. The problem is the bottom leaves are always yellowing and then drying out. What's wrong? What should I be doing?

WHEELS, Canora, SK, Canada

THE PLANTS ARE SUFFERING from a lack of nitrogen (N). The plants are moving the nitrogen from the lower leaves to new growth. To eliminate this deficiency, use a high-nitrogen fertilizer. All fertilizer packages list three numbers on the packages in the same order, N-P-K. A high-nitrogen fertilizer will have an N-P-K of 10-5-5 or 5-1-1. You can also foliar feed by spraying the leaves with a dilute solution of soluble fertilizer. The plants absorb the fertilizers through their stomata.

For more on N-P-K, see "Ideal N-P-K" in chapter 4, section B.2.

NITROGEN DEFICIENCY

ED'S TIP   **MAGNESIUM FOR YELLOWING**

Plants were grown in expanded clay pellets under a 400-watt HPS lamp. They were fertilized with General Hydroponics vegetative formula. All of the plants showed symptoms of magnesium (Mg) deficiency.

Deficiency symptoms were yellowing beginning at the edge of new leaf growth and then over the entire leaf, leaving only the veins green; twisting of new growth; and growth slowing or stopping.

Magnesium is the center element of chlorophyll, where photosynthesis takes place. It is not mobile in cannabis once it is part of the chlorophyll molecule. It must be supplied continually. At the first sign of a deficiency, Epsom salts should be used.

The magnesium-deficient plants were

Mg DEFICIENCY

Photo by Ed Rosenthal

sprayed to dripping once with a solution of 1 teaspoon per gallon of Epsom Salts (MgSO$_4$), which was also added to the water in the rate of 1 teaspoon per gallon. The new growth exhibited no signs of deficiency.

YELLOWING LEAVES II

I pull 20 clones per week. After 3 weeks of continuous light they go into flowering for 8 weeks then harvest. I was blasting them with Peter's 20-20-20 the first 3 weeks then switching to 5-50-17. My top bud would be tiny while the side buds would be nice and fat.

I decided to try organic and used mushroom compost, bat guano, bone, blood and kelp meal. Now the plants are a foot shorter, and producing gigantic buds. The fan leaves are yellowing 4 weeks into flowering rather than 6-8 weeks as they were before. Should I be concerned about the early yellowing?

LUCKEY MONKEY, Tacoma, Washington

IF THE FAN LEAVES are yellowing and dying from the bottom of the plant moving upward, the plants are suffering from nitrogen (N) deficiency as the available N is transferred to the new growth. This is perfectly acceptable at 6 weeks but is going to slow growth during the next 3 weeks. Feed the plants with some water-soluble organic fertilizer such as fish emulsion or a guano high in nitrogen. Use the solution a couple of times.

YELLOWING LEAVES III

> I have ten plants in my garden. They are all in enriched potting soil in 6-inch pots and are about a foot tall and bushy. This week the leaves on the bottoms of the plants started turning yellow and it is progressing. Should the plants be doing this?
>
> SUNNY, Burnaby, BC, Canada

THE PLANTS ARE SUFFERING from a nitrogen deficiency and may be in too small a container. They should be repotted into a 12-inch-container and fertilized with a balanced fertilizer.

For info on fertilizers, see chapter 4, section B.2.

C. BRANCH PROBLEMS

DEAD BRANCHES OUTDOORS

I have had pretty good luck for a number of years growing and budding clones under lights and then regenerating them and putting them outside in the spring.

One perplexing thing happens to a few plants each year. Some of the branches coming off the main stem die. This can affect up to half of the plant, while the rest of it continues to grow well. This can happen during any part of the growth cycle, even while the plant is budding. I see no evidence of damage above ground. All I can think of is insects or rodents underground. What do you think is causing the problem?

SIERRA FARMER, Reno, Nevada

THE BRANCH IS BEING attacked by a caterpillar, which bores inside and then chews the pulp. To find out who the culprit is, look where the necrosis starts. You will probably find some sort of borehole or puncture where the caterpillar entered the stem. It is probably extremely small. Then with a razor-type edge slice the stem. You will find damage and perhaps even the culprit.

One solution is to dust or spray the plants with a *bacillus thuringiensis*-based insecticide, available at your local nursery. It contains a bacterium that causes plague in caterpillar populations. It is completely harmless to other organisms.

For more on caterpillars, see chapter 10, section A.3.

D. PLANT PROBLEMS

LEGGY PLANTS

> I am using fluorescents because they give off less heat than the high power bulbs. My problem is that when I set the lights to bud cycle the buds are thin and leggy. Do I need more lights?
>
> RSA, W. Upton, Massachusetts

THE PLANTS ARE NOT receiving enough light. In order to grow tight dense buds the plants need more intensity. An HPS lamp or high-watt compact fluorescents could solve the problem.

For more on plants' lighting needs, see chapter 2 and chapter 6, section D.

LANKY PLANTS

> I'm growing using a constant flow system and 1,000-watt HPS. I force flowering when the plants are 12 inches. Then they go into a major growth mode. Two weeks after I cut the light, they grow to 4-5 feet tall. Once they begin flowering, the stem cannot support the large buds and they fall over.
>
> I see photos of plants are short and compact. Why aren't mine that way? What is going on?
>
> PERPLEXED, Oregon

YOU ARE PROBABLY GROWING an equatorial sativa strain. They stretch out when they are forced to flower at short height. The compact plants that you see are the result of years of breeding. They are mostly hybrids of sativas with indicas, which grow only 10-25% taller once they are forced.

Use bamboo stakes to support your plants. For the next crop switch to a commercial variety bred for indoor growing.

> For more on pruning, see chapter 6, section B.
> For more on plant size and forcing, see chapter 6, section C.
> For more on the differences in varieties, see chapter 12.

TINY PLANTS

My plants are growing under a 400-watt metal halide (MH) lamp. They are over two months old but only a few inches tall. The leaves are small and dark green. What's the matter with them?

TOMMY R., Bronx, New York

THE SOIL THAT YOU are using is much too acidic. It probably has a pH under 6. Under these conditions many of the nutrients in the soil are insoluble and unavailable to the plant. Adjust the pH using pH Up, available at many garden stores. The plants will respond almost immediately and begin rapid growth.

Photo by Ed Rosenthal

E. BUD PROBLEMS

STRETCH AT BUDDING

I think I am having a stress problem with my plants. The flowering plants stretch instead of budding compactly. Some plants develop male traits near the end of the cycle and stop the budding process.

I am growing in a closed-off closet with the dimensions of 3.2'x 3'x 7'. The space is lit with a 400-watt high pressure sodium lamp. We have made sure that no light comes in the room during the night cycle. I keep the ballast on the other side of the closet. A stand fan is set at low to circulate the air. We are using a drip system.

When the light goes on the temperature quickly rises to 85-90° F. What are we doing wrong?

S.S., Hull, QC, Canada

THE PLANTS ARE SUFFERING from heat stress. The temperature is 10-15 degrees too high. This causes lanky, running buds. The male flowers at the end of flowering are characteristic of many varieties and are an indicator of ripeness.

One way to keep the temperature down is to open the closet door to promote air and heat exchange. Another possibility is to convert the light reflector to an air-cooled model.

For info on controlling heat, see chapter 3, section A.2.
For info on hermaphrodites, see chapter 11, section B.

AMMONIA-SMELLING BUDS

I just tasted my friend's homegrown. The stuff smelled like ammonia. What caused this?

A.C.F., Gainesville, Florida

THE ODOR IS CAUSED by anaerobic bacteria, which are active in the absence of oxygen. Ammonia is one of their waste products. Anaerobic decomposition quickly destroys chlorophyll, leaving buds tan or brown colored.

Your friend probably was holding wet bud in a plastic bag. Soon all the oxygen was used and the anaerobic bacteria became active, feeding on the pot.

> *For info on molds, see chapter 14, section C; chapter 10, section B.3.*

WHY WEED TASTES BAD

Why is schwagg so nasty tasting and smelly?? Where has all the skunky smell gone to?

BELDARR, Clayton, New York

THERE ARE SEVERAL KINDS of schwagg; grade-B Mexican and other varieties that just don't have the genetics, improperly grown, harvested or cured sinsemilla and mistreated weed.

Much of the pressed Mexican weed imported to the US is genetically inferior material. If you took seeds from this weed and grew it out under ideal conditions, it would still be mediocre. The slightly sweet odor and taste of the fresh material is fermented out during processing. When the damp material is pressed together, anaerobic bacteria, which function in the absence of oxygen, attack the vegetation. They turn it brown by destroying the chlorophyll, odor and taste. The bacteria release ammonia, detectable by its astringent, pungent odor.

Bud that is stored in a baggie and moved in and out of pockets soon turns bad. Polyethylene attracts the THC glands leaving the inside of the bag covered with glands by the time a quarter-ounce is used. As the buds break up from handling and are exposed to air, potency, taste and odor are lost. The crumbs at the bottom of the bag, which started out as bud have been reduced to schwagg.

For more on storage, see chapter 7, section F.

LOW QUALITY

I've been having some low potency lately, how can I improve my product?

GOING CRAZY, Internet

NO MATTER HOW GOOD a gardener you are and how well you grow your plants, the most significant factor determining the quality of the product is the genetics of the plant. If you start with a low potency plant you will produce low potency bud. The easiest way to improve the quality of your produce is to start with the highest quality strains. Only they have the potential to grow the finest bud.

For info on genetics, see chapter 1, section A.1; chapter 11; 12.

F. PROBLEMS OVER GENERATIONS

GENETIC DRIFT?

I have had a clone garden growing continuously for 3 years. When I started out, the plants were sticky with resin and very smelly. In the last year they have lost their odor and some of their glands.

I started with seeds and then regenerated the plants several times. Then I took cuttings from the stinkiest plant and regenerated those plants. Then I used one plant for cuttings. The buds that matured on this plant were normal. The problems started in the next generation. The buds had lost something. I know because I compared them with other buds from my "bud library." Since then, things have gotten worse.

I grow using a nutrient film technique with a recirculating mist spraying the hanging roots. My fertilizers and all other conditions have remained the same. I suspect some sort of disease, but my friend says the plants are suffering from genetic drift. What do you think?

JUDD, Fresno, California

THERE IS SOME GENETIC variation among clones that may be noticeable after many generations. It occurs at a very slow rate as a result of mutations.

I don't think this is your problem. There are two reasons. I suspect your plants are suffering from a viral infection. The problem came on very quickly, not over a period of time, and the characteristics that are affected are probably controlled by more than one gene (although there could be a "master control gene" involved). Second, the situation has continued to deteriorate; the problem is not stable. If it were a genetic problem, the plants would have developed the new characteristics and then remained that way. These plants are continuing to deteriorate, a result of a growing infection.

Unlike animals, plants don't have a defense system to fight infections. Once the plant is infected, it may continue to grow. The infection spreads to

> Annual plants beat infections by reproducing sexually, producing seed that is uninfected. Cloning circumvents this protection.

the new growth. Depending on the virus, plants can sometimes continue to grow even though they are infected. They often change in appearance, lose vigor, and become less productive when they are infected. Annual plants beat infections by reproducing sexually, producing seed that is uninfected. Cloning circumvents this protection.

To rid the garden of the infection, which is obviously spread either through water or air, all of the equipment must be sterilized using hydrogen peroxide or another agent. All surfaces should be washed down and all systems thoroughly flushed using sterilizing agents. Then new plants from seed can be started.

> *For more on viruses, see chapter 1, section B.2; chapter 10, section B.1.*

Photo by Ed Rosenthal

G. HYDRO PROBLEMS

ALGAE IN HYDRO SYSTEM

In the clay medium and nutrient tank in my hydro system there is always algae growing. How can I eliminate this?

X-RAY, Oregon

Green Algae is forming on a few wicks. What can I do to prevent it?

THE BUG-MAN, Tallahassee, Florida

ALGAE NEED LIGHT and moisture to grow. Since you cannot deprive them of moisture, you must eliminate sources of light such as light transmitting tubing, tanks and containers. One way to do this is to cover the hydro area with reflective material which bounces the light back up to the plants rather than letting it penetrate to the root area. Some people make collars using Mylar or aluminum foil to prevent light getting to the planting medium.

Adding a $1/2\%$ hydrogen peroxide solution to the planting mix every three days will keep all algae in check. Using a UV-C water sterilizer that is made for hot tubs will also keep the water clear.

WICK SYSTEM'S GREEN WATER

I'm using the wick system in my garden from your book *Easy Marijuana Gardening*. The water in the reservoir turned green after a few weeks. I drained it, cleaned the reservoir with H_2O_2, and refilled it. It has turned green again and so have the wicks. I'm thinking algaecide is probably a bad idea. Would a lid over the reservoir do any good? I'll need a big lid and might not be able to find one. Hopefully the green water is okay? Do you have any suggestions?

RAYZ HELL, Romulus, Michigan

A LID OVER THE water would be a great idea. Green algae requires light for photosynthesis. Cutting off the light eliminates them. The tank can be covered with a sheet of black plastic or cardboard.

GREEN PERLITE

I am using perlite as a growing medium for my hydroponic garden. The problem is that it turns green.

HEMPTECH, Fallsburg, New York

PERLITE'S CREVICES HOLD NUTRIENT-RICH water that makes an ideal home for algae. To prevent algal growth, the top of the medium should be kept dry. Ebb-and-flo systems should be set at a shallower flood level and drip emitters should be placed under the surface. Another way to prevent growth is to place black shadecloth or reflective Mylar over the medium's surface.

A ¹/₂% hydrogen peroxide solution will also keep the algae in check. It should be added every 3 days.

WRONG WATER

I started six plants indoors. Shortly after planting they started developing brown dead spots (necrosis), wilted leaves and dead tips. The plants are all different strains.

I fertilize with commercial fertilizer and softener-conditioned water. Two plants have already wilted and died.

Any suggestions?

FATALE, East Lawrencetown, NS, Canada

YOUR PLANTS ARE DYING because of the softened water. The water is adjusted by adding various mineral salts, which make the water unsuitable for garden use. The minerals affect the plants by increasing the electrical conductivity of the water. This makes it harder for plants to draw water and causes them to wilt. The dissolved minerals drawn into the plant with the water are poisoning the plant by messing with the availability of calcium.

To save the plants, rinse the containers with fresh water so the minerals are flushed out of the container. Then irrigate with nutrient–water solution adjusted to a pH of 6.2.

If you need a water softener, the water is probably high in calcium and may be high in other minerals too. If it is too high in mineral content, it is unsuitable for the plants. To find out just what is in your water, call your water company. They will send you the results of their tests. If the water has a high mineral content, solutions for a healthy crop include customizing the fertilizer, reverse osmosis filters that remove minerals from water or buying bottled water with low mineral content.

> *For more on watering, see chapter 4, section D.*

WRONG PH

I have a small garden of eight indoor plants in a 2' x 4' growing area with a 1,000-watt metal halide bulb. I am using a commercial soil and have adjusted the water to a pH of 7.0-7.5. My babies are only 2-3 weeks old and the earlier ones have turned pale yellow with no warning. The others are starting to yellow at the tips so I used a 10-15-10 fertilizer with a cup of urine per gallon for the higher N. I also added some Epsom salt in case they were missing some Mg. It has now been 3 days of foliar feeding and using the mix for watering and they have not responded. How could this happen? I want to be a good father but might lose my little ones.

GANJA, Internet

THE PRIMARY PROBLEM THAT your plants are experiencing is the unavailability of nutrients caused by too high a pH. As the pH edges up to neutral, nutrients become less soluble. Solubility decreases drastically in the alkaline range, which is over 7 pH.

You have given the plants a heavy dose of fertilizer. It would be toxic if it became soluble. First flush the containers using water with a pH of 6.2-6.5. Test the ppm of the run-off water with a ppm meter. When the runoff measures below 1,600 ppm, you can stop flushing. Irrigate with pH-adjusted water until the leaves start turning lighter green. Then start using a complete fertilizer containing micro-nutrients. The new growth will be normal. Don't expect much recovery of old growth. In the future keep the pH at around 6.2.

For more on pH, see chapter 4, section D.

OVERFERTILIZATION

Photo by Ed Rosenthal

H. OUTDOOR PROBLEMS

IMMATURE OUTDOOR PLANT

I have a five-month-old sativa plant growing outdoors in the ground and she is just starting to bud. I don't think she will mature before frost.

Will she finish flowering if I bring her inside under fluorescent lights? How should I do it?

YANN, Rennes, France

IF THE PLANT WILL only experience a light frost but will still get days of bright sunshine and fair weather, it might be wiser to cover the plant in the evening to protect it from the elements and remove the cover early in the day. A sheet or horticultural insulating cloth can work.

Adjusting outdoor plants to indoors requires meeting their needs—minimal damage to the root system and bright light. These conditions may be hard to meet. Moving a large plant from the ground to an indoor situation should be considered a last resort.

It is much easier to move small plants than large ones. Large plants are hard to deal with because they are difficult to light and their large root system is hard to dig up and easily disturbed.

> *For more on flowering times, see chapter 5; chapter 7.*
> *For more on sativas, see chapter 12, section A.1.*

RAIN DAMAGE

What is the best thing to do when your plants get beaten down in the rain?

BILL, Bartow, Florida

PULL THEM BACK TO an upright position and support them using stakes or other supports if that is feasible. If they are very large or won't stand up easily, you may let them lie while making sure that the roots are securely in the ground. Fill with soil any holes caused by torn up rootballs. Place a cloth tarp under the plant to keep the buds from touching the ground. Woven cloth will allow water to drain and help prevent mold. Spread the branches out so that light reaches them and they can continue to grow. The branches will soon grow vertically to face the sun.

> *For more on rain and plants, see chapter 7, section B.*

SMOKY FOREST

> **I am growing some plants in the forest. Unfortunately, they have been growing under a thick blanket of smoke from fires since the beginning of the flower period. Will the smoke reduce harvest?**
>
> TYRONE SHOELACES, Internet

YES. THE SMOKE REDUCES the amount of light the plants receive. Since green plants use light to energize photosynthesis, this reduction in light from the amount they normally receive will reduce the growth rate. In addition, the contents of the smoke may affect plant growth. Solid particulates from the smoke form layers of dust and grime embedded with toxins and ash on the leaf surfaces. The smoke clogs the leaf stomatas and absorbs light. Although the air contains high amounts of carbon dioxide (CO_2), which would ordinarily be useful to the plant, it also contains volatile unburned hydrocarbons, sulfur dioxide and carbon monoxide, all of which damage plant tissue.

Expect reduced yield. By the way, why would you want to smoke these buds embedded with poisons? This "Poison Bud" isn't worth the health risks.

BUDLESS POT

I have a garden with ten plants in my backyard. I transplanted them when they were two months old, in May. It's late September and my plants aren't flowering at all. What's wrong?

R. OF R., St. Petersburg, Florida

MARIJUANA FLOWERS AS IT senses the advent of autumn. It does this by chemically measuring the number of hours of uninterrupted darkness during each 24-hour cycle. When enough hours of darkness accumulate each day, the plant accumulates a critical level of hormones that change its growth cycle from vegetative to reproductive. The number of hours of uninterrupted darkness required to induce flowering ranges from 8-10 hours for many indicas and other high-latitude plants to 12-14 hours for equatorial varieties.

Marijuana is very sensitive to interruption of the dark period. Even a short blast of light can upset a plant's flowering cycle. You have probably been turning the lights on in your garden fairly regularly and the plants have responded to the interruption of the dark period by continuing vegetative growth.

Another possibility is that you are growing a very late equatorial variety that does not begin to flower until late September or October.

Even if the plants are flowering, an interruption of the dark cycle can cause smaller, looser buds, and delay maturation. If the light interruptions continue regularly, the plant reverts to vegetative growth.

For more on dark cycle, see chapter 6, section D.3.

FLOWERLESS WINDOW POT

I am growing a plant in my window. It's three years old and fills the whole window, but it hasn't flowered. What's wrong with it?

NO NAME, No location

NOTHING. THE PLANT IS probably a female. A male would have flowered by now. For the plant to flower, it needs a 12-hour daily period of darkness. Even turning on the light for a second means the count has to start again. Apparently you use the room at night and turn on the lights.

> *For more on triggering flowering, see chapter 6.*

THE WIND

> For three years, I've been growing a good Afghani variety. It grows really well here along Lake Erie, New York. My problem is that the winds wreak havoc on my plants, sometimes twisting them right off the stalks. Is there any way of producing a stronger, thicker main stalk? I've tried securing the plants with strings but like I said, they really grow here. I have neither the time nor the string for the job.
>
> D. P., New York

TRY PUTTING A 2'x 2' or even a 2'x 4' stake in the ground and securing the main stem to that. The branches can also be secured to it. Some growers have used bird netting to support plants in various ways.

10

PESTS & DISEASE

A. PESTS

B. VIRUSES, FUNGI & MOLDS

C. SOLUTIONS

RELATED TOPICS
Diagnosing plant symptoms: chapter 9 Troubleshooting.

MORE ABOUT

Viruses: chapter 1 Seeds & Clones, section B Clones &
Potency; chapter 9 Troubleshooting, section F Problems
over Generations; chapter 11 Genetics & Breeding, section D Generations & Stability.

Molds: chapter 7 Harvest; chapter 14 Paraphernalia & Use,
section C Cannabis Consumer Tips.

A. PESTS

1. ANTS

ANTS ON THE PLANTS

I have a lot of ants all over my plants. Will they do any damage? What are they doing?

THE SILVER DRAGONS, Auckland, New Zealand

ANTS IN THE PLANTS

I have ants running around all over my garden. Are they attracted by the sweet smell? Should I let them live in peace or should I exterminate them?

NORTHERN STONER, Ft. St. John, BC, Canada

THE ANTS ARE MAKING nests in the planting medium of the containers. This messes with the roots. They are aphid ranchers. Aphids suck the juices of the plants and concentrate the sugars in a "honeydew." The ants squeeze the aphids to harvest the honeydew.

Ants protect aphids from predation by other creatures. Aphids harm plants in three ways: they suck vital juices from the plant, their "honeydew" promotes infections, and they are often vectors for disease, spreading bacterial and viral infections.

Although it may seem as if the ants are everywhere, once you follow the trails, you will probably find that the ants are only colonizing a few containers or a few holes in the garden.

The ants must be eliminated. There are many ways to do this without using poisons. Mixes of sugar, boric acid and diatomacious earth can be placed in the ants' path. The substances coat the ants' exoskeleton and puncture it so the creatures dehydrate. A sticky barrier can be placed on the stems of the plants so that ants cannot climb up. Nurseries sell Tanglefoot® made for this purpose. Ant colonies are exterminated professionally using a solution of pyrethrum poured into their holes. Ant bait is also very effective.

277

Cinnamon is by far the most effective ant killer/repellent. It is both repugnant and fatal to ants. As you sprinkle it or water it into the soil, you will see the ants scurrying out of their nests. With a spoon, sprinkle ground cinnamon, the regular spice type that you can purchase at the grocery store, on the top of the planting medium. Then make a drench using 2 rounded tablespoons of ground cinnamon per gallon of hot water. Let the water cool to room temperature then add a liquid pyrethrum insecticide into the solution as directed. A surfactant such as Coco-Wet® will make the solution more effective. Use the solution as a drench.

Beneficial nematodes should be added to the medium. These microscopic creatures attack various insects including ants and help prevent their return.

To keep the ants out, the perimeter should be lined with an inch-wide barrier of diatomaceous earth and cinnamon powder. If the ants have encouraged an aphid infestation, be sure to treat for aphids once the ants have been eliminated.

A. 2. APHIDS

APHIDS

I didn't look at my plants much for about two weeks. When I finally had a chance to examine the plants I found colonies of $1/16$-inch pale green insects all over the stems. They had a thin head and wide body that is sort of pear shaped. What are they? Do they damage the plant? If I need to get rid of them, how should I do it?

STELLA, Red Bud, Illinois

YOUR PLANTS ARE INFECTED with aphids. These insects come in a range of colors including, white, brown and black as well as various shades of green. They have a proboscis, a straw-like mouth, which they use to pierce the stem and suck its juices. They reproduce very

quickly, often in colonies that are composed only of females reproducing parthenogenetically (without males). Aphids are herded by
ants, which eat the honeydew exuded by the insects.

Aphids can quickly devastate a plant and must be dealt with
immediately. Some populations are resistant to pyrethrum, but
it should be tried as a quick knockdown. Botanigard™ and
Cinnamite™ are effective sprays against aphids, as are fatty-acid-
based (soap-based) insecticides. If it is feasible, the aphids can
be washed off the plants using water. This will not eliminate
them, but it will prevent much of the damage caused by the large
numbers. They can also be controlled or eliminated using predatory insects.

A. 3. CATERPILLARS

RAPACIOUS CATERPILLAR

I have plants outdoors. My plants are about one week away
from harvest and all of a sudden I noticed some of the top
flowers are dying. They look dry and discolored. Upon further inspection I found a larva of some sort, just eating
away! It was camouflaged and looked just like a leaf. What
do I do to save the rest of the flowers?

KES, Redding California

TINY CATERPILLAR

I have a caterpillar that is getting the best of my green
ladies. The pest in question is 1-2 mm long, is off-white and
crawls around on the top side of the leaves. It sucks them
dry little by little. The affected areas brown out. There are
little black specks and honeydew on the leaves.

These pests really took off when the air-cooling system
broke down and the temperature rose from 70-78° F to

80-92° F during the lit periods. The humidity went up 20% due to the heat. What should I do?

CHRONICSTER, Hills, California

REMOVE ANY CATERPILLARS YOU see. Then look to see if there are any others around that you can hand-pick. Then it's time to move from mechanical removal to chemical or biological warfare.

Pyrethrum is a concentrate of a natural plant pesticide produced by a plant in the chrysanthemum family. It is extremely effective against caterpillars and grubs. Spray it onto the plant and the critters will stop munching and die. Pyrethrum is not harmful to warm-blooded animals, but can harm cold-blooded animals such as reptiles and fish. (Maybe it would be effective on some of our politicians.) It should never be used near a stream or lake.

Pyrethrum remains effective for just a short time once it is used and it comes in organic formulations. It is used for a quick knockdown. Check instructions of the individual brand because there are different formulations. Most brands can be used very close to harvest.

Bacillus thuringiensis (BT) is a bacterium that causes a plague in many insects including grubs and caterpillars. It is specific to insects and completely harmless to anyone who isn't one. There are several brands. Dipel™ is one of them. Once it is sprayed on the plants, the insects ingest it. They get sick, stop feeding and die within a very short period of time. Upon the insect's death, more bacilli is released, ready to infect once again.

Botanigard™ is an insecticide composed of a fungus that infects many insects. It is very effective but takes 2-3 days to work. Both the BT and Botanigard can be used with the pyrethrum.

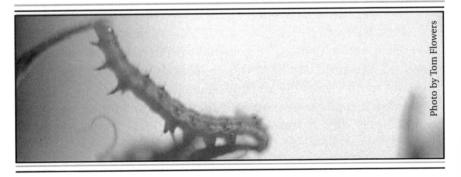

Photo by Tom Flowers

CORN BORERS

My outdoor garden was seriously set back by the presence of European corn borers. The garden is located in a rural agricultural area. The corn borers drill a little hole in the lower stalk, then eat their way up to the top branches, where they feed on new growth. The only plants that survived had some sort of predator that ate the corn borers. What can I do to stop them?

S. A., Address Unknown

BORERS ARE A TYPE of caterpillar, also in the lepidoptera family, and they can be treated in many of the same ways as other caterpillars. Borers climb up the stem and then bore inside. They can be stopped using a physical barrier of sticky tape. It prevents them from reaching the upper stem, where they bore inside. There are several ways to apply the tape. Tanglefoot® can also be used.

Tanglefoot® is a sticky spreadable substance with a consistency similar to petroleum jelly. It's available at garden shops and nurseries. Insects can't cross these barriers. Small mammals don't like them, either. Don't spread sticky substances directly on the stem because it may harm the plant.

Bacillus thuringiensis, often known as BT, is a bacterium that infects only lepidoptera-type insects, moths and butterflies. Find the corn borer hole and use a dropper or straw to spray inside the stem.

It is considered totally safe for food crops. Soon after borers ingest the BT, they stop eating and die from disease. In the process, they release more of the BT bacterium, which infects more chewing pests. BT is completely harmless to all animals other than butterflies and moths. It remains effective until it is washed off the plant by rain or spray. It is available at most nurseries under the brand name Dipel™. If it is not available at your local nursery, you can order it on the internet.

281

Pyrethrum is a natural insecticide found in chrysanthemum-type plants. It is available as a powder or a spray at nurseries. It is a very potent pesticide that eliminates caterpillars including borers. It remains effective for several days then must be re-applied. It is harmless to warm-blooded animals (including humans) but is lethal to fish and most invertebrates.

A. 5. DEER

DEER PATROL

I plant in a clear-cut in the middle of a forest. It was replanted a few years ago and the trees are all 4-8 feet high. I have flown over in a small plane and it was difficult for me to tell the pines from the mature plants.

I plant late in the season because of the deer problem where I live. When I planted early in the season, the deer ate the new growth. Then I tried starting later, in July when there is plenty for them to eat. So far, no trouble. But I am sure they are going to come back to munch in September. Are there any commercial sprays that I can use to discourage them from munching the buds?

HERB HEAD, Augusta, Georgia

THERE IS ONLY ONE deer repellent spray registered by the EPA for use on edibles without a warning.

Deer-Off™ is made from food-grade organic ingredients and creates both odor and taste barriers for deer, squirrels, rabbits and other mammals. It is somewhat rain resistant. The company claims that it was the most effective of 25 products tested at Rutgers University.

Two readers reported that it was an effective deterrent to deer browsing. They both said that they sprayed the ground and plants near the garden to create a barrier zone surrounding the growing area. The plant leaves were also sprayed.

The spray comes in quarts and concentrates.
Tel. 800-800-1819 ▪ Web site: www.deer-off.com

READER TIP ▸ **MOTHBALL FOR FOREST PESTS**

I'm writing to tell you about an inexpensive pest control for all forest animals. I found that mothballs placed around the perimeter of the garden kept the animals out.

I grew a plant about 3 feet from a deer trail. When the plant was about 2 feet tall, the deer ate it down to its stem. After I placed the mothballs around it, it was never bothered again. It turned into a beautiful 5-foot-tall indica.

MOTH BALL BELIEVER, Smithville, West Virginia

READER TIP ▸ **MOTHBALLS FOR DEER**

Two years ago I had a garden in a forest clearing. Even with invisible nylon string and later a plastic deer fence, the plants were constantly being nibbled. I figure I lost half the crop to some bucks and does and a few rats.

Last year my friend told me to use mothballs. I hung them from trees at about 4 feet and placed them in little cups on the ground near the plants. The result was not one bite, not one nibble from either pest species. A few mothballs doubled the garden yield.

MOTHBALL MAN, Burlington, Vermont

THANKS FOR YOUR TIPS. Apparently mothballs aren't just for moths anymore. They stop pests from chewing on leaves as well as cloth.

FUNGUS GNATS

I have fungus gnats in my garden. How can I get rid of them?
I have drained my plant's soil and changed the water, but
that didn't work. Please advise.

MR. CHOKER, Internet

WATER "LICE"

We are using a drip system in a soilless mix. The other day
we moved a plant and saw hundreds of tiny white bugs in
the water standing at the bottom of the pail. They are very
quick and constantly jump around in the water and tend to
collect into colonies. What are they? Should we kill them?

BUDDY, Internet

THE LITTLE WHITE BUGS in the water are immature fungus gnats.
They suck on the roots and are vectors for disease. Once they
mature they eat plant debris and continue to spread pathogens.
They should be eliminated.

Fungus gnats are black, about $1/16$-inch long and look a lot like
fruit flies. They hang out near the planting medium. They are vectors for disease. They and their pupae, which live in the planting
medium, eat decaying organic matter. In their travels, they are likely to pick up pathogens from an infected plant and transfer it to the
next one.

The insects are attracted to the color yellow. One way to determine whether the garden is infected is to hang up a yellow sticky
card. If the garden is infected, some of the pests will stick to it.
There are several ways to kill them. All of these pest killers listed
below are harmless to you and your warm-bodied pets. They are
all organic and are suitable for use on food crops. Many of these
products are available at garden shops, indoor grow stores or over
the internet.

- Beneficial nematodes are tiny worm-like creatures that feed on many kinds of soil insects and larvae. They are very effective against gnat larvae. The nematodes come as a dry powder that is added to the water. They can be re-introduced as a prophylactic once every 4-6 weeks. Many nurseries and indoor grow shops carry them.

- Botanigard™, which was also mentioned in relation to grubs and caterpillars, works on gnats as well. It contains a living fungus that infects and kills soft-bodied insects. The fungus is not interested in other life forms. It's sort of like athlete's foot gone super bad. It comes as a liquid that is added to the water.

- Gnatrol™ has the bacterium *bacillus thuringiensis israelensis* as its active ingredient, which causes plague in gnats. It is harmless to other creatures. Gnatrol™ comes as a liquid concentrate. It is very effective because the bacteria remain alive for a couple of weeks, plaguing new larvae as they emerge from the eggs.

- Pyrethrum is a pesticide made from a chrysanthemum-like flower. Pyrethrum is toxic to fish so it should never be used in a way that will lead to contaminating a water source. Once pyrethrum is used it remains active for just a short time before it deteriorates. A spray will eliminate the flying gnats. It comes in a spray that can be used as a bomb, a liquid concentrate or a powder. If you use the bomb, leave the room for a few hours. It's not that the active ingredient is harmful, but it's just not good to breathe propellant fumes. The concentrate or powders can be prepared and watered into the soil to kill the larvae.

MEALY BUG INFESTATION

After several successful indoor growing seasons, my garden has a mealy bug infestation. I have changed the soil, tried Safer's soap, pyrethrins, predators and Malathion®. Malathion® is the only thing that seems to work, but it devastates the plants. What can I do?

DESPONDENT, Los Angeles, California

MEALY BUGS ARE ABOUT $^1/_8$-inch to $^1/_4$-inch long, white and are covered in a cottony web. They are very slow reproducers; a cycle takes just short of a month. For this reason, they are generally little threat to cannabis since it is a fast growing, short-lived plant.

If there are only a few bugs present, or a branch is infested, the insects can be wiped off with a sponge or Q-Tip or the branch can be cut away. A group can be sprayed with a 25% alcohol solution and then wiped off the leaf with a sponge.

If the infestation is more intense, the treatment should be done in stages. Use a spray made from mixing neem oil diluted as directed into herbal tea composed of 1 tablespoon each mixed Italian seasoning, ground cinnamon and cloves, four big cloves fresh crushed garlic, and 8 ounces denatured alcohol. Add water to make a quart.

Boil the water. Place it in blender with all ingredients except oil and alcohol. Blend and let stand 30 minutes. Add alcohol and horticultural oil as directed. Mix in and strain. Use as a dip or spray every 3 days.

This treatment will eventually get rid of the bugs and will immediately knock down their population, resulting in less harm to the plants.

Cleanliness is essential to be sure that the infestation is not carried over to new plants. First, the clones should be totally cleaned. The clone area should be isolated and kept totally clean.

Before new plants are moved to the next area, that area should be totally free of infected plants and should be given a thorough cleaning. First, wipe down the room with detergent. Once it has been thoroughly aired, give it a second round with a 1% hydrogen peroxide solution. This will kill anything that might be hanging out. Your garden should be bug-free at this point.

Since insects and other pests do not spontaneously generate, they must have invaded from somewhere. Check cracks and openings and perhaps the perimeter of the space for possible points of entry. Also, develop a protocol such as changing your clothes from outside to prevent carrying the pests in. It is very easy to brush against a bush, pick up a pest and then drop it off in the indoor garden.

A. 8. MITES

MITES

> My plants were doing great. Then they started getting these tiny brown dots on the leaves.
> The plants look really sad. What's happening to my garden?
>
> MARCO, Internet

THE SMALL BROWN DOTS on the top of the leaves indicate places where spider mites have stuck a proboscis to suck plant juices. You can see the $1/32$-inch long creatures on the undersides of the leaves. They look like little black or brown dots. Watch for a minute or so and you will notice them moving. They are not insects, but are related to spiders. These plant suckers reproduce quickly and have large families. They can rapidly ruin a garden if they are not controlled. When the colony has grown a bit, the mites build webs and can be seen walking on them.

First try using pyrethrum. The problem is that many populations of mites are immune to it since it has been used so much. The few hardy mites that survived previous sprays of the poison passed on their genes. If pyrethrum doesn't work, try Cinnamite™. It's made from cinnamon and kills mites on contact. Soap and fatty-acid sprays are often effective, too. Neem-oil sprays also eliminate the pests.

MITES

My garden has a small mite infestation. I would like to use a natural means of dealing with them. What should I do? I was thinking of some sort of predator.

BUD MAN, Kansas City, Missouri

MITES FOR MITES?

I have a spider mite problem on my plants and I've heard that I should use predator mites to take care of the problem. If I use the predator mites how will they affect my plants?

C. B., Warren, Michigan

THE PREDATORS SUGGESTED FOR control of these plant suckers are predator mites. Several species of predator mites are available from mail-order companies. Each of them thrives under different conditions. When predators are used successfully, they form a balance with the plant eaters, resulting in small quantities of each, with minimal damage to the crop, and even possibly some benefit. Predator mites eat only other mites. They are not interested in your plants and will not feed on them. Introducing predator mites is a solution that has minimum impact on your garden.

Not every introduction of predators produces control. Success may depend on several introductions of different varieties. Mite predators do best under humid conditions as a result of their diet of relatively dry meat. The plant eaters, which drink lots of plant juice, prefer a drier environment.

Predators may not be the answer. Perhaps you should aim for total eradication of the mites. This may not be that difficult to do if the garden or its parts are periodically closed down. Then the system can be thoroughly cleaned, the room washed down with a sterilizing hydrogen peroxide or bleach solution and new uninfected plants introduced to the space.

READER TIP **KILLING MITES**

I found a great way to kill mites on clones and small plants. I add 2 heaping tablespoons of cornstarch per cup of water and dip the clones or spray the plants, paying particular attention to the undersides of the leaves and also the top of the growing medium. The water evaporates quickly leaving the cornstarch to dry and mummify the suckers. If you spray the plants daily for three weeks, you will be rid of the pests.

HARRIET T. HEMPSTER, Lansing, Michigan

GOOD IDEA FOR CLONES and other small plants, Harriet. I would add just a dash of detergent to spread the water quickly. Also, you could make a "tea" by brewing a quart of boiling water over a tablespoon each of ground raw onion, ground garlic, mixed Italian seasoning, ground cinnamon and ground cloves. Mix this tea with the cornstarch and detergent and add 8 ounces denatured alcohol. It is a powerful general pesticide.

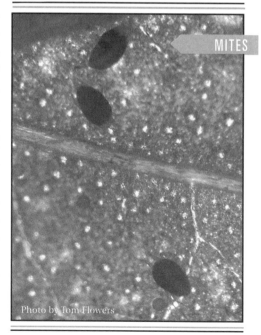

MITES

Photo by Tom Flowers

MITES & PEST SPRAY

> I have an indoor closet garden. About two weeks into my first crop I developed a problem with mites. Those little suckers had their webs all over my buds. I found "Purge" in my local pet supply store.
>
> I am now into my third harvest, and I have not had a problem with mites or any other pests since I used this product. I have noticed absolutely no side effects, but just bug-free, healthy plants.
>
> THE EXTERMINATOR, USA

T.E. SENT ME "PURGE'S" label. It is for use in automatic dispensers and activates about every 15-30 minutes. Its active ingredients are listed as pyrethrins 0.975%, piperonyl butoxide 1.950%, and N-octyl-bycloheptane dicarboximide 3.050% and 94.025% unlisted "inert" ingredients.

It is listed for use in food handling and food preparation areas of restaurants and processing plants, dairies, schools, hotels, supermarkets, daycare centers and other people-oriented areas. This means it is considered rather non-toxic. Even so, it does come with a statement of cautions and hazards.

It sounds like an interesting way of ridding a place of pests.

MITES NEAR HARVEST

> My garden is infested with spider mites and only has two weeks left. Will the webbing on the buds from the mites affect the potency or have any other effect? How can I get rid of them this close to harvest?
>
> GREY BOY, Longmont, Colorado

YOU WOULDN'T WANT TO eat vegetables that are covered with mites. Why would you want to smoke them? I don't know whether it's harmful to smoke them, but it certainly isn't pleasant and smells bad, too. Here are some suggestions:

Spray the plants with neem oil that is certified for food plants. Neem oil is a natural insecticide and miticide that comes from a tree and is available over the internet.

Many races of mites are resistant to pyrethrum but some populations are devastated by it. Pyrethrum foggers and sprays are available at most nurseries. Pyrethrum is a natural miticide/insecticide produced from chrysanthemum-type plants.

Mites have a habit of moving toward the top of the plant. After harvest, turn the branches upside down to eliminate some of the mites because they will move to the top and can be removed.

A. 9. THRIPS

THRIPS

When I hold my leaves up to the light I see little trails but I can't find any eater. What's going on?

PICKLES, Evansville, Indiana

YOUR PLANT IS INFECTED with thrips, which are tiny insects ($1/16$-inch long) that get into the leaf tissue and mine it. These insects don't reproduce as fast as many, and if the plants have only a few weeks before harvest and there is only a small infection, you can do nothing. However, if the plants are young, these pests should be dealt with. They can be treated with pyrethrum, Botanigard™ or Cinnamite™.

Biological control of thrips can be effectively maintained using a combination of beneficial nematodes and pirate bugs. These predatory insects are available from Nature's Control (www.naturescontrol.com), other insectaries and some garden shops. The nematodes eat any thrips larvae and eggs that are in the soil, while the pirate bugs eat the thrips themselves. The pirate bug, *Orius sp.*, is a predatory bug about $1/20$-inch long. Both nymphs and adults possess a "piercing-sucking beak" with which they pierce holes and suck their victims dry. Orius prefers thrips larvae, but adult thrips are also killed. Each adult Orius can eat 5 to 20 thrips larvae per day, and with higher thrips infestations, even more are killed. This combination of pirate bugs and nematodes is a very effective control. One application of the beneficial insects is all that was needed to clean up the infestation.

A. 10. WHITEFLIES

WHITEFLY ATTACK

My plants have been attacked by whiteflies. What should I do?

G. V., Columbia, North Carolina

WHITEFLIES ARE ABOUT AN $1/8$-inch long and are completely white. They can be seen flying off plants when they are shaken. These insects pierce the plant and suck its juices. They are vectors for disease and exude a sticky, sugary concentrate of the plant juices that often promotes mold. The insects reproduce quickly.

There are several ways to eliminate whiteflies from the garden. The easiest way is to introduce a parasitoid. Encarsia formosa is a parasitic wasp that lays its eggs in the whitefly pupae. Once the egg is laid in the whitefly pupae, found on the underside of leaves, the pupae dies and turns black. The wasps are not social and don't make nests. They are so tiny that once you release them you will probably not see them again. The wasps spend their entire lives living off whiteflies. They take a few weeks to control the whiteflies, so if you are dealing with an intense infestation it may be best to use an insecticide first to bring the population down, and then use the wasps to control the immature pests.

The natural pesticide pyrethrum, which is derived from a cousin of the chrysanthemum plant, is very effective at killing the insects. The pesticide is available as a spray or bomb. The spray does not affect the eggs however, so it should be used every 3 days to catch the insects as they emerge from their juvenile states.

Botanigard™ is an insecticide composed of a fungus that attacks a broad range of insects. Once the insect comes in contact with it, the fungus grows into the insect's body and kills it in a few days. The fungus attacks only insects and is not harmful to humans or pets. It is available as a concentrate and is sprayed on the plants.

Cinnamite™ is an insecticide/miticide derived from oil of cinnamon. This has been shown to be deadly to mites and many insects including whiteflies. It is safe for humans and pets.

Pyrethrum, the insecticide from a chrysanthemum-type plant is effective against thrips. It is deadly to all cold-blooded animals such as reptiles and fish, but it is safe for warm-blooded animals such as humans, other mammals and birds. It's available at most plant and garden shops.

A. 11. MULTIPLE PESTS

SUMMER PEST EXTRAVAGANZA

I have two 1,000-watt lamps in a 100-square-foot grow room in a shack on my property. My problem is that now that summer is here, the insects have invaded. My plants have infections of the big four: mites, aphids, white flies and thrips. Luckily, my crop is about to be harvested at the end of July. Should I put in a new crop and fight the insects or wait for a few months? How should I preserve my plants since I don't want to restart from seed?

HIGH SWATTER, Wilkes Barre, Pennsylvania

IF YOU RE-PLANT THE garden in mid-summer shortly after harvest, it will probably be attacked by insects, just as the present crop is infected. In many situations there is no way of keeping the creatures out. From your description, there would be a constant battle between you and the pests for the plants. However, you can put up a pretty good fight.

Spray the plants with a combination of Cinnamite™ and neem oil to control the mites. The combination will act as a repellent and miticide. It may also affect the thrips and aphids.

Add Botanigard™ to the mix to kill the aphids. Botanigard™ is a fungus that attacks soft-bodied insects, including aphids, thrips and white flies.

Use Encarsia formosa to take care of whiteflies. This tiny solitary parasitic wasp lays its eggs in the immature whitefly. The wasps soon keep the population in check and will continue to stay active as long as new whiteflies invade.

The thrips will probably be eliminated using the neem oil, Cinnamite™ and Botanigard™. To kill their pupae, add beneficial nematodes into the soil. These predators attack insects in the soil where the thrips larvae live.

In the fall, the cold weather returns and insects stop invading from the outdoors. You may wish to hold off replanting until then. You will miss a crop, but have freedom for the rest of the summer.

READER TIP ▶ **NEEM SOLUTION**

I've been dealing with the problem of bugs, in particular spider mites and aphids, for three years and have tried various insecticides such as pyrethrums and kelthane, but ultimately decided against the use of any chemicals on something I was going to smoke. For several years I depended on green lacewings for aphids and predatory mites for the spider mites. These bugs were very expensive because I had to continuously re-introduce them to keep their numbers up. The mites performed badly under high temperatures. After two weeks, the lacewings flew away or into the light although I put up a shield.

After seeing a documentary on TV regarding the controversy of an American company trying to patent products from an Indian plant called the neem tree, I did an

internet search and discovered a lot of debate on the effectiveness and uses of the plant. The oil from the seeds of this tree disrupts the hormonal balance of most insects, rendering them sterile. The oil has no effect on humans. In fact, in India neem oil is used as an ingredient in popular toothpastes and other hygienic preparations.

I found a product "Nemesis," which is 100% neem oil. I have been using it for 6 months now and find that by mixing just 5 ml (1 teaspoon) in 500 ml (a little less than a pint) of water and spraying plants the plants about once a month, the bugs cannot take hold. I also add 15 ml (1 tablespoon) to my 50 liter (11 gallon) reservoir which has completely stopped all grow media bugs as well.

I highly recommend that anyone out there with bug problems try neem oil. It has saved me a lot of headaches without chemicals.

MIKE, Sydney, Australia

THANKS FOR YOUR TIP, Mike. I'm sure that many people will use the information in your report. There are many sources for neem oil. DynaGrow offers 100% neem oil. Other sources can easily be found by searching the web.

MITE DAMAGE

Photo by Ed Rosenthal

B. VIRUSES,
FUNGI & MOLDS

CUTTINGS & VIRUSES

I've been an indoor grower for seven years and started experiencing nutrient uptake problems about two years ago. I think that a virus is my problem.

What strategies can I use to eliminate the problem? Does bleach kill the virus? How do these infections spread, through the water or air?

JOHN, Dayton, Ohio

VIRUSES SPREAD IN SEVERAL ways: air, water, plant pests and physical contact with infected plants or animals. Many changes in the characteristics reported by growers are the result of infections. These include reduced odor and yields, lowered potency and problems with growth and nutrient uptake.

Typical responses of plants are to isolate the infection by growing tissue around it, planned death of infected parts and seed production. Viruses are much less likely to infect seed than other plant parts, so the next crop starts off uninfected.

There is no cure for an infected garden or its plants. To be rid of the infection, the plants must be destroyed. The garden must be thoroughly cleaned. All walls and floors should be wiped down with a hydrogen peroxide solution. All instruments and tools should be thoroughly washed or boiled and then sterilized. The planting medium or substrate should be discarded. All tables, containers, trays, lines and pumps should be thoroughly washed, wiped and flushed with sterilizing solution.

As I mentioned, seeds are usually free of infection. Another plant part that is usually infection-free is the meristem growing tip.

296

The tiny growing tips are often used for tissue culture (cloning starting with a few cells).

There are several ways to lessen the chance of garden infection:

1. Filter all air coming into the room. This also lessens the chance of insect or pest infection. Mites, aphids and other pests sometimes ride on air currents.

2. Don't go into the indoor garden after working or brushing through plants outside. Infections of all kinds can hitch a ride on you or your clothing.

3. Recirculating water is a master vector for infection. Add hydrogen peroxide to the water periodically or use a UV-C sterilizing unit, which are manufactured for aquarium and laboratory use and easily fitted into recirculating systems.

4. Never introduce a clone into your system without a quarantine period of at least two weeks. Many growers have had gardens ticking along until they introduced a clone holding a pest or infection. One example is a grower who introduced a single clone with a known nutrient uptake disorder to his garden. Within months, the space had to be sterilized.

For more on viruses, see chapter 1 section B.2; chapter 9, section F.

Photo by Pepper Design

POWDERY MILDEW

> Our new clones have a gray mold growing on them. Is there
> a cure? We think it's a spore because it's quite dry and puffs
> when you touch it. We have been picking the infected
> leaves off but nothing has changed. It continues to spread.
> Apart from the affected leaves the growing seems to be
> continuing fine. We are surprised because we keep the
> room quite dry using a dehumidifier.
> Can we cure this or should we start again?
>
> ANONYMOUS, Internet

POWDERY MILDEW IN PLANT DNA?

> I've been cloning a strain for some time. Last year it
> became infected with a powdery mildew. I assumed it was
> the environment and diligently sprayed clones and any
> older infected plants with natural defense. When I intro-
> duced the strain to a new environment with other plants
> the mildew returned. Is powdery mildew a strictly environ-
> mental problem or is it possible that the mildew was incor-
> porated into the plant's DNA?
>
> STILL FRUSTRATED, Internet

YOUR PLANTS ARE SUFFERING from powdery mildew. This fungus
occasionally attacked marijuana crops previously, but in 1999 more
aggressive strains appeared. Since then it has become more common in both indoor and outdoor gardens. The reason for this is that
the mildew has evolved to accept cannabis as a food source. The
problem will probably get worse as Canada allows more industrial
hemp to be grown. There are many species of powdery mildew, and
to my knowledge there has been no research on which one(s) are
attacking marijuana. Although the mold you saw was grayish, powdery mildew spores are most often white.

Unlike many molds and fungi, powdery mildew thrives in moderate temperatures of the low 70's F and about 50% humidity. This is unfortunate, because those are the same conditions ideal for growing cannabis. An infection is not an indication of poor gardening practices, just that the spore came in contact with an environment in which it could grow. As you noted, the spores are easily airborne, and float around. Out of sheer numbers and percentages some of them are going to land on an opportune surface. The spores are in the air and are endemic, so it is hard to prevent plants from being attacked. During the winter there are fewer spores in the air since there are none growing outside and the spores have been cleaned from the air by rain.

Powdery mildew DNA is not incorporated into the plants' DNA. Although bacteria and viruses can sometimes deposit DNA in other organisms, fungi and molds generally do not. The reason your plants indicated the disease is that they were re-infected. Once an infection has occurred, rather than waiting for signs of a re-infection before taking action, fungicides are used as prophylactics.

When a plant is attacked, it becomes a vector in spreading the disease because of all the spores that grow at the leaf surface. Removing the plant by pulling it out exacerbates the problem because the spores become airborne.

We have ways of dealing with powdery mildew, which of course, lead to its complete control, if not extermination. Here are some products that I have found effective for powdery mildew. All of them are labeled for vegetables and are considered non-toxic.

- AQ10 is a biofungicide consisting of the fungus *ampelomyces quisqualis*. This fungus is a hyperparasite that colonizes the powdery mildew infection and kills it. It is listed by the Organic Materials Review Institute (OMRI) for organic crop production. Manufactured by Ecogen, Inc.

- Cinnamite™ is labeled for mites, aphids and powdery mildew. It is very effective on each of these pests. It is an extract of cinnamon, cinnamaldehyde. It is available through the internet and in some stores. Manufactured by Mycotech.

- Milk in a solution of 80% water and 20% skim milk kills powdery mildew. It is very effective and can be used repeatedly to keep the mold from attacking.

- Neem oil is a natural protectant produced by the neem tree originally used by people in India. It is effective for use against mites and insects, as well as an effective fungicide and a general tonic. It also encourages plant health and vigor. It is packaged by a number of manufacturers.

- Plant Shield® contains the beneficial living fungus trichoderma harzanum strain T-22. This fungus forms a symbiotic relationship with plant cells at the leaf surface. It protects the leaf and attacks organisms that have colonized the plant. The predatory fungus attacks molds such as botrytis (gray mold), powdery mildew, pythium, rhizoctonia and fusarium wilt. These molds attack the leaves, stems and roots of plants. The fungus is harmless to humans, pets, and beneficial organisms and is considered organic. Manufactured by Bioworks, Inc.

- Potassium bicarbonate is an alkaline compound that works by changing the micro-environment from acidic to alkaline. Fungi and molds prefer an acidic environment, so their growth is stopped and their organs collapse. Some brand names are Armicarb®100, KaliGreen® and Remedy®.

- Serenade® is the fermentation product of a bacterium, *bacillus subtilis*. The toxin doesn't affect animals. It has several modes of action. It attacks many types of fungi and molds, and competes with them for nutrients and resources. It also activates the plant's equivalent of the immune system, system-active resistance. Serenade® is absorbed by the plant and translocated, making it even more effective. The toxin does not affect animals. Manufactured by AgraQuest.

■ Sodium bicarbonate, otherwise known as baking soda, is used in the same way as potassium bicarbonate and is quite effective. It should not be used repeatedly because it causes a build-up of sodium, which can harm the plants if present in excess.

To prevent the problem from reappearing, the plants should be treated with one of these products every 7-10 days. Treating the plants after the symptoms appear and the fungus is reproducing is much less effective.

B. 3. MOLDS

BUD MOLD HEARTBREAK

I am growing a stupendous variety, both indoors and out. It produces very fat, dense buds that are almost circular nuggets, which form in pairs all the way up the stem. The problem is mold. It grows rapidly, starting from the inside growing out.

My indoor garden is in a basement and rarely gets above 68° F. My outdoor garden matures in mid-October, when the dew sets heavily. What can I do to stop the heartbreak of mold?

MARK, Cornelius, Oregon

THE TIGHT CREVICES OF the nearly ripe buds provide an ideal environment for mold to develop.

If you raised the temperature of the indoor garden to 75° F, the temperature would be above the mold's ideal. Just by raising the temperature, the relative humidity would decline. Using a dehumidifier dries the air, making conditions even more inhospitable for the mold. Dehumidifiers raise the temperature while removing moisture from the air. They nearly always stop mold development.

There are a couple of innocuous chemical treatments that can protect both indoor and outdoor gardens. They are benign and non-poisonous.

Since molds prefer acidic conditions and do not grow well in an alkaline environment, a change of pH using either potassium bicarbonate or pH Up can be used to prevent mold from growing or stop it from spreading. Plant Shield® creates a biological barrier to organisms attempting to colonize the leaf. Rain rinses these treatments from the buds, so they must be reapplied if the buds experience rain. The pH Up solution should be adjusted to 7.5.

MOLD

How can I prevent mold on my indoor marijuana buds?
K-9810, Trinidad, California

MOLD THRIVES UNDER MOIST, dark, cool, acidic conditions. A dense bud is a perfect environment for them. Once moisture gets trapped between the folds of tissue, it is hard to dry out. However there are several things you can do.

In the grow room, mold should be fairly easy to control. Since it requires moisture in order to grow, making sure that there is constant air circulation and low humidity creates an unsuitable environment for mold. There are several ways to keep the humidity low in the growing space.

In dry areas, just ventilating the room and exchanging spent CO_2-depleted, moist air for fresh, dryer CO_2-laden air solves the problem. During winter, cold air holds little water as compared with warm air. Once it is heated, it is considered dry rather than moist. Using this air to ventilate the room keeps the humidity low.

Air conditioners condense water as they cool. Dehumidifiers heat the room as they condense water. As soon as the humidity goes down to 50-55% the mold problem will cease.

For more on outdoor mold, see "Rainy Harvest" in chapter 7, section B.

BASEMENT PREPARATIONS

I have a potential super-discreet grow room in the base-ment of my new house. A heavy door leads to a crawlspace that opens to the room. The room has electricity and is big enough to grow a fair bit of reefer. Its small windows are practically hidden from the outside.

The only problem is the dirt floor. When snow melts in the spring, the floor becomes wet. The room has been dark, cold and damp for a while. It is probably infected with molds and fungus. Do you have any suggestions as to how I might go about sanitizing the room so that my future plants don't become infected with mold or fungus?

JOKER LIPS, Thunder Bay, ON, Canada

PLACE A BRIGHT LIGHT in the space and dry it out using a dehumid-ifier or room dryer. The dehumidifier draws moisture from the air, which will dry out the walls and floor. After the space has lost its mustiness, it is time to sanitize. Spray the space with hydrogen per-oxide, which is a sterilizing agent, and baking powder, which has anti-fungal properties.

Dealing with the flooding floor takes some ingenuity. Place plastic shipping pallets on the floor to create an air space, and then cover them with a plastic tarp. Then make a flooring of $3/4$-inch out-door-grade plywood. To keep the earth dry during wet periods you could set up 4-inch ventilation ducting with an inline pump. The tubing could ventilate out the window, removing moist air.

Use air-cooled lights to prevent the room from heating up too much and fans in the windows for cooling. If the room gets too humid, dry it out using a room dehumidifier or air conditioner depending on the temperature.

C. SOLUTIONS

THE MAGIC OF HYDROGEN PEROXIDE

When and how much hydrogen peroxide should I use in my hydroponic solution?

STIGGY, Internet

HYDROGEN PEROXIDE (H_2O_2) is a powerful oxidizer that can be used to destroy fungi, molds, bacteria and other infectious agents and pollutants. Adding it to hydroponic water helps plants by destroying infectious agents and adding oxygen to the roots' environment.

Hydrogen peroxide is an essential ingredient in maintaining a clean growing room. It replaces chlorine bleach, which is antiseptic, but harmful to breathe and bad for the environment. When H_2O_2 is added to reservoirs, it slows the growth of algae and other water organisms so equipment needs cleaning less frequently. Soil and water-borne diseases such as pythium and other stem and root rots occur at much lower rates in hydrogen peroxide–enriched water. Hydrogen peroxide creates an oxidative reaction, so microorganisms are unlikely to develop tolerance.

There are many ways to add H_2O_2 to the water. A measured amount every 3 days is the crudest method of enriching water but is still effective. A smaller measured amount daily evens out the peaks and valleys of oxygen in the water. Another method is to use a drip similar to IV bag that delivers a measured amount continuously.

Hydrogen peroxide keeps infections in the garden to a minimum and stimulates root growth by increasing the oxygen content of the water. It degrades over 3 days into free oxygen and water. Some of the oxygen dissolves in the reservoir water and is used by the roots. The water is enriched with $1/2\%$ hydrogen peroxide. Hydrogen peroxide is sold diluted to 3% in drug stores. Drugstore H_2O_2 is used at the rate of 1 part to 5 parts water. Some indoor garden shops sell 10% hydrogen peroxide. Ten percent H_2O_2 is used at the rate of 1 part in 19 parts water.

Three percent hydrogen peroxide is used topically to sterilize cuts and infections. Ten percent H_2O_2 burns skin.

ZeroTol® is a peroxide-based commercial sterilizing agent used in the greenhouse industry. Its active ingredient, HO_2, also breaks down into oxygen and water, but it is a hazardous oxidizer similar to concentrated acid. It is used at the rate of 1 part per 100.

READER TIP ▶ ANTIBACTERIAL SOAP

I've used antibacterial soap on my outdoor produce garden. The plants seem to love it when I spray the leaves. I have had less trouble from bugs and diseases. I haven't noticed any bad effects on yield or taste of fruit.

SOUTHWEST, Manasota, Florida

THANKS FOR YOUR TIP, Southwest.

READER TIP ▶ HOMEMADE PEST CONTROL

I have been using a homemade pest control with excellent results. To a quart of water I had 5 drops of 35% food-grade hydrogen peroxide (equivalent to 50 drops or $1/2$ teaspoon 3.5% hydrogen peroxide) $1/8$ teaspoon hemp seed oil and one drop of dish detergent. Shake well. The spray kills mites and virtually all other pests.

Y., Seaside, California

READER TIP ▶ WATER SPRAY FOR INSECT CONTROL

I control aphids in the grow room by blasting them with a water spray every other day for a couple of minutes. To prevent the container from getting drenched or aphids washing onto the medium, I place a plastic sheet over the container before I blast. Then I take them into the bathtub and spray them. I check the plants daily and blast them when necessary.

After the second week of flowering I stop spraying, but until then the plants are kept totally pest free using just water. I've read about using soapy water and insecticide, but I prefer not to put those things on my plant when plain water works.

I didn't know if this rough treatment would hurt the plants. The odd leaf gets damaged, but it produces a thicker stalk and stronger structure, more like an outdoor plant. I think they are also producing larger flowers.

VERY HIGH E., Dorset, England

THANKS FOR THE TIP, Very.

READER TIP   SURGICAL TAPE REPAIR

I have a solution that could prove useful to growers. I was training one of my plants, bending it ever so carefully when I heard that dreaded snap like a piece of celery. I had decapitated one of my prized green friends. I wrapped the fracture with some 3M Micropore® surgical tape that I had left over from a knee operation. The tape is fibrous, like adhesive gauze, so it holds moisture and breathes well. I sprayed the bandaged area several times a day with water with a couple drops of SuperThrive® in it. I am happy to report that a healthy cola has appeared above the damaged area.

PLANT CAST, Internet

THANKS FOR THE INFORMATION. It is much appreciated, not to mention useful.

11 GENETICS & BREEDING STRATEGIES

A. GENETICS

B. HERMAPHRODITES
1. HERMAPHRODITE EXPECTATIONS
2. ACCIDENTAL POLLINATION
3. USE IN BREEDING

C. POLLEN COLLECTION

D. GENERATIONS & STABILITY

E. MARIJUANA'S PLANT FAMILY

RELATED TOPICS
Indoor/outdoor varieties: chapter 12 Varieties, section A.2
    Specific Varieties.
Sativa/indica: chapter 12 Varieties.
Stress and hermaphroditism: chapter 6, Plant Life Cycle,
    section A Sexing; chapter 9 Troubleshooting, section E
    Bud Problems.

MORE ON
Seeds: chapter 1 Seeds & Clones.
Regeneration: chapter 7 Harvest, section C Revegetation &
    Mothers.
Cloning methods: chapter 1 Seeds & Clones, section B.2
    Cloning Methods.
Viruses/genetic drift: chapter 1 Seeds & Clones B.2 Cloning &
    Potency; chapter 10 Pests & Disease, section B.1 Viruses.

A. GENETICS

GENETIC DIFFERENCES

I have four old outdoor females. One's buds are fat, two are regular size and one has puny buds. I fertilized all of them with Miracle Gro™. Would a certain nutrient have made the puny bud bigger?

ANGIE, Internet

YOU TREATED ALL OF the plants the same and gave them nutrients equally but one plant outperformed the others. Difference in bud size is a criterion for judging plants. From your standpoint, that plant was genetically superior.

Rather than have the puny plant catch up with extra supplements, that additional input will be better spent on the superior plant. Not knowing the garden conditions, I hesitate to give advice on what that might be.

BUD GENETICS

Suppose a plant had two buds. If one is more potent and smokes a little better than the other one, would the seeds from the better bud have better genes?

GREEBS, La Habra, California

MAYBE. EITHER THE ENVIRONMENT or the genetics could create the difference. One bud may have been shaded or have faced other environmental stresses that affected its quality.

The difference could be genetic, but this is a less likely explanation. On rare occasions, a branch has a mutation, which usually occurs at the node. This mutation will be transferred to the seed.

BREEDING FOR BUDDING

I recently saw a plant that grew buds right out of the stem of the fan leaf. Buds also grew out of the middle blade of the fan leaves. Have you ever seen this before? Is it possible to breed for this characteristic?

BURNT !!!!, Toledo, Ohio

YES. THIS CHARACTERISTIC CAN be bred into a strain. First try crossing the plant with a male of the same strain. See if any of the plants have the characteristic. If they don't, take a male resulting from the cross and pollinate the mother with it. Keep backcrossing to the mother until the progeny exhibits the characteristic.

HERMAPHRODITE

Photo by Ed Rosenthal

PURPLE PLANTS

Is there a secret to getting plants to turn purple or is it simply a matter of genetics?

K2, Florida

SOME VARIETIES TURN PURPLE with no environmental trigger. For instance, I recently saw a purple skunk growing next to green skunks in a warm Swiss field in July. In Australia, there are purple sativa hybrids bred from Southeast Asian varieties. This characteristic appears in indica and sativa varieties.

Some varieties turn purple only upon experiencing a cold period that causes them to "purple up." This is also a genetically determined characteristic; it occurs when the roots are cooled below 50° F.

> *For more on purpling, see "Identifying Purple Plant" in chapter 12, section A.1.*

FRUIT FLAVORED POT

I read that some people grow flavored pot including blueberry, coconut and pineapple. How are the flavors created? Did the growers use extracts or essences?

P.J.J.F., Hamilton, ON, Canada

THE FLAVORS WERE NATURAL odors and essences that the plants produced. They were the result of breeding and luck. No artificial flavorings or ingredients were added. The odors are the result of essential oils and other aromatics. Some of them may be common to many plants.

B. HERMAPHRODITES

1. HERMAPHRODITE EXPECTATIONS

AGE & HERMAPHRODITISM

I have noticed that after one or two rejuvenations, male flowers appear on normal female plants. Also in my greenhouse, after 8 or 9 months male flowers appear on the lower branches. Is this normal and how can I control it?

KINE KEEPER, Spokane, Washington

IT IS NOT ABNORMAL for plants to develop male flowers as they age. These should be considered stress related since they appear well past the plant's normal lifespan. These flowers contain no male genes so seeds produced from their pollen produce female plants only.

> For more on hermaphroditism from stress, see "Mostly Hermaphrodites" in chapter 6, section A.

HERMAPHRODITIC SELF-POLLINATION

If a plant has male pods and fertilizes itself, will the seeds be female seeds only?

J B SLANGSHOT, Moultrie, Georgia

IT DEPENDS ON WHY the plants are hermaphroditic. If the plant produced male flowers as a result of stress there is a good chance that most of the progeny of the self-cross will be female. If the hermaphroditism is a hereditary trait some of the plants will be female and some hermaphrodite.

Unless you have had experience with the particular plants you are growing, there are few indications whether the plant is hermaphroditic naturally or as the result of stress.

BREEDING HERMAPHRODITES

Marijuana cultivation books give different advice regarding male flowers on female plants. One book said don't breed, another said to breed to the host plant. What's right?

HEMPTECK, Elmira, New York

HERMAPHRODITIC PLANTS HAVE GENES for hermaphroditism. They should not be used for breeding because they will pass these genes on.

HERMAPHRODITE SEEDS

One of my six outdoor female Nebulas went hermaphrodite after the third week of flowering last summer. What is likely to grow if I plant seeds from this hermaphrodite?

RICHARD, Spain

THE PLANT WAS A genetic hermaphrodite. None of its sisters turned hermaphroditic under the same conditions. Its progeny are likely to have the same characteristic. Seeds from crossing a hermaphrodite with another female plant will be either hermaphroditic or female. Seeds from the hermaphrodite crossed to itself will be mainly hermaphroditic.

TAKE THE HERMAPHRODITES?

A friend has a few hermaphrodites that popped up in his high intensity indoor garden. He asked me if I wanted them for my yard and indoor garden. The buds are great, but aren't hermaphrodites like a black plague in the garden? I don't have any plants now. Is it worth the risk or should I just get better plants?

KRISPY, Internet, USA

GENERALLY SPEAKING, HERMAPHRODITES ARE a problem in the garden and should be removed as soon as they indicate. However, there are situations when hermaphroditic plants can be used. First, the plant's hermaphroditic characteristics should be examined. Some hermaphrodites produce a single branch with male flowers that is easily detected and removed. Other plants, probably the majority, produce individual clusters of male flowers throughout the plant. These are the most dangerous and should be removed from the garden.

> Generally speaking, hermaphrodites are a problem in the garden and should be removed as soon as they indicate.

Since you have no plants now, a hermaphrodite garden would not be dangerous. To prevent the male flowers from pollinating the females you will have the tedious chore of checking for male flowers every other day, before they open.

Plants that are not especially prone to hermaphroditism are induced to produce male flowers due to environmental stress. This may be the case with your friend's plants. Sometimes plants that remain totally female outdoors produce male flowers under lights. If you have the time and space you could try growing them outdoors.

SEEDS FROM ENVIRONMENTAL HERMAPHRODITES

This is my second medical marijuana crop. Unfortunately, I stressed out the first crop by not having the lights on a timer and doing the best I could (give or take an hour or two). I wigged out the poor plants so bad they became hermaphrodites. I did not take cuttings, but I have a lot of these seeds from hermaphrodites. I read in one of your books that seeds from induced hermaphrodites will have a tendency to be female, but a friend said that I shouldn't plant these seeds because they are bad. Could you please advise?

ADDIE M., Seattle, Washington

SINCE THESE WERE KNOWN females and the hermaphroditism was induced by environmental conditions the seeds have no genes for either maleness or hermaphroditism. Although the females produced male flowers, the pollen on those flowers contained only female genetics, no *y*-chromosomes or male genes. Thus the seeds are all female.

HERMAPHRODITE POLLEN

> I had three female plants. At the end of flowering, one tiny bud had a few male flowers. I collected the pollen from them. If I use it, will the resulting plants be female or hermaphroditic?
>
> MR. X, Kennabeck

THERE IS A GOOD chance that the few male flowers have all-female pollen. The resulting plants will all be female. Male flowers appear at the end of flowering on unpollinated plants of some varieties. This pollen produces female plants.

B. 2. ACCIDENTAL POLLINATION

HERMAPHRODITES

> I have two plants that I put into flowering cycle (12/12) about three weeks ago. One plant has scattered male flowers among the female buds. The first plant shows no sign of male flowers. I have separated the two plants to prevent the "good" female plant from being contaminated by the pollen of the second plant. Do I need to do this? Are male flowers viable on a primarily female plant?
>
> CLUELESS, El Paso, Texas

MALE FLOWERS ON FEMALE plants produce viable pollen. This pollen can fertilize the female flowers of the same or other plants. Pollinated bud has much less useable weight than unpollinated and is considered undesirable. Hermaphrodite plants should be destroyed as soon as their true nature becomes apparent.

> For more on pollination, see chapter 6, section A; section C, this chapter.

HERMAPHRODITE PROBLEMS

> I got some great genetics from British Columbia and after weeding out the males I found two hermaphrodites after 5 weeks of a 12-hour light cycle. They managed to pollinate all the females to one extent or another. After reading what you have already published, I have three questions. Can I regenerate the seeded females? Will the seeded females have a higher tendency toward becoming hermies? What are the environmental conditions that induce hermaphroditism?
>
> LAND OF THE CHEAP KILOWATT, Internet

THE FEMALE PLANTS CAN be regenerated by leaving vegetation on them and placing them under continuous light. They will have no more tendency to become hermaphrodites than they did the first time they flowered. You can assume that if they were pure females the first time around they will remain that way when they are flowered after being regenerated. All kinds of stressors induce plants to become hermaphrodites. These include irregular light cycle, water stress and some chemicals. Hermaphroditism is also a genetic trait that indicates even without stress.

Your plants were genetic hermaphrodites. They were the only two plants in the garden that produced male flowers. If the flowers had been stress induced, more of the plants would have been affected.

B. 3. USE IN BREEDING

NEEDS HERMS TO SAVE STRAIN

I have a variety that's a lot like BC Pineapple bud, which is killer. I want to take a break for a year or two but don't want to lose the strain. How can I force these female plants to hermaphrodite? Will the seeds produced be exact duplicates of the mother?

READER, Oregon

GIBBERELLIC ACID CAN BE used to induce male flowers on female plants. The plants produced both male and female flowers. The pollen is fertile as are the female flowers. This means that the plants can be self-fertilized or that the sprayed females can be self-crossed or crossed with sprayed or unsprayed females.

Another way to produce male flowers is to let the plants over-ripen. At some point they will produce some male flowers. The seed resulting from pollinating a plant with pollen from a forced male is viable. Because they contain only female genetic material, all seeds created from this cross will be female.

> The seed resulting from pollinating a plant with pollen from a forced male is viable. All seeds created from this cross will be female.

You might consider cloning the plants and placing them in suspended animation. Cuttings are exact genetic duplicates of their clone mothers and are the only way to preserve the exact genetics and characteristics of the plant.

Seeds, even if they are the progeny of the same plant, do not have the same exact genetic make-up. The reason for this is that genes come in pairs. They may consist of the same or different versions (alleles). The pollen grain and ovum may contain different alleles of the gene. Hybrid plants contain many pairs of genes with dissimilar alleles, so a plant's progeny will not be homogeneous.

However, there will be plants that have characteristics close to the clone mother's. The most desirable of these plants can be cloned or used for breeding.

> *For info on other ways to perpetuate a variety from seed, see section C, this chapter.*

READER TIP ▶ **CREATING HERMAPHRODITES**

I have found an easy way to make sure that female plants produce "all female" pollen.

When shifting from vegetative stage to flowering, turn the lights off for 36 hours. Then turn them on, using the normal flowering regime. All the plants will produce pollen.

SALLY SATIVA, Georgia

THANKS FOR THE OBSERVATION, Sally.

BREEDING FROM FEMALES

We are starting our breeding program and we have a few questions. We are using clones that we bought or traded with other growers along with a few varieties that we purchased as seed. The varieties from seed were all hybrids so we decided to self-cross them to get more uniform plants. We are in our third generation now. With each generation the plants look more alike, but the yield has gone down. Why is this happening?

The varieties from clones are only females. We are successful at producing stress-induced hermaphrodites using heat. We bring the temperature in the rooms up to about 38° C (100° F) and maintain that temperature for a few days so we could get female pollen from the plants, but we were told that using induced males for breeding is not a good idea. What do you think? If we can't use the female pollen for breeding how should we go about it?

SPICY TOM, Concord, California

THE ORIGINAL BREEDING STOCK was a hybrid and exhibited hybrid vigor. The plants that you are inbreeding through self-crosses are showing lower yield each generation because the genetic pool is becoming more homogeneous. This is to be expected. With rigorous selection your variety will be very stable in another generation or two.

Using stress-induced pollen from female plants for breeding purposes is not a good idea. When inducing pollen from females, not every plant in the population produces it. The plants most likely to produce the pollen have more of a tendency to hermaphroditism than the plants that are not induced. By using these plants each generation, you are inadvertently selecting for hermaphroditism. The female-to-female cross is best used only for the last generation that is to be used for production. These plants are much less likely to be naturally hermaphroditic than are the group resulting from several generations of female-to-female crosses. If you must use female–female crosses, make sure to pollinate flowers of plants that resist hermaphroditism.

Another way to begin a breeding program with a clone is to cross the clone with a male from a similar variety to create a sexually heterogeneous population. Then backcross the resulting male with the mother. In six generations you will have a stable variety that is ready to be bred and has less than 2% of the male's genetics.

Once the varieties are stable, that is, plants from a batch of seeds grow uniformly, the plants are ready to be crossed. The homogeneous genetics of each line has resulted in uniformity at the cost of hybrid vigor. By crossing two inbred lines, hybrid vigor will be restored and the F1 plants will be uniform because they are genetically similar. This F1 line, which is to be used for production, is a good candidate for a female-to-female cross. All the resulting plants will be uniform and female.

SELF-CROSSING'S GENETICS

I will be away for about three months and I need to pre-serve my genetics while I am gone. I don't wish to leave clones unattended during that time so I thought about making seeds. I have read about sex reversal from female to male and I think that might be the answer. Will the seed from pollinating a female plant with its own chemically-induced pollen produce a plant that is a genetic replica of itself?

HAPPILY GROWING, Hampton, Florida

VEGETATIVE REPRODUCTION SUCH AS cloning produces an exact genetic duplicate of the plant because there is no recombination of genetic material. With sexual reproduction, which results in seeds, there is a recombination of genetic material. During the reproductive process, the pairs of chromosomes separate and individual chromosomes reassemble in random order, so that each pollen grain or embryo sac is left with half (haploid) a set of chromosomes. During this process, the genes of each pair of chromosomes are exchanged randomly. The seeds that result from crossing the plant by itself are not identical. However, the plants will be similar because the gene pool was limited.

C. POLLEN COLLECTION

COLLECTING POLLEN

What is the best way to collect pollen from male plants isolated from the females?

D.G., Kent, Washington

THE EASIEST WAY TO collect pollen is to lay the plants or branches down horizontally in a space with no draft. Spread the branches over wrapping paper or newspaper and then cover this with paper. As the flowers open, the pollen drops onto paper. After all the flowers have opened, any pollen that dropped on the leaves should be shaken onto the paper. The pollen should be collected and placed in a container with a moisture desiccator and kept in the refrigerator.

STORING POLLEN

How should pollen be stored to keep it viable?

SAYHEY JOHN, Internet

POLLEN SHOULD BE STORED in glass containers such as small tubes or glassine bags in a sealed container with a desiccant, placed in the refrigerator. This will keep it viable for at least a month. It can be stored in the freezer for extended periods using the same technique—sealed in glass tubes or glassine envelopes inside a glass or metal container with a desiccant.

D. GENERATIONS
& STABILITY

MATURING SEED

I pollinated a Northern Lights female with a powerful indica/sativa hybrid and the seeds have been growing for two weeks. When do I determine when the seeds are mature?
NORTHERN CROSS, Vancouver, BC, Canada

IT TAKES **20-30** days for seeds to mature once the flowers are pollinated. Maturity times vary by variety, light and temperature. The brighter the light, the faster the seeds mature. They are ready when the pod cracks open revealing brown seed.

For more on seed maturity, see chapter 1, section A.

HYBRID TO STRAIN

When crossing two strains how many generations is it necessary to breed to get a homogeneous, true breeding strain?
RED & BUD, Mt. Pleasant, Texas

WITH PROPER SELECTION, YOU can develop a fairly uniform strain five or six generations after the cross. Of course, one must define "uniform strain." Seeds from Dutch companies are fairly uniform. Northern Lights, White Widow and Ice, are all distinctive varieties. However, a hundred seeds from any of them would produce plants with differences in maturity, yield, taste, potency and a host of other characteristics.

It is difficult to get more uniformity in cannabis for several reasons. First, many of the original landraces that modern varieties were developed from are quite variable. The weather at the 30th parallel along Himalayan foothills varies from year to year. If they were homogeneous, the population's survival would be endangered, as all the plants would react to conditions in exactly the same way. By having different reactions as a result of a heterogeneous gene pool, survival is more likely no matter what weather conditions prevail in a particular year. Plants that originate from the same area, such as any pure indica variety, are likely to produce plants with varying characteristics. Equatorial sativas are not likely to have as much genetic variability.

Before a landrace is used to create a hybrid it should be inbred for generations to eliminate variability. Only then will commercial strains have true uniformity.

The best way to run a breeding program is to develop a set of goals and then to choose plants closest to those objectives.

STABLE GENES

I bought Bubbleberry, Valley Girl and Juicy Fruit seeds in Holland. None of the varieties displayed stability. Nor was the taste the same as what I had tasted in Holland. I figured it's because they are being grown in rockwool. So I thought I should change to an organic system. What do you think? How do I get the tastes I experienced in Holland?

RESIDENT INDICA, Minneapolis, Minnesota

YOUR METHOD OF GROWING, using hydroponic fertilizers in rockwool had little effect on the taste, odor or potency of the bud. These factors exert subtle, not gross, influences on the aroma and flavor. A Bubbleberry should still taste like a Bubbleberry. Rockwool is the most popular growing medium in Holland and it is likely that some of the bud you smoked there was probably grown in it.

There are several reasons why you haven't gotten the flavors and odors you expected. These plants are hybrids of hybrids and the varieties are variable. It takes generations of inbreeding and breeding parallel lines to stabilize a variety. I don't think that seed breeders are doing this in a disciplined way.

Since Bubbleberry has been adopted by a number of seed companies, there are now variations between the different lines. Also, some breeders have small growers produce seed for them. If these gardens are not centrally regulated, there will be differences in a company's seed.

> *For more on rockwool, see chapter 4, section C.2.*
> *For more on varieties and stability, see chapter 12.*

SAME VARIETY

I purchased some seeds in Amsterdam from a single variety. The nine plants that germinated all look different. Is this possible? How come the plants of the same variety all grow in different patterns?

D.M.A, Odense, Denmark

THE VARIETY THAT YOU are growing is not a stabilized variety but a hybrid bred from unstabilized hybrids. The result is extremely variable plants. Take clones of all of them. After harvest, select the plants you like best and continue those lines. Eliminate the others.

SATIVA

HYBRID SORTING

I took my seed stock from a large Afghani-Skunk bud. The resulting plants had different characteristics. One was indica dominant, with wide leaves and a high calyx-to-leaf ratio. Another had dark green leaves, but had thin leaves on Christmas-tree-shaped plants typical of a Colombian, leafy buds and a few male flowers. Three looked like sativa-dominant hybrids, with long hairs and an irregular shape, typical of Northern Lights. Three were in the Afghani-Skunk genre, but each was slightly different from the others.

Do I have an unstable strain? Should I grow another strain that is less dysfunctional?

J.GOODBUD, North Carolina

YOU DON'T HAVE A strain at all. The bud that you had was the result of several hybridizations. The male that pollinated the bud was also the result of hybridization. When these two hybrids crossed, many different combinations of characteristics resulted. This is to be expected because each plant's heterogeneous background created a lot of variables. Each of these plants had individual growth habits, harvest dates and bud character. Most of them are also probably pretty good. I don't see a dysfunction there.

Take cuttings of the plants that you like and propagate them into a population for next year. This will give you a known quantity. Produce seeds from your favorite plants.

F1 & F2 HYBRIDS

I just bought Jack Herer seeds in Amsterdam. I was told that they are F1 hybrids. When these seeds are crossed with each other or another strain they would produce F2 hybrids, which can lose characteristics of the original strain such as potency or yield. Is it possible to produce stable seeds from this variety?

HIGH AS A KITE, San Gabriel, California

JACK HERER IS AN F1 hybrid bred from four stabilized hybrids. When you grow it, you will find that each plant is distinctive. The plants have different shapes, height (growth patterns), ripening times, yields, tastes and highs.

You cannot grow Jack Herers from seed the way you would a packet of heirloom tomatoes. You expect the tomato plants to be uniform, and they are because any hybrids used for parentage were stabilized by selective inbreeding for many generations. They are a variety with a particular set of alleles. When they are crossed to produce hybrids, the resulting plants are uniform because they have mostly pairs of genes with the same or similar alleles. The plants have hybrid vigor.

Marijuana breeders have some problems producing stable varieties. The reason is that without sex reversal, inbreeding is more difficult since only one sex indicates many of the desirable characteristics. Choosing the best male for breeding requires both wisdom and intuition. Another problem is that the seed companies do not have the room to grow out the thousands of plants required to run a comprehensive breeding program.

The best way to use seeds from most of the hybrids is to grow the plants out and choose the ones you like. Eliminate weak plants and specimens that don't fit your growing profile. For instance, plants that grow too tall should be eliminated. Get rid of all the males and all but the best plants. Only these plants will be selected for your version of the Jack Herer strain.

INDICA

F2 HYBRIDS

I recently mentioned to a seed dealer that I planned to produce seed from the seeds he sold me. He responded in a letter stating, "There is a problem with producing seeds from
the varieties I sold you. The seed company told me that all
of their seeds are F1 hybrids. This means the seeds (you
produce) will not have the characteristics of the parents.
Instead they either go back to their original wild state or
they are not very viable." In researching this, I noted that
the Seed Bank stated in their catalog, "The F2 generation
has tremendous variation among the progeny, and the heterosis also disappears." Why is the second generation of
seeds not as strong as the first?

CANOER, Address Unknown

THE F1, OR FIRST hybrid generation has great uniformity because
all of the plants received half their genes from each of two stable
varieties. These varieties have similar alleles. The genetic makeup
of the resulting plants is very similar.

The F1 hybrid generation plants all have versions of genes similar to each other, but each pair of alleles is dissimilar because they
come from two different varieties. When these plants are crossed,
all different combinations of alleles occur in the F2 generation, so
there is no uniformity. Regarding any given characteristic, whether
maturation time, odor, or quality of the high, plants will exhibit the
range that were characteristic of the two varieties that were originally crossed. Since the alleles are all mixed up, a given plant might
exhibit one characteristic from one side, and another from the other
side. A third characteristic might fall somewhere between the two.

Rather than the term "wild" your correspondent might have
used the term "varied."

Heterosis refers to "hybrid vigor," a phenomenon that occurs in
F1 hybrids. Hybrids exhibit increased vigor, growth and yields as
compared with either parent. The F2 generation will also exhibit
hybrid vigor.

BACKCROSSING FOR IDEAL STRAIN

I have three strains. The best one is a very fast finishing Skunk #1 derivative. It was inbred until I found the clone mother I was looking for. It is very potent, has a pungent odor but a sweet taste, and it turns purple almost all over with fall's cool nights.

The second strain is an indica that finishes after the Skunk. It isn't that strong, but has an extremely high gland count with enormously swollen gland heads. It looks like it's covered with a quarter-inch of snow. From these two plants I would like to develop a strain with the Skunk's qualities but the gland density and size of the indica.

I have no pollen because both of these clone lines are female only. I do have a NL5 male and was going to pollinate each of the females with it. I am not interested in this plant's qualities but would use it just to produce seed with genes from my two favored varieties. How should I go about doing this?

So far the only thing I have done is to make crosses of the Skunk and Indica with the NL5.

Is there any way to get the plants to go hermaphrodite so that I can cross them directly?

CRYSTAL SKUNK, Oswego, New York

ALL OF THE NEW seeds have about 50 % of their genetic material from the NL5. If crosses were made of the two different hybrids, the resulting seeds would have 25% of their genes from each of the favored varieties and 50% from the NL5. That is not what you had in mind.

To get past this problem, start backcrossing each hybrid to its mother. The second generation will have 75% of its genetic material from the desired variety. Each time a new generation is backcrossed to a pure plant, the amount of NL5 material in the resulting seed is halved. With random selection, after five generations, 96.875% of the genetic material would be from the desired originals. Since you are selecting, you can get very close to the original mother after about four generations.

When the two backcrossed varieties are hybridized, the amount of total NL5 material increases to 6.25%, half from each variety, but still an acceptable level. Then a series of backcrosses with the Skunk are conducted. Selection is based on closeness to the desired traits.

PLANT WON'T SEED

A friend gave me some cuttings of a hybrid called "Saqueena," which has been cloned for the past ten years. They are now flowering under a 400-watt HPS. The plant produces a few male flowers. However, a friend told me that he's tried to breed it but was not able to get it to produce seed. How can I ensure that a few seeds are produced at harvest time?

TOAST, Gainesville, Florida

THERE ARE THREE WAYS that you can try to produce seeds from this plant. They are crossing the plant by itself, using the pollen to fertilize another plant, or using pollen from another plant to fertilize Saqueena.

There is a limited amount of pollen available from the few male flowers, and the flowers may yield small amounts of pollen, so it should be conserved. Opening buds can be removed from the plant and placed between two clean sheets of paper so the pollen doesn't drift with a draft. The pollen collected on the paper is painted onto young stigmas (the white hairs sticking up from the ovary) using a watercolor brush. If the plant will not cross itself, there may be a problem with either the pollen or the female flower. You can try using this pollen on another plant or using pollen from another plant on the female flowers of your target. In either case, you could then make a series of backcrosses. Several generations of backcrosses with the original plant will create an approximation of the original.

For more on collecting pollen and self-crossing, see sections B and C in this chapter.

VIRUSES & SEXUAL REPRODUCTION

If a female plant is carrying a virus and is pollinated with pollen from an uninfected male, will the virus pass on to the seed? Do clones carry a virus from plants that are infected?

DAVE, Columbus, Ohio

A CLONE FROM AN infected plant carries the virus. The only exception to this is tissue cuttings, taken from the growing tip, which contain uninfected cells.

Seeds from infected plants are usually uninfected. Seeds or seedlings become infected when the roots come in contact with the virus in the soil, rooting medium or water. Uninfected seeds are one of the advantages that fast reproducing annual plants have over species that reproduce asexually or only after years. With annuals, each year starts with uninfected plants.

I visited a garden infected with a virus that caused the leaves to become distorted as the plants entered flowering. It also resulted in smaller buds with less odor but undiminished potency. The chronic infection became more destructive as generations of clones succeeded each other. Eventually the grower used old seed, produced before the infection, to restart the garden. The equipment was not sterilized and these plants eventually exhibited symptoms of infection, though not as seriously as the set of plants which had carried it for several clone generations. Seeds were produced from the second clone generation, which was already exhibiting more serious degeneration. These seeds were uninfected.

For more on viruses over generations, see chapter 9, section F; chapter 10, section B.

E. MARIJUANA'S PLANT FAMILY

GRAFTING TO HOPS

I am interested in grafting marijuana plants to hops, but can find no information on how to do this. Would the grafted marijuana still produce THC?

SMOKIN' CHOCOLATE BUNNY, Miami, Florida

ANY LIBRARY HAS BOOKS on grafting plants. Just follow the instructions they give you. Expect disappointments. Grafting is a fine art and success comes with experience.

The marijuana scions will produce the same quality marijuana that they ever did, since they retain their characteristics.

MARIJUANA & HEMP

Can I plant marijuana plants in the middle of ordinary hemp or will they be pollinated? Will this decrease potency? By the way, people grow a lot in Slovenia.

TOMAO, Celje, Slovenia

MARIJUANA PLANTED IN A hemp field will be pollinated by the hemp. The buds will be potent but will not yield much because they will be well seeded. They can be used for rubbing hash or making water hash. The next generation will have more potency than hemp, but will be much weaker than its high-grade mothers.

12 VARIETIES

A. DEFINING VARIETIES
1. INDICA & SATIVA
2. INDOOR & OUTDOOR STRAINS

B. SPECIFIC VARIETIES
- HAZE
- NORTHERN LIGHTS
- SKUNK
- THAI
- WHITE WIDOW

RELATED TOPICS

Creating a variety: chapter 11 Genetics & Breeding, section D.

Jack Herer variety: "Late Planting Up North" in chapter 5 Outdoors & Greenhouse, section C.2 Fall.

Mexican varieties: chapter 7 Harvest, section A.3 Real Garden Scenarios.

Varieties from tropical climates: chapter 5 Outdoors & Greenhouse, section D.1 Tropical Climates.

MORE ABOUT

Outdoor varieties: chapter 5 Outdoors & Greenhouse.

Specific varieties: chapter 11 Genetics & Breeding.

A. DEFINING VARIETIES

DEFINING VARIETIES VISUALLY

With all the hybridizing that's been done in the last twenty years, is it still a safe bet to look at a group of young plants and say that those with the shorter, wider indica-type leaves will produce a more indica-type high, and those with narrower leaves will smoke more like a sativa?

AL, Mackenzie, BC, Canada

USUALLY. IT SEEMS THAT the genes for indica morphological characteristics such as wide-webbed leaves, compact stature and distinctive odor are probably on the same chromosome and probably located close to each other. If that's the case, then indica looking plants are much more likely than others to have other indica characteristics. Conversely, sativa looking plants are more likely to have sativa-like buds and highs.

The first word in my answer is, "usually." Although the genes are located close to each other they are not related. Through selective breeding, using a sharp eye and keen intuition, these characteristics can be separated. Some of the new hybrids are not really varieties. A packet of seeds will yield plants with a range of characteristics. Choose the ones you like and clone them. They become your variants of the variety.

INDICA SATIVA

A. 1. INDICA & SATIVA

GROWING SATIVAS

All the seed companies seem to sell only indicas and indica/sativa hybrids. How come they don't sell sativa varieties such as Colombian Punta Roja, Thai, Kerala, Panama Red and Oaxacan?

NO NAME, Clarksburg, West Virginia

MOST SEEDS ARE SOLD for use in indoor gardens. Indoor growers look for fast maturing, compact plants that grow and ripen well under lower light conditions. Plants such as Early Pearl, the Whites and Northern Lights, that are primarily indica/sativa hybrids, do better under these conditions and mature in a much shorter time than sativas.

The varieties you have named—Colombian, Thai and other sativas—would be unruly plants in an indoor garden. They would have an internode length of 3 inches or more and would take 6 months to mature if forced to flower at germination. Meanwhile they would grow to a height of up to 8 feet.

Even outdoors, indica/sativa hybrids are preferred. Growers look for plants that are compact and mature earlier. Sativas have the potential to be the legendary 10-foot giants with 6-foot diameter. They are easy to detect and mature late, in November through January, too late outdoors for most regions of the country. In contrast, indicas do not usually grow above 5 feet tall and ripen between August through October.

IDENTIFYING PURPLE PLANT

I have a plant 5 feet tall that has long, thin leaves with purple stems from the main stalk to each leaf. What causes this? The plant just started flowering in late March, (equivalent to late September in the northern hemisphere) much

later than other varieties. Is this plant a tropical variety?

Mo, Waikato, New Zealand

THE PLANT SOUNDS LIKE a late flowering sativa. The purpling is caused by a pigment, cyananin. The presence of this pigment is genetically determined. In the variety that you have, the purpling occurs without regard to environmental conditions. In other varieties it occurs only after cold weather, when potassium becomes temporarily unavailable to the plant.

> *For more on purple plants, see chapter 11, section A.*

EQUATORIAL SATIVA

I am growing an equatorial sativa and have had problems with it that I have not encountered with indicas and commercial hybrids that I grew before. I forced the plant when it was a foot tall and it began developing flowers about three weeks later. However, they began as wispy clusters and have gotten only a little larger. It is now three months later and the plant is 5 feet tall, still with these small flower clusters, which show no sign of ripening. What's going on? What should I do about it?

GOLD GROWER, Washington, D.C.

WHILE INDICAS AND COMMERCIAL indica/sativa hybrids are short-day plants and flower when they are exposed to a long uninterrupted dark period, equatorial sativas use other cues to determine flowering. At the equator, there is not much variation in day length throughout the year, so this would not be a good cue for the plant, unlike conditions in higher latitudes. Instead, the plant depends on its height and possibly moisture conditions to determine flowering time.

You have experienced the reason why people do not usually grow sativas indoors: they take a long time to mature, grow gangly, do not produce much bud, and the bud they produce tends to be loose and runny rather than tight and compact.

Here are some things you can do to spur ripening:

- Cut the light back to 10 or 11 hours, leaving the plants in darkness for 13 or 14 hours daily. Even though equatorials do not respond to lighting cues as forcefully as higher latitude plants, they do show some response to it.

- Cut back planting medium moisture if possible so that the plant is in a dryer environment. Less moisture in the soil is sometimes a cue for plants to mature.

- A more drastic measure is to pollinate the flowers using pollen from a male flower. Once pollinated the plant will stop producing flowers. Instead, the flowers will start to produce seed. First the stigmas, the two hairs on the pistil, will begin to wither and withdraw into the ovary, which starts to swell as the seed begins to grow. The capitate glands that cover the surface of the leaves and ovary begin to swell as they fill with THC produced near the leaf surface. At this point, about a week after pollination, it is time to harvest the buds.

The best way to grow pure sativas is either in a greenhouse or outdoors. The reasons for this are that they need an extraordinary amount of light to produce dense, tight buds. They tend to be gangly and tall, and they take a long time to mature. Start the plants indoors about a month before they are to be transplanted into greenhouse or outdoors in the spring. As soon as they are transplanted, start forcing them by placing an opaque cover over them daily so that they receive only 12 hours of light each day.

An easy way to do this outdoors is to build a frame to hold black polyethylene so that it covers the plant yet provides an air space. The problem with black plastic is it absorbs the light and heats up. White/black polyethylene is available from some grow stores. It solves the problem by reflecting the light, yet remaining opaque. The cover should be placed over the plants in the late afternoon, as soon as the plants have received 10 hours of light.

Forcing the plants in late spring or early summer has many advantages. The plants, which take 90 days to mature, will be flowering during mid-summer and mature in early fall. Ordinarily they would ripen between November and January. By forcing them early, they flower when the sun is at its most intense, making the buds tighter and more compact.

In the warmer parts of the country, southern zone 10, sativas can be started either in spring or early summer and forced, or they can be left to flower in the fall after growing into 6-12 foot tall specimens. Another planting strategy is to put the plants in the ground in early September, as the daylight hours dwindle. They will soon start flowering as they grow and will mature as usual in late fall or early winter.

> *For more on ripening, see chapter 7.*
> *For more on the flower forcing and factors that trigger flowering, see chapter 6.*

A. 2. INDOOR & OUTDOOR STRAINS

BREEDING OUTDOOR PLANTS INDOORS

I am trying to adapt some plants to ripen here by the end of August. If I grow only outdoors then I have only one breeding crop a year. In order to speed up the process I have decided to breed indoors as well. How should I go about regulating day length in the grow room. Do I have to simulate summer and fall temperatures?

MR. BRIGHTLIGHT, Edmonton, AB, Canada

IN ORDER TO RIPEN by the end of August, the plants have to be triggered to flower 8-10 weeks, or 55-70 days earlier, depending on the variety. The 70-day variety would have to trigger by June 22, the first day of summer and the longest day of the year. The 55-day variety must trigger on July 12, still in the long stretch of summer.

In Edmonton at 53 N latitude, there is a dark period of 7 hours on June 22 and 7 1/2 hours on July 12. Presuming that you are growing seeds from 70-day plants that are normally started indoors, set the timer for continuous light until the plants are about a month past germination. Then turn the light back to 7 hours of darkness and wait 10 days for any sign of changeover from growth to flowering cycle in any of the plants.

Any females that indicate are likely to ripen in the time limit. Increase the dark period by 30 minutes, simulating July 12, eight days after the nights start lengthening. Wait two weeks to see if any additional plants trigger. The rest of the plants will ripen more than a week after August 31 and are not good candidates for breeding. As far as this program is concerned, they should be discarded unless no suitable candidates meet the mark. If not, choose the earliest suitable plants for further breeding.

Pollen from early male plants should be collected and saved, along with carefully preserved leaves of the males for examination and trial. Clones should be taken of both male and female candidates. The plants should be flowered out and tested. Only plants with the best qualities should be preserved. High yield, strongest potency, enjoyable flavor are typical qualities to select for. Selected plants will become part of the new breeding stock.

The 55-day plants should also be tested under 7 hours of darkness, the same amount as on June 22. Only the plants that flower under these conditions should be used. If none of the plants flower under this regimen, the dark period should be increased by 15 minutes for 2 weeks. This simulates the dark period in Edmonton on June 30. The latest plants can be forced for harvest September 1 is July 12, when the plants would have a dark period of 7 1/2 hours.

Once plants are selected, either regenerated females or their clone daughters should be pollinated. The seeds from these plants should then be grown out and given the same regimen. Choices are made only from plants that flower within the selected time frame or close to it. This time a higher percentage of plants will flower early.

For vigor, it is best to start with at least two lines from different parentage with the same breeding goals. After several generations of inbreeding the plants of each line, you will be closer to your goal of early flowering. However, as the plants become more inbred they lose their vigor. Crossing them with the other line will create an F1 hybrid with renewed vigor and stamina.

The temperature in the grow room will not significantly affect the development or ripening of the plants. Outdoors, cool temperatures and cloudy skies delay ripening.

> *For more on ripening, see chapter 7.*
> *For more on breeding techniques, see chapter 11.*
> *Sunrise/sunset hours are listed in appendix B.*

SAVE THE PLANT

I have this incredible plant that grows big, fat, round buds both indoors and out. First I grew it from seed and flowered it indoors. Then I regenerated it and placed it outdoors in speckled shade, where it grew great. My problem is that I am about to harvest it, but I don't want to lose the genetics. The plant is too big to dig out and bring back indoors. What should I do?

MISSISSIPPI RIVER GROWER, Kansas

TAKE CUTTINGS FROM THE plant before the flowers mature. The best branches for cuttings are ones with immature flowers. These branches are often found near the bottom of the plant, but mature flowers can also be used. Remove most of the flowers from the branch, leaving only a few leaves. Dip the cutting in rooting hormone and place it in sterile planting mix, rockwool or Oasis® cube. Root it as you would any cutting, under vegetative flowering cycle. Within a few weeks the cutting will root and vegetative growth will appear.

> *For more on saving genetics, see chapter 11.*
> *For more on regeneration, see chapter 1, section B.1; chapter 7, section C.*

NZ SEED BLUES

> I live about 150 miles above the 45th latitude. We're frost free until late April or early May. I like to harvest as early as possible.
>   Most of what's grown in this country is from Thai sticks that were abundant in the early and mid-70's. Most people here grow whatever seeds they find in good dope. There's a definite shortage of seeds.
>   What would be a good variety to grow here? We need a potent early maturing variety that stays short.
>
> CHRIS, Christchurch, New Zealand

THAI IS A LATE season variety and has a hard time ripening under the waning autumn sun. It is a sativa with a unique independent history.

The best plants would be short season indicas such as the indoor plants that are prize winners in the Amsterdam Cannabis Cups. These plants are extremely potent, start flowering early, ripen quickly and stay relatively short. They can be planted in early to mid-summer so that they stay in the ground only a short time.

Some seeds sold in Holland are for plants acclimated to the Dutch latitude. These plants, such as William's Wonder, do very well outdoors at high latitude.

> *For more on obtaining seeds, see chapter 1, section 1.*

VARIETIES FOR THE HOT

> I live almost right on the tropic of Capricorn (23 S latitude). The soil up here is good but I don't know how well the weed would grow in a hot climate. Water is no problem at all.
>
> GROWER, Newman, West Australia

GROWERS IN YOUR AREA have two problems. The first is to find a good plant that will grow through the season without flowering prematurely. The second is to prevent mold that can attack tight buds when the humidity gets higher.

Seed breeders have concentrated on developing small, fast maturing plants. When these plants are placed outdoors in the tropics, even during the long day season, they start flowering without getting a chance to develop a good infrastructure.

When they develop super-tight buds in high humidity, the deep crevices become an ideal environment for molds. These varieties are extremely difficult to grow except during the drier season, but then the short days force flowering.

The solution is to grow high quality equatorial varieties. Central Africans, Colombians, and Thais will all respond favorably to the conditions in your area. They start flowering in February but continue to grow into 7-15 foot (2-4 meter) giants. They will ripen in late June, in mid-winter. The buds will tighten up, but they won't be as dense as indicas. Sativa/indica hybrids will ripen a month earlier than the sativas and will not grow as tall.

Some commercial varieties respond well to these conditions. Haze, Skunk, and boutique sativas are suitable for winter cultivation. Look for varieties advertised as late maturing with a large sativa presence.

Varieties with even a small sativa presence will grow 50-80 inches (125-200 cm) during the long season. During the short-day period, they grow 20-40 inches (50-100 cm) tall.

> *For more on breeding for characteristics, see chapter 11.*

NORTHWEST VARIETIES

What varieties would be good for the climate in southwestern Washington?

NOT TOO EXPERIENCED, Vancouver, Washington

MANY OF THE NEW indoor varieties including the Skunks, White series, Mitey Mite strains and Northern Lights variations will do well throughout the northern half of the country. Some Afghanis and other indicas as well as fast maturing Durbans will also flower in time.

The plants will start to flower in the last weeks of July, ripening in September. The advantage of the indoor varieties is that they tend to be compact with dense buds that usually ripen fairly early in the season. The plants do not get too large so they are not so conspicuous.

In the southern half of the country, the plants will stop growing vegetatively soon after they are placed outdoors, even in mid-summer because of the shorter days.

> *For more on timing the harvest outdoors, see chapter 5, sections C and D.*

NEEDS DOMESTIC MEXICAN

I have used marijuana for years now due to my disability. I've found that really good Mexicans help me more than indicas for my particular needs.

I have a problem growing Mexican varieties where I live, in northern California at 5,000 ft. elevation. It gets too cold to get nice, tight, ripe buds. Where in the US would be an ideal place to get tight, ripe buds from sativas?

SANTA MARTA RED, Chester, California

TO GROW MEXICAN IN your area, you should force it to flower in mid-June so it will be ready in mid-September. To do this you would have to put shading over the plants 12 hours daily. This can be done in a greenhouse or by moving the plants indoors each evening.

Late maturing varieties will mature in southern California, and California's Central Valley, which stays warm well into November. They will also work in Florida, other parts of the southeast and along the Gulf Coast. Basically, these varieties are suitable in mild or very temperate areas such as the US West and Gulf coasts. However, in a greenhouse with shading, you can grow long season varieties anywhere in the country.

For more on Mexican varieties, see chapter 7, section A.3.

HYBRIDIZE WITH FERAL

I'm growing in Japan. There is wild sativa strain growing in Hokkaido and I am thinking of crossing my Dutch and Canadian strains with it for outdoor growing. Is it worth the effort?

TRIP MAKER, Kanazawa, Japan

HOKKAIDO IS AT ABOUT 42 degrees latitude but the feral cannabis growing there is likely fairly psychoactive. It sounds like a good candidate for cross-breeding because the strain is already acclimated. Try using the outdoor strain both as a pollen donor and to produce seed. Outdoor-adapted Canadian seed should finish quickly there. Fast indoor strains will also finish in early to mid-autumn.

Kanazawa, at 36 degrees latitude, with temperatures mediated by the Sea of Japan, might also be a good area to try some of the "indoor" varieties outdoors, with September and early October harvests.

I don't know if anything is growing there, but if there is feral hemp in southern Kyushu, at 31 degrees latitude, or in the small southern islands, it is likely to be quite psychoactive.

For more on crossing and stabilizing, see chapter 11.

B. SPECIFIC VARIETIES

DISSIMILAR HAZE

I'm growing Haze from Willy Jack seeds. I noticed that the plants are not all similar. Out of 10 seeds only 2 of the 6 females seemed like sisters. Is that normal for a strain? In the last weeks of flowering I've noticed a few pollen sacs on one particularly good plant. Should I try and pollinate this one plant to get seeds because this is a nice short plant with good bud compared to some of the other plants that are way taller and have longer node lengths or should I just pluck the male flowers off? If I do get seeds will there be a chance that they will be similar to the mother?

DAVE, River Drive Park, ON, Canada

THERE ARE SEVERAL DIFFERENT crosses that are called "Haze." All of them are crosses of sativas such as Mexican, Colombian, Jamaican and Thai. The different groups that developed Haze varieties worked for years inbreeding the original stock. They are large, late maturing plants. They have the traditional sativa conical Christmas tree shape and thrive under an unclouded sun and warm temperatures during the summer. Most importantly, they need a long warm autumn in which to develop their colas. Haze was bred in California and was adapted to the unique climatic conditions including a long autumn.

One group south of Santa Cruz developed a strain that was heavily influenced by several varieties of early 1970's Colombian, as well as Jamaican and Thai varieties. The plants grow 8-14 feet tall with a diameter up to 8 feet at the bottom. These plants were adapted to the coastal conditions, heavily mediated by the nearby ocean. During the summer, the coast is shrouded by fog in the morning. It burns off by noon and returns between 5 and 6 PM. The wind direction changes around Labor Day, bathing the land in full sun from morning to night as the day shortens. Unless storms come, there is a 50–50 chance the weather will remain like this until harvest time, just before Halloween.

346

There were other groups in Humboldt, Mendocino, and the Central Valley who grew their own adaptations of Haze. Often starting with another breeder's plants, each breeder added his/her own sativa varieties and expertise to the mix. All of these plants were called "Haze." If indica was added, which happened quite a bit, the resulting plants were not looked upon as Haze. All Hazes have a long maturation period, usually in late October or November. It is an exuberant plant that turns sunlight into exceptional growth. It is unsuitable for indoor cultivation.

When Haze seeds arrived in Holland, the breeders saw the potential of the plant, but only if it was tamed. Maturation time had to be shortened. Its unruly growing traits had to be restrained. The solution was to cross the plant with it's early maturing cousin, indica, to make it a shorter, earlier plant that could be used indoors and outdoors in areas with a shorter growing season. In order to maintain sativa characteristics, Haze was backcrossed to itself.

Willy Jack breeds in southern Canada, so he's probably adapted

Photo by Ed Rosenthal

the plant a bit to his conditions. His "Haze" was probably crossed with an indica more than once so indoor growers could taste some of its sativa qualities in an indoor plant. The taller plants, with longer internodes, are more like the original Haze. The reason that no two plants look alike is that this is a hybrid of hybrids. First generation (F1) hybrids are uniform because they have a similar assortment of genes. When hybrids are crossed, the genes, and thus the characteristics, are sorted in a random way. No two plants have similar sets of genes and no two plants look alike. It takes about six generations of inbreeding from the F2 hybrid to develop a homogeneous strain.

The advantage of starting with high quality plants with different characteristics is that one of them may match the environment. The variety of plant types provides a selection. If several plants are special, they will provide you with variety. Don't worry about the plants you don't like. You have purchased unique genetics for a few dollars.

The six females that you have all look different and your favorite one is a hermaphrodite. Unfortunately the plant should not be considered a candidate for breeding. You are left with several plants from which to choose.

> For more on F1 and F2 generations, see chapter 11, section D.
> For more on hermaphrodites, see chapter 11, section B.

NORTHERN LIGHTS

> I am growing some Hawaiian Indica and Shiva Skunk hybrids and plan to use them in my breeding program. They are both Northern Lights hybrids. What should I expect from the next generation?
>
> LIPSLEY PHAST, Te Kopura, New Zealand

SHIVA SKUNK IS A cross of Skunk #1 and Northern Lights #5. Hawaiian Indica is a cross of a Hawaiian sativa female and a Northern Lights male.

Skunk #1 is described as a stabilized indica/sativa hybrid. It produces large, moderately thick buds. The internodes (the space between each set of leaves) are intermediate. The odor is sweet rather than skunky. The flowering time is listed as about 50 days, but it usually takes 65-70 days. It has a lot of sativa characteristics but is more controllable—it doesn't grow that tall, responds quickly to flower forcing and does not require excessive light.

Northern Lights #5 is a very powerful, almost totally indica plant. At some point in its history an indica was crossed with a sativa and then backcrossed to its indica mother. Several other indicas entered the picture. The result is a plant with short internodes with a very stocky stem. The buds are large, dense and rounded. It has a powerful skunky odor and a dense smoke, which expands in the lungs. It is ripe 60 days after starting forcing.

The Shiva Skunk is a blend of two very powerful varieties, an indica and a stabilized indica/sativa hybrid. It is versatile, produces short stocky plants with large buds and has a powerful indica high. It matures in about 65 days. Because both of its parents are indicas, the F2 hybrids will show some differentiation, but it will not be extreme.

Hawaiian Indica is a true sativa/indica hybrid. It has intermediate internodes and a tendency to continue to grow vertically after flower forcing if the plants are less than 20 inches tall. The buds aren't quite as dense as indicas and the smell is sweeter. It requires more light than most indoor varieties and is not well suited to tight sea of green gardens because it has strong branching and longer internodes. The F2 hybrids will all have different combinations of sativa and indica characteristics.

When F1 plants are crossed for F2's, they can be used in two ways. The first is to choose a specific exceptional plant for cloning to start a monocrop garden. The plants can also be used for breeding a specific plant type or developing a perfect plant, which is then inbred to develop more consistency and stability so that it is considered a variety.

For more on F1 and F2 generations, see chapter 11, section D.

SKUNK #1

I bought some Skunk #1 seeds from the Sensi Seed Bank. The salesperson said that it was extremely similar to the original. When I grew it, it had a strong odor, but was not at all skunky. Also, its leaves were more sativa-like than indica-like. What gives?

Tom, Oakland, California

SKUNK #1 WAS DEVELOPED by the former proprietor of Sacred Seeds. This variety was the first stabilized hybrid offered on the seed market. It is approximately 25% Thai, 25% Afghani and 50% Mexican, probably Oaxacan.

A Thai male was crossed to an Afghani female. A female from that cross was pollinated by a Mexican male. All Skunk #1 results from that cross. Those seeds were germinated and individual plants were bred to each other for several generations, until the plants developed uniformly.

The cross is apparent. The leaves are sativa-like. It is a mid to long season plant and takes up to 90 days to mature indoors.

Skunk is the name of a generic group of pungent varieties that are either indicas or heavily indica hybrids. They have an odor highly reminiscent of a skunk.

Skunk #1 was given that name only because skunky plants were the rage in the mid-1980's, when the variety was popularized, but it doesn't have a skunk-like odor. Once people grew it, they didn't mind that its odor was not overpowering.

Skunk #1 revolutionized indoor growing. It was uniform, controllable and highly adaptable; one of the first "90-day wonders." Up until that point, indoor growers were attempting cultivation of stash seeds, mostly Mexican and Colombian, which never ripened properly and took six months to finish. This was the first of the reliable indoor varieties. Outdoors, the plant adapted well, drawing from all its parents to thrive in many adopted environments.

Although Skunk #1 is a little old-fashioned now, being considered a rather long 80-90 day indoor harvest and a October-November, late season harvest, it did revolutionize American growing.

SKUNK DEFORMITY

I have been growing Skunk #1 from the original Seed Bank for the last ten years. After I received the original seeds, I planted a seed crop. I germinated plants from the new seeds and then started cloning, taking clones from each new generation of plants just as they go into flowering. Only on a few occasions, when I moved and when the plants were badly infected with insects have I restarted from seeds.

I have a three-stage garden that starts with clones rooting in rockwool. From there the plants go into stage two, vegetative growth, in 4-inch rockwool cubes. When they are about 15 inches tall, they go into flowering. The blocks are placed on rockwool pads, spaced two per square foot.

The cubes and pads are individually drip irrigated from pre-mixed concentrate injection systems. The water is used only once, and I drip till one-third of the water drains to avoid salt build-up. I have tried all different concentrations of nutrients, from 500-1,750 ppm. That never seemed to make a difference either when the plants were healthy or now. I currently maintain solution at about 600 ppm.

For the past four years my garden has suffered from a problem that I have been unable to identify. It starts just as the plants are placed into flowering. First, there is a slight deformity of the new growth. The leaves are slightly twisted and unshapely. Then during flowering the buds grow smaller with each succeeding clone generation. My last harvest was half that of the one three clone generations ago.

When the problem first appeared I thought it was a phosphorus deficiency and I increased levels. That seemed to help for a while, but the problem reappeared.

I had an "expert" look at the plants and he said that the plants looked like they were suffering from nutrient deficiencies of iron, manganese and phosphorus. However, he said, it is not that these minerals are unavailable from the water–nutrient solution, but that the plant is unable to

absorb them. He suggested a dilute foliar spray to amelio-
rate but not solve the problem.
   What's wrong with my plants?

SHARKBAIT, Auburn, California

I SPOKE WITH SEVERAL breeders who have experience with the variety for breeding. They all noted that Skunk has a tendency toward a
slight deformity at the beginning of stage three, when the plants are
placed into flowering. This may be similar to the deformity you
describe.

The plants are probably suffering from a viral infection. The
virus' activity increases over time, so the plants' condition deteriorates. Cloning in some way helps the virus increase its expression in
the cells.

If your plants are all infected, any clones taken from them will
also be infected. Only tissue cultures taken from the growing tip
will be uninfected. Most of the time the viruses don't transfer to the
seed. However, if the plants from the seed have a very noticeable
deformity, perhaps they are infected also. Another possibility is
that the infectious agents left a residue or degenerative permanent
mutations.

The only way to make sure to get rid of this problem is to close
the growing area down and clean it thoroughly using steam, hydrogen peroxide (H_2O_2) laboratory detergent or other antiseptic
cleansers. The rockwool should be considered permanently contaminated and removed from the grow room. It could probably be
used for other crops since the disease is probably specific to
cannabis. All of the irrigation lines leading to and from the rockwool must be thoroughly disinfected or replaced. The floors and
walls should be washed down and disinfected. Then restart with
new seeds.

For more on viruses, see chapter 10, section B.

GROWING THAI

From four old Thai seeds I grew a female plant vegetatively under four 4-foot cool-white fluorescents. Then I flowered it, changing the tubes to deluxe warm-whites. Female buds grew in layers for two months. Then male flowers began appearing out of the tops of the buds. Is the plant trying to seed itself or is this being caused by light stress?

COLABUD, Hardwick, Vermont

MANY PLANTS ARE NATURAL hermaphrodites, especially if they remain unpollinated throughout flowering. Many indicas develop male flowers that open just as the plant ripens. Since this occurs at ripening it does not harm the crop.

Thai plants are known for their erratic growing patterns. Just as one branch ripens, another grows a new set of flowers. The flowering period can take six months or longer. The hermaphroditic patterns on these plants can be just a few male flowers hanging under a female bud, or on the other extreme, entire branches of male flowers. Although some Thai plants can be considered female, most of them grow some male flowers.

Under some circumstances, such as equatorial conditions with continuous warm weather and days that vary little by season, some Thai varieties become short-lived perennials. That is, the lower branches mature but new flowers continue to grow on upper branches.

For info on hermaphrodites, see chapter 11, section B.
For info on stress-induced male flowers, see chapter 6, section A.

WHITE WIDOW HERMAPHRODITES

The White Widows in my garden are growing male flowers on the bottom branches. The flowers don't affect the high at all and result in just a few very big seeds.

The plants are under a 150-watt HPS. The temperature ranges between 77-78° F. Are these flowers the result of environmental stress? Will the plants from these seeds be female or hermaphroditic?

GOTTAHIT, Internet

THE WHITE FAMILY IS not usually hermaphroditic, so the male flowers are probably stress related. If that's the case, then the plants resulting from this pollen will be all female since male chromosomes were not involved. However, these females will have the tendency to hermaphrodite under stress conditions.

For info on hermaphrodites, see chapter 11, section B.
For info on stress-induced male flowers, see chapter 6, section A.

13 CANNABIS & HEALTH

A. MARIJUANA & HUMANS
1. THC
2. HEALTH RISKS: MYTH & FACT
3. CANNABIS PROCESSING & HEALTH
4. PREGNANCY & PARENTING

B. MEDICAL MARIJUANA & SPECIFIC CONDITIONS

C. MARIJUANA & PETS

A. MARIJUANA & HUMANS

1. THC

THC & EVOLUTION

I recently read about a receptor for THC found on the surface of the brain cells. One of my friends claims that this shows that humans and cannabis must have evolved together. Why else would we have those receptors?

I think this hypothesis is flawed because humans evolved in Africa while cannabis evolved in Asia. Also, because cannabis is psychoactive in other animals. What's your opinion?

ANDY, Columbus, Ohio

SINCE PLANTS AND ANIMALS are part of the same ecological system, they have affected each another in the course of evolution.

One example of this co-evolution is the arsenal of chemicals that plants have developed to protect themselves from animals. For instance, estrogen, one of the female regulatory hormones, is produced by several varieties of yams. The reproductive cycle of insects and other animals that munch on this food are interrupted so that fewer predators emerge in the future.

After a receptor for THC was found in the brains of several vertebrates, a scientist, Dr. W.A. Devane, isolated the substance that the body produces which locks onto the receptor. He named it "anandamide," the Sanskrit word for bliss. Most researchers think that all vertebrates produce it. Receptors for anandamide have been found all over the body.

While anandamide may be ubiquitous among vertebrates, cannabinoids are unique to cannabis. No other plant produces a similar chemical. The inevitable next question is what do the cannabinoids do for the plant?

I think the cannabinoids protect plants in several ways. Cannabinoids are found on the surfaces of the entire plant in

357

increasing quantities as its investment in reproduction increases. This could indicate that cannabinoids play a protective role. I have observed insects trapped in the smelly resin and also noted that some insects seem to be repelled by the odor.

Mel Frank hypothesized that one purpose of the high concentration of cannabinoids surrounding the flower and developing seed is to protect against larger predators such as birds and mammals. He reasoned that animals that have been affected by cannabinoids avoid the flowers and immature seeds. The animals eat the seeds only when they are mature and drop from the plant.

I think your friend has the cause and effect reversed. You could say that as a result of co-evolution, cannabis produced cannabinoids, which protect it from predators by getting the munchers high—a state which most animals do not like. Rather than humans developing receptor sites as a result of contact with cannabis, cannabis produces cannabinoids, at least in part, as a result of its contact with vertebrates.

Cannabinoids may serve the plant in other ways, too. High THC variety clones grown under higher levels of UV-B light produce higher amounts of THC. This clue may indicate that THC protects the plant from these destructive rays.

> *For more on THC, see "Advice on Storage" in chapter 7, section F.*

THE TERM "MARIJUANA"

Why did Americans start using the term "marijuana"? When did it happen?

KRUSTY, Oregon

IT WAS FIRST USED by law enforcement and the pothibitionists at the turn of the century to describe the "loco-weed" used by Mexicans and Chicanos in the southwestern US.

The term "marijuana," which was used in Mexico, was imported for two reasons. First, if it had been called by its common name, hemp, people would not have been alarmed by its use. Second, many law enforcement authorities were unfamiliar with "Indian hemp" and learned it by the name the users called it.

A. 2. HEALTH RISKS: MYTH & FACT

MARIJUANA & YOUR LUNGS

I have two questions. Is it true that no one has died from cannabis directly? What are the chances of contracting lung cancer or emphysema from smoking the herb? I don't smoke tobacco.

CONCERNED CANNASSEUR, San Jose, California

THE US GOVERNMENT HAS published reports by the Drug Awareness Warning Network (DAWN) since the late '70's. They collect statistical data on drug use including morbidity. No annual report has ever reported a death caused by marijuana use.

I spoke with Dr. Donald Tashkin of UCLA Medical School who told me of findings from several recent studies he has done on long-term marijuana smokers.

Dr. Tashkin and his coworkers found that "marijuana may not be a risk factor for emphysema and it does not accelerate the natural diminution of lung capacity associated with aging."

They also discovered that, unlike tobacco, marijuana smoke stays in the central airways but does not get into the peripheral passageways for some unknown reason, possibly due to the larger size of the particles.

In the central passageways, where marijuana smoke is held, there is a similar deposition of smoke residue. In biopsies of these lung cells taken from long-term marijuana smokers, he "found injury to the cells at least as marked as in cigarette smokers." The cells had certain pre-cancerous abnormalities regularly found with cigarette smokers. Tashkin thought this was interesting (read alarming, Ed) because he was comparing 3 joints to 22 cigarettes daily.

Among the indicators he used were three genes that regulate growth and are normally overexpressed in tobacco smokers. When these genes function abnormally, their ability to suppress uncontrolled cell growth is impaired. This presages tumor and cancer growth. He found that these genes were also overexpressed in marijuana smokers. People who smoked both marijuana and tobacco had the most extensive genetic damage.

The US government has published annual reports on drug statistics since the late '70s. No annual report has ever reported a death caused by marijuana use.

He mentioned that benzopyrene, one of the byproducts inhaled from the burning cigarette or joint, affects the p53 gene. This gene helps regulate growth and suppresses unregulated growth such as cancer. When this gene functions improperly, tumors happen.

Tashkin is also concerned that the receptors for THC are found on the T-cells, macrophages and killer cells, as well as other cells that are involved in immune response. He thinks that THC may suppress both the immune system and its surveillance system, which tells the body to get ready to deal with a problem.

One of Tashkin's colleagues took a variety of mice that are susceptible to cancer and pre-treated them with massive dosages of THC. Then they injected tumor cells. The cells grew much faster in the mice that were pre-treated with the THC. To Tashkin, this is an indication that THC might suppress immune response.

Tashkin does feel that many of the worst effects of marijuana use are the result of the pyrolytic compounds. If an inhalant were available that worked well, this might be a suitable method of delivery. A study of medical inhalant users found that most of them get only a small percentage of the prescribed dose because of improper use.

Tashkin also thinks that a vaporizer would be more suitable than smoking the substance. All of these problems are resolved when marijuana is ingested rather than inhaled.

When I spoke about this with California NORML director Dale Gieringer, he reminded me about one of the few studies comparing morbidity between marijuana and non-marijuana users, reported in "Ganja in Jamaica" by Vera Rubin. She showed that marijuana users have a life expectancy a few months longer than non-smokers, which is a statistically significant figure.

> *For info on vaporizers, see chapter 14, section B.*

LOWERS IMMUNE SYSTEM?

I have read that pot lowers your immune system to colds and other infections. Also, that smoking pot makes your cold last longer. However, I find that smoking joints helps out when I'm sick and I always feel better after toking up. I find that marijuana outperforms many of the synthetically produced prescription drugs.

STONED AND HEALTHY, Geraldton, ON, Canada

THERE IS A LOT of debate in the scientific community as to whether or not marijuana lowers the T-cell count and impairs the immune system. In both in vivo and in vitro studies, marijuana was shown to impair the immune system slightly. For instance, the Kaiser study, conducted in California, showed that marijuana smokers had more colds and they persisted longer than in a partially matched group of non-smokers.

On the other hand several studies found that marijuana smokers had higher counts of T-cell and other immune system indicators. Certainly marijuana is not a major creator or vector of infection or organic problems.

A study of 65,000 men and women who were members of an HMO found no statistically significant association between marijuana smoking and death. Dr. Stephen Sidney, senior epidemiologist with Kaiser-Permanente published the results of his research in the April 1997 issue of the *American Journal of Public Health*. This study shows that marijuana cannot be too harmful, since it does not increase the death rate.

As some correspondents have mentioned, some people have peculiar allergic reactions to marijuana, or certain types of marijuana, or even certain parts of the plant. My feeling about that is, if something doesn't agree with you, don't do it or use it.

People who have lung problems or bronchitis should be very careful about irritating their lungs. Certainly marijuana smoke has irritants and affects the lungs, as Dr. Donald Tashkin explains in "Smoke Particulates," (next page).

One thing that is hard to measure or run controls on, is a person's state of mind. Although the "pure science" medicos of the mid-twentieth century denigrated the importance of a person's mental state in prognosis, opting instead for chemical reactions, researchers now know that a happy, positive attitude helps people heal. Fifty million people in the US who use marijuana in spite of the legal risks are proof that a sizeable minority of adults feels the herb has a positive effect on them.

PROPAGANDA

A letter to the editor of my local newspaper said that smoking marijuana could "cause damage to the pituitary gland, lower resistance to disease and cause birth defects."

It continued that when pot smokers get the munchies, they crave "sugar-laden foods and an unusual thirst for alcohol." The letter also mentioned kidney disorders, elevated blood sugar levels and insulin imbalances.

Will smoking marijuana be harmful to my health? Does it have long-term effects on the body? Are any of the assertions in the letter true?

GANGSTER OF BUD, Windsor, Utah

THERE ARE ABSOLUTELY NO peer-accepted research papers showing that marijuana affects the pituitary gland or causes birth defects. A study by Kaiser Permanente Medical Center in California showed that marijuana smokers do get more colds but that marijuana use does not affect morbidity rates.

There is no research supporting marijuana as a cause of kidney disorders, insulin imbalances or major changes in blood sugar levels. From personal observations of people using pot, I would say that it makes them more aware of their hunger.

There is no evidence that marijuana causes any permanent change in brain organization or metabolism. Studies of marijuana users in both third-world countries and the US show little difference between pot users and non-users in achievement levels and most other sociological indices.

There are no deaths reported from marijuana use, and it has a very low emergency room treatment rate for its effects. When compared to other recreational drugs, such as alcohol or tobacco, or with many sports such as skydiving, tackle football, skiing or mountain climbing, marijuana has to be considered safe. The Drug Awareness Warning Network (DAWN) statistics, compiled by the US government, track deaths from all drugs annually. Marijuana has yet to make the list. There has never been a death reported from the use of marijuana. No other herb or drug has marijuana's safety record.

The letter writer is totally misinformed and has no factual basis for his/her assertions. To quote Dr. Lester Grinspoon, noted marijuana author and legalizer, "Marijuana does cause hysteria in people—those opposed to its use."

Write the newspaper and challenge the writer to show any scientific support for his position. She just doesn't have it, because it doesn't exist.

SMOKE PARTICULATES

I have a friend who has a 5-foot bong. He's a swimmer. When the entire bong chamber filled with smoke, he drew it all in. Then he held it for about 50 seconds. When he exhaled, there was virtually no visible smoke. What happened to it?

BILL'S FRIEND, Santa Barbara, California

IF THE SMOKE DOES not come out, it must remain in the lungs. The solid particulates and other unhealthy products of the burn are not good for the lungs.

Dr. Donald Tashkin, a prominent researcher at UCLA is studying this. He told me "80-90% of the solid particulates stay in the body. The fine particles, with a median size of about one micron, are caught mostly in the periphery of the lungs where they are taken up by the alveolar macrophages—scavenger cells that gobble the particles up. The particulates are held here for long periods of time—months, or even years, as succeeding generations of scavenger cells ingest the debris released by dying macrophages. Some components of the particulates, including THC and other cannabinoids, are absorbed by the lungs and enter the bloodstream.

"The larger particles are caught in the mucus lining of the central airways. The cilia, hairlike filaments projecting from the lining cells, use a waving action to move the particles up to the mouth, where they are mostly swallowed."

I have noticed that heavy cannabis smokers produce a lot of mucus and they either spit it out or swallow it. I suspect that this higher production of mucus is the body's response to the frequent smoke intake.

Vaporizer users do not produce the large amounts of mucus that marijuana smokers do. This is because they aren't inhaling all the burn residues inhaled in smoke. Instead they are just inhaling the evaporated cannabinoids.

> *For info on vaporizers, see chapter 14, section B.*

BODYBUILDING

I have been smoking marijuana for seven years, using at least two joints a day. Recently I got involved in bodybuilding. I read that smoking the herb thwarts efforts at building body mass. Is smoking pot incompatible with bodybuilding?

HIGH LIFTER, Chicago, Illinois

MANY ATHLETES USE MARIJUANA. I asked some gym-going marijuana users what they thought about it. Some said that it detracts from their concentration, so they don't use it before exercising. Others said they always got high before working out because it helped them get through it. One said his mind could wander while his body stayed on autopilot.

A racquetball enthusiast said he loves to play high, but not stoned. He said it doesn't affect his game much, but made it more fun to play. It's well known that competitive bikers, basketball players and snowboarders frequently use marijuana.

There have been no studies on marijuana use and muscle mass. However, marijuana use does not affect muscle development in the general population, so it is not likely to affect your training goals. Marijuana may affect body mass. As you know, the munchies are one of marijuana's well-known side effects. Eating a properly balanced high-protein diet when you get the munchies may help you build mass. The endogenous cannabinoids, the ones the body produces, play a fundamental role in regulating feeding.

DRY MOUTH & RED EYES

How come I get dry mouth and blood-shot eyes when I smoke?

LINDA, Ames, Iowa

I have been a regular smoker for two and a half years. Pot has always made my eyes red, but lately it's been ridiculous. They get totally bloodshot after about two hits. Strangely, my left eye gets much redder than the right. Visine doesn't usually work, so I can't smoke if I'm going out in public because people are very concerned and ask about it. What causes this redness? Is it unhealthy and can it be avoided?

ANDY, Marquette, Michigan

THERE ARE THREE BASIC physical reactions to cannabis. You mentioned one of them; the others are tachycardia (a speeded heartbeat that usually diminishes with tolerance) and cottonmouth.

Bloodshot eyes are the result of dilation of the capillaries in the eye, so they become more visible. Marijuana "relaxes" the vessels of the blood system. This lowers blood pressure in the eye.

Cottonmouth is the result of the THC itself, not smoking it. You get the same effect when you eat it. Not only does the mouth become dry, but the throat as well. I have seen no research on this subject.

Extremely bloodshot eyes, especially with the asymmetry that you mentioned, are a signal. The blood vessels are dilating too much. Your body is saying this isn't good for you, sort of like an allergic reaction.

MARIJUANA & METABOLISM

My 18-year-old girlfriend smokes all the time. She is a vegetarian and eats a lot. She is very skinny. She visited her doctor to make sure she didn't have a metabolic problem. He told her that THC causes fat not to remain on the body. Is this true?

HEMP, Glendale, California

THE DOCTOR IS MISTAKEN or s/he is deliberately misleading the client. Can you imagine if the doctor's claims were true? Eat all you want, smoke pot and stay slim? There would be many fewer fat people in the US and many people would be using it for diets. Everybody would want the stuff and it would immediately be legal.

Marijuana is recommended for symptomatic relief of anorexia and bulimia. Certainly it would not be indicated for these problems if one of its contraindications were possible weight loss. The doctor's statement is off the charts.

The reason your girlfriend is so slim is that she is eating a low-fat diet and metabolizes carbohydrates very well. The doctor should be confronted about the misleading statement. Personal prejudices have no place in the delivery of medical care.

DREAMING

> I smoked pot almost every day for two years. A bong hit
> was enough for me. I don't think I dreamed but a few times
> during the 730 days.
>   I stopped smoking after I closed down my grow room. I
> have no problem without pot; however, I dream every day
> since then. I don't have nightmares or bad dreams, but they
> are very vivid.
>
> TETSUO, Osaka, Japan

THE NATIONAL ACADEMY OF Sciences (NAS) study of marijuana,
released in 1999 found that the REM (rapid eye movement) sleep
period was reduced 18% in marijuana smokers and eye movement
was reduced 49%. When marijuana use stopped, the withdrawal
symptoms included an increased period of REM sleep, up 49%,
while eye movement increased 67%.

These statistics indicate that pot interferes with dreaming,
since the REM sleep period is when dreams occur. The NAS study
also found that other withdrawal symptoms included increased
irritability and reflexes and a mild agitation.

According to California NORML director Dale Gieringer, one
Freudian psychologist complained that potheads don't have
dreams, at least ones they can recall.

VOMITING

> Sometimes when I smoke pot I end up spewing chunks. Is
> this normal?
>
> DTL, Chicago, Illinois

No, IT IS NOT normal. It is an allergic reaction. Your body is telling
you to stay away from this substance.

HEADACHES WITH HIGH

Every time I smoke pot I get a terrible headache as I am coming down. Why does this happen and what can I do to stop it?

THE HAPPY HEMP, Johnstown, Pennsylvania

PERHAPS THERE IS A constriction of the blood vessels in your brain when you are coming down. This would cause a headache. I don't know why this happens to you.

Some people are sensitive to certain types of marijuana or perhaps even to chemicals or fertilizers used in the growing technique. Some varieties may be pleasant for them but others leave them with a headache.

If you regularly have headaches with marijuana use, consider it an allergic reaction of some sort. Your body is telling you not to use it.

A. 3. CANNABIS PROCESSING & HEALTH

HASH & HYGIENE

Some fellows I know swallowed Indian charas (hash) while traveling over there. It was wrapped in layers of plastic. They pooped it out back here. It smells a bit dodgy. I've had Afghani smuggled this way before, but it was packaged in special bags intended for internal use, and smelled perfectly okay.

Is there any sort of health risk smoking this charas? What about eating it?

THE DUCK, Cairns, QLD, Australia

YOU HAVE BEEN SMOKING some real crap. Now you are thinking about eating it? Maybe pot does rot your brain!

If it smells like crap there is a reason for it—because it's contaminated with crap. Throw this crap away.

A. 4. PREGNANCY & PARENTING

GENETIC DAMAGE?

Does marijuana use produce genetic damage?

M.V., Lacey, Washington

THE NATIONAL ACADEMY OF Sciences (NAS) summed up marijuana and health research in its report, "Marijuana and Health" published in 1982. On pages 101-102 it stated, "extensive testing with delta-9-THC using three established tests for mutagenesis failed to detect any mutagenic effect, or any effect as an inhibitor of DNA repair (Legator et al., 1976; Glat et al., 1979; Zimmerman et al., 1978). Then the paper cites other research that confirms these results.

The section continues, "Does marijuana cause chromosome breaks? The weight of the evidence from in vitro cultures of human cells and from in vivo animal and human studies is that neither marijuana nor delta-9-THC causes chromosome breaks."

Finally it states, "Studies that have reported chromosome breaks or gaps in cell cultures of users of marijuana have largely been carried out on multiple drug users, and the breaks and gaps may be due to other factors associated with a life of heavy drug use." (Gilmour et al., 1971; Herha and Obe, 1974).

These findings have held for the last 20 years. There is no new research that contradicts this research.

Marijuana must be benign. The government has spent billions of dollars funding researchers who are trying to show toxicological effects of marijuana. They have not been successful. With all this research, they would have found something if it were there.

Marijuana has been popular in the US for the last 35 years. If it were so harmful, we'd see the statistics regarding hospitalizations and the death rate. Marijuana use doesn't seem to affect the public health negatively.

MARIJUANA DURING PREGNANCY

I used to smoke marijuana every day, but gave it up when I decided to become pregnant. At 6 months, morning sickness returned and my weight gain was already 10 pounds under normal. Not being able to eat left me feeling weak and stressed out. We already have a two year old and a four year old. So I smoked for one month during parts of the sixth and seventh months. It relieved me of the nausea and I was able to eat well.

Is there any way for the doctors to discover whether I had smoked during my pregnancy when I deliver? What are the consequences?

CONCERNED MOMMY, Pensacola, Florida

Can I smoke marijuana when I'm pregnant or will it affect the baby?

JILL, New York City

YOUR USE OF MARIJUANA to control nausea is an accepted medical remedy for the condition. Since you smoked it between one and two months before delivery, if you were tested, it would not indicate positive, especially since your use was limited.

Unless a woman or her spouse showed indications of use or talked about drugs with her doctor, she would not be tested. In many states, it is illegal to test a person against their will, but the baby might be tested. In the unlikely event that you or the baby tested positive, the legal ramifications vary county by county, state by state.

Marijuana has been used for thousands of years to control the discomforts of pregnancy. Aside from nausea, it is also used to relieve muscle spasms, so in states where a medical defense is permitted, this medical application should come up. It has also been used for childbirth, both to alleviate the pain and to ease the labor.

No study has shown any increase of birth defects from the use of marijuana. "Executive" or organizational skills of babies whose mothers smoked marijuana are normal. Dr. Peter Fried has studied children of mothers who used cannabis during pregnancy, comparing them with a control group of non-cannabis users. He found that the children of mothers who indulged had a higher IQ, but he attributes this to environmental factors, not the marijuana. In some studies "marijuana babies" weigh slightly less than non-smoker's babies, but in others, they weigh more, so no conclusive link could be established.

BREAST-FEEDING MOM

I'm a breast-feeding mom of an eight-month-old baby. I get stoned about three times a week, taking only two hits at a time. How does that affect my baby?

NAME WITHHELD, Montmouth, Oklahoma

WITH VERY HEAVY SMOKING, minute amounts of THC pass into the breast milk. Pot smoking by breast-feeding moms has never been associated with any problems of development.

Breast-feeding babies of alcohol-imbibing mothers do not suckle as long and gain weight slower. Marijuana does not inhibit breast-feeding and weight gain is normal.

The main problems you and your baby face are the extremely harsh laws in Oklahoma. For instance, simple possession of marijuana in the presence of a child can get you 20 years, cultivation for personal use, 70 years or more.

My wife and I have toked up since our late teens. We now have four children.

Since we smoked on a daily basis, we didn't believe there would be any problems so she didn't quit during pregnancy. She found it helped her with morning sickness and we stayed high all the time. She took no other drugs, nor alcohol, aspirin or other pain relievers.

Our children are all healthy and have no problems, either physical or mental and are all well adjusted. My 10-year-old son is in an enrichment program and maintains a 3.75 GPA, and the other kids show similar signs of thriving.

Pot isn't the substance that reefer madness politicians would have you think it is. We find it to be a great stress reliever.

MERCURY, Alaska

THANKS FOR SHARING YOUR life experiences with us, Mercury.

B. MEDICAL MARIJUANA & SPECIFIC CONDITIONS

PRESCRIPTION FOR POT

I get migraine headaches a lot and have even been given a prescription for drugs that didn't work. I have noticed that when I smoke pot the headaches went away and stayed away. How do I approach my doctor about a prescription?

A.S., Modesto, California

ACCORDING TO THE PROVISIONS of Proposition 215, California's medical marijuana provision, a recommendation from a doctor is required for an affirmative defense for possession or cultivation of marijuana. The recommendation is used in place of a prescription, since they are illegal according to federal law. The 9th District Court ruled that doctors have a constitutional right to recommend marijuana to patients.

You owe it to yourself to get help from your doctor. On your next visit you should bring up the fact that you experienced relief from migraines while using marijuana and that you feel it is the most effective drug for the medical problem. Then ask if s/he would recommend marijuana for the problem if it were legal to do so. If s/he says yes, ask if s/he would sign a note saying something like, "I recommend marijuana to my patient for the relief of his migraine headaches."

If you are uncomfortable approaching your physician, there are organizations that can help you find out more about medical marijuana use and offer risk assessment and preparatory materials for speaking with your doctor. Once such resource is the nonprofit organization Americans for Safe Access. Visit their website at www.safeaccessnow.org, or call 510-486-8083 for assistance and referrals to other sources of information that can help in your area.

INSULIN DEPENDENT

What are the effects of marijuana on insulin-dependent diabetics?

MARC, Internet

MARIJUANA HAS NO EFFECT on diabetics, either insulin or non-insulin dependent. Marijuana does not affect the blood sugar level. The main danger for diabetics is going off their prescribed diet because of increased appetite.

READER TIP ▶ **HIGH BLOOD PRESSURE**

Cannabis has had a number of good effects on me. It has lowered my blood pressure after I was diagnosed with high blood pressure three years ago. I've given up the prescription medications because the herb is all natural and does not damage the kidneys like the man-made synthetics.

When I told my doctor he didn't tell me to quit but he didn't advocate use either.

CANNABIS CANNISUR, Santa Clara, California

THANKS FOR THE INFO, Canna. The overall effect is to lower blood pressure after an initial increase of both heart rate and blood pressure.

LIVER PROBLEMS

I have cirrhosis of the liver (not from drinking) and I was smoking pot while waiting for a liver transplant. Recently my doctor said I should stop using it. He said it was too risky to use because it contains "who knows what." That advice came from a doctor who seemed to have his mind fixed about this "drug" and could not even pronounce it right. I left the hospital that day disappointed and angry because there's no research and nobody knows if it would be too risky for me to use it.

I did not tell the doctor that I grow a beautifully healthy marijuana plant indoors and I do know what goes in it. No one else's hands are touching it. Also I know my body does not lie and when I smoke pot I'm so in touch with each organ inside me.

I don't use marijuana just to get stoned. I use it during my meditation, almost in a religious way and it does wonders. It also helps me with the stress in my entire body.

Do you have any information about what marijuana does to the liver?

HELEN, Seattle, Washington

POT DOESN'T AFFECT THE liver. People with cirrhosis, hepatitis and other diseases that affect the liver can use it.

Although your cirrhosis was not the result of alcohol, many sufferers have an alcohol problem. Many recovering alcoholics have found that cannabis is a good substitute for alcohol cravings.

Your doctor might have been concerned about contamination. Since you grow your own you know that is not a problem.

STEM FOR SLEEP

I have many allergies and I react to THC with bummer trips from smoking leaf or bud. However, I found that smoking a chunk of stem $1/8$"x $1/8$" x $1/4$" makes me sleep like a baby. I don't get a headache from it, and get no hangover in the morning, which is more than I can say for over-the-counter snooze pills.

Only the stems of fresh plants seem to have any effect. I have tried dried imported stem from a hemp shop and it does zilch.

Why does this work? Would my smoking stems show up on a piss test?

LASHER, San Francisco, California

I HAVE NO IDEA why the stem would affect you differently than the leaves or buds of a plant. If it works you should continue using it. The stem has the cannabinoids of the same quality as the leaf and bud, just in smaller quantities.

In Switzerland several nursing homes use sachets of low-grade marijuana leaf for aromatherapy. A small "pillow" containing several ounces of whole leaf is hung on the headboard. Patients find it easier to fall asleep and to sleep through the night.

The THC in the stem would indicate on a piss test.

For more on drug tests, see chapter 8, section B.1.
For more on processing the plant, see chapter 7, section G.

ULCERS

I have a peptic ulcer and was taking a drug called "Pepcid" until I found out that prolonged use can cause liver and kidney damage. By accident I found that smoking a marijuana cigarette relieves my stomach pain almost immediately for some time. Do you know of any medical information on the subject?

NATURAL RELIEF, Lowbanks, ON, Canada

MARIJUANA IS NOT CONSIDERED a treatment of choice for ulcers in the medical books. However, it does calm the nerves and relieve spasms, so it is reasonable that it provides you relief.

ALZHEIMER'S DISEASE

My 50-year-old aunt is in the final stages of Alzheimer's disease. Has cannabis ever been shown to be useful in preventing or alleviating symptoms of the disease?

GARY, Internet

THERE IS NO INFORMATION in the literature that shows that marijuana prevents or alleviates symptoms of Alzheimer's disease.

MARIJUANA FOR ALLERGIES

I suffer from severe allergies and have tried all the drugs from the doctor's bag. Nothing worked.

I have noticed that if I stay high I'm not as miserable as I used to be. Is marijuana an effective alternative medicine for allergy sufferers?

J.T., Sebring, Florida

APPARENTLY MARIJUANA IS AN effective medicine for your allergies. Because of your experience you are an expert on the subject. Marijuana does dry the sinus cavities, even when it is ingested rather than inhaled. Some of the relief you experienced may be the result of this.

Photo by Pepper Design

C. MARIJUANA & PETS

PET CAT ON DOPE

One day my girlfriend offered her cat one of the lower leaves from a live plant, and she ate it with gusto, and then looked up for more. Ever since, she seems to live for weed. She spends much of her time waiting outside the grow room, begging to get in, always hopeful for a handout of two or three fresh leaves. Between crops she sniffs forlornly around the empty closet. I try to keep a supply of dry leaves around for her so she won't be too deprived. Do you suppose our furry friend actually likes getting high on the THC in the leaves?

CONCERNED PARENT, San Diego, California

CATS ARE DRIVEN BY the pleasure principle; that is, they tend to repeat behavior that gave them pleasure. Obviously your cat was able to figure out that these leaves made her feel good, and that she would get high whenever she ate them.

As a concerned parent are you aware that your cat may graduate to harder drugs? Many a cat started on pot but turned to catnip when their humans realized the cost savings. Hopefully, with her private garden that you maintain for her, this will not be Miss Fifi's fate.

MEDICAL CANNABIS FOR FIDO

My dog was diagnosed with cancer and is undergoing chemotherapy. He lost his appetite so I give him a marijuana tincture several times a day. At first he resisted the medication, now he cooperates with the routine. Has he learned to like getting high? Do you think I can get a 215 ID for my pet as his caregiver?

DOGSITTER, San Francisco, California

IF HE IS COOPERATING with the treatment he must like it, or at least its effects. Some cats and dogs seek marijuana in one form or another but an animal's cooperation may result from their trust in you as their caretaker. He doesn't find it too unpleasant or he'd show his displeasure in one way or another.

California's Proposition 215, the medical marijuana initiative, makes no provision for use of medical marijuana by animals so I doubt that you can get a vet to provide you with a recommendation in writing. Make sure that your dog is aware of the consequences of his use. Make sure that he doesn't discuss his medication with strangers. He must remain very discreet.

14 PARAPHERNALIA & USE

A. BONGS, PIPES & JOINTS

B. VAPORIZERS

C. CANNABIS CONSUMER TIPS

RELATED TOPICS
Effects of smoking on health: chapter 13 Cannabis & Health.
When is marijuana ready to consume: chapter 7 Harvest,
    section E Drying & Curing.

A. BONGS, PIPES & JOINTS

BONG INTENSITY

Does the size of the bong affect the intensity of the high?

CHRIS, Palatine, Illinois

YES. THE VOLUME OF the bong determines how much air is "conditioned" or "smokafied." If the volume is small, not much smoke gets inhaled when the carburetor is released, allowing a free flow of air. Bongs with larger volumes hold more smoke so more gets to the lungs of the inhaler.

The configuration of the bowl and the pipe may also affect the concentration of the smoke. I know of no research conducted on this subject.

The bigger the chamber that holds the smoke, the more smoke that you can draw into your lungs once the carburetor is opened. When more smoke-filled air is drawn in, more THC gets into the lungs and is absorbed by them. This increases the intensity of the high.

BONG ALCOHOL

I own a glass bong, which I sometimes fill with vodka. I was told that vodka absorbed some of the unwanted particles while leaving the good stuff in. Is this true or is the alcohol absorbing some of the THC?

A.M., Mt. Lawley, Australia

THC IS ALCOHOL/OIL soluble and is not as soluble in water. The result is that the alcohol allows more of the non-psychoactive substances to pass while dissolving THC.

It would be better to use water, in which the THC is less soluble, but which does dissolve many of the harmful gasses and non-psychoactive smoke particles. A recent study conducted at the Research Triangle found that water pipes filled with water collected a higher percentage of THC than solid particulates, making an unfiltered joint safer as far as solid particulates go. Gas absorption was not tested. Presumably, alcohol would fare even worse on these tests.

In a conversation with Dr. Donald Tashkin of UCLA, he expressed concern not only of the irritants in the smoke but also of the hot air that he felt was not healthy for the lungs. Water pipes filled with ice cool the air and solve that problem.

CLARIFYING BONGWATER

A few years back, you stated that it was better to use warm water in a bong since it filtered out more of the water-soluble non-psychoactive chemicals. Recently you stated that the THC becomes sticky and is more likely to stick to the sides of the pipe or float on the water's surface when hot water is used. What's the scoop on hot versus cold water?

CONFUSED BONG OWNER, Denver, Colorado

BOTH COLD AND WARM water capture equal amounts of the larger particles, namely ash. Cold water captures fewer non-psychoactive water solubles, because many of them are less soluble in cold than warm water. THC oil is also much less soluble in cold than warm water. In hot or warm water more of the oils are captured in the water. They float on the surface if the water is left undisturbed. Warmed THC is more viscous and less hardened than cold THC. Viscous THC is more likely to stick to container and tube walls than cold, hard material. More of the non-psychoactive compounds will stick to the surfaces too.

Cold water is best because hot air is not good for your lungs. Cooler smoke is less likely to irritate them. In addition, more of the warm viscous oil is likely to stick to container walls.

BROKEN BONG

I recently attempted to clean my 4-foot Graffix bong with some alcohol, as a friend suggested. When I did this my bong started making popping noises. As I held it in my hands it started shattering into dozens of little pieces. I had used alcohol on other bongs with no ill effects.

What do you think caused this? What would be the appropriate way to clean my long bong in the future?

BUMMED WITHOUT BLUE, Bossier City, Louisiana

THE PIPE SHATTERED BECAUSE the alcohol quickly cooled the surface of the plastic inside the pipe while the rest of the plastic stayed the same temperature. Shrinkage in the cool area caused enough tension to cause the pipe to break.

READER TIPS **GLASS CLEANING**

I am writing in response to "Broken Bong." The bong probably broke because it had a hairline crack. Alcohol can cool the surface very quickly. Perhaps a sudden change in temperature caused his warmed Graffix to break.

EMBRACE HAYEK, DeKalb, Illinois

I too have experienced bong wreckage using caustic chemicals on plastic smoke tools. I learned my lesson and it's changed my cleaning habits forever.

I now use a glass pipe, not plastic. Cleaning is easy. Pull out the stem and gasket, and then block the open hole with tape so that it's watertight. Fill the bong with water above the level of the encrusted resin. Drop in 2-4 Efferdent Denture Cleaning Tablets. As the tablets bubble, hold one hand over the top of the bong and shake the water around. Repeat this a few times until the tablets are completely dissolved. Let the solution sit until the build-up is gone or overnight in extreme cases. Then brush the walls. Voila! A sparkling clean instrument. I think it's safe because people use it for their dentures.

HYDROBIONIC, Santa Cruz, California

I use glass bongs and clean them with Soft Scrub and a bottle brush. I also use wooden Q-Tips that work great on the stem. The Soft Scrub works almost immediately. There's no overnight wait.

A, McGrath, Alaska

I clean my bongs using hot water, Dawn detergent, and a washcloth. Pipe cleaners are handy for cleaning out the stem and an old toothbrush works well for cleaning the bowl.

BUCK ALEISTER GROWLITE, Columbia, Missouri

I use Citra Solve, which is made from the oil of citrus peels, to clean my bong. It gets everything out. Make sure to rinse the bong thoroughly several times.

NO NAME, San Diego, California

I use Spic and Span with hot water. Swish and brush it clean, then rinse with cold water.

SUE W. Long Beach, California

Let your bong soak in Simple Green for about five minutes. Then take a Q-Tip and gently rub the side. Rinse and you're done. Simple Green is biodegradable, non-toxic, non-flammable and non-abrasive. It's bong safe, and environmentally safe.

DAWN, Coral Springs, Florida

KEEPING GLASS PIPES HEALTHY

Glue a piece of cork to the ashtray using silicon or white glue. You can tap the ashes out of the bowl onto this friendly surface without fear of breaking the glass.

TAJI LLAMA, Placerville, California

THANKS FOR THE TIP, Taji.

DEFINING SPLIFF

My friend and I have a disagreement about what a spliff is. I say it is a cone-shaped roller. My friend says that it is any joint rolled with two papers to make it longer. Who's right?

VICE ONE AND B HEAD, Hudson, New York

YOUR FRIEND SMOKES A long joint. You smoke a spliff.

THE ROACH

Did the roach get its name from looking like a cockroach?

THE RHINO SHAKERS, Orange, California

THAT SEEMS RIGHT TO me. One fellow told me that it originated in New York's Lower East Side (East Village) during the hippie era, where roaches and marijuana were common denominators in most apartments. I know that's not true because the Mexican Revolutionary song "La Cucaracha," discusses the "cockroach" that Pancho Villa needed to smoke before he could start his day. It's ironic that preschool children are taught this ballad as well as "Puff, the Magic Dragon."

I think that the term "roach" originated as a result of the visual similarity between the insect and the unused portion of a joint. They are about the same size and the joint end is often discolored brown and black.

B. VAPORIZERS

VAPORIZER FACTS

Do vaporizers work? Does the taste element fall away? Do they reduce the health risks?

THE COUNT, Zurich, Switzerland

VAPORIZERS WORK BY HEATING marijuana to the point that THC evaporates and becomes a gas. This temperature, about 380° F, is too low to cause a burn so the solids and pyrolytic compounds in the smoke stream are eliminated.

The airstream vaporizer is clear, carrying only the cannabinoids and essential oils, but not all the other compounds created by a burn.

Vaporizers allow people to inhale the cannabinoids in marijuana without subjecting the inhaler's lungs to harsh smoke. There are no carcinogenic compounds created so inhaling vaporized air is much safer than inhaling smoke.

VAPORIZER RUMORS

I've read that vaporizers have absolutely no ill effect on your health. I have heard rumor, however, that the oil that sticks to the top of the dome harms your lungs. Is this true?

A CONCERNED CONSUMER, Internet

VAPORIZERS WORK BY HEATING marijuana to the point where the THC evaporates but not so high that it burns. Then the evaporated THC is inhaled leaving behind all the vegetative matter. Since there is no burn, no smoke or other pyrolitic materials are inhaled.

The ingredients in the smoke are not good for your lungs and are implicated in both short- and long-term damage. The vaporizer allows you to inhale only cannabinoids and essential oils, eliminating the inhaling of smoke.

As it travels in the airstream through the tubing, the evaporated gasses condense into small droplets of viscous oil. This is what is inhaled. In this form it is probably still not good for the lungs, but certainly a lot cleaner than smoke consisting of burn products. You wouldn't want to inhale smoke from a pile of burning leaves, but that's essentially what you are doing when you smoke marijuana. Vaporizing marijuana is a way of inhaling THC and other cannabinoids in a fairly pure form.

VAPORIZING TEMPERATURE

At what temperature does THC vaporize?

ARON, New York City

THE CANNABINOIDS VAPORIZE IN the 375-400° F. The exact temperature varies a bit depending on the cannabinoid, the altitude and the barometric pressure.

CONSIDERING VAPORIZING

My friend tried a vaporizer in Holland, which he said is the best way to inhale. Other friends who have tried it said they were disappointed. What do you think?

INTERNATIONAL HEMPSTER, Internet

VAPORIZERS ARE VERY EFFICIENT delivery systems because all of the THC is released and none is destroyed in the fire. Inhaling it is a unique experience. There is no incoming rush of smoke, which signals the hit size, just a subtle, perfume-like taste drifting down the throat. The vapor expands in the lungs, and a large hit can result in a series of coughs.

Like Pavlov's dogs we have learned to associate the rush of smoke with highness. When your friends did not get that signal they probably did not feel they were getting the whole event, and did not float as easily into the high.

C. CANNABIS
CONSUMER TIPS

WHITE MOLD

I recently procured some reefer that has a white mold growing on it. What is it and can it be harmful?

JD, Scotia, New York

THE WHITE MOLD IS an infection. The mold may be benign or may produce harmful or poisonous chemicals. You should treat this material in the same way you would moldy food—throw it out. Risking your health is just not worth the high.

MOLDY WEED

I grew a few plants this past summer, with unbelievably good results. I hung the plants for two weeks and cured the buds in large canning jars after that. I was inspecting the buds today and noticed that the tips of the crystals have little balls on them. Some buds have translucent fuzz growing on them. Is this mold as I suspect? Perhaps just a very advanced stage of ripening?

BRIAN, Internet

YOUR FIRST GUESS WAS correct. There is mold growing on your buds, rendering them useless. The reason it started growing on the buds was that they contained moisture. The mold spores were floating in the air or already on the bud. With the correct temperature, nutrients and moisture the spores activated. After growing on the nutrient in the vegetation they produced fruiting bodies, which is what you observed. It is not safe to ingest or smoke unknown fungi or molds.

MOLDS & BACTERIA

I store bud in my freezer in containers injected with carbon
dioxide. I am worried about smoking marijuana with
harmful bacteria, fungi or molds on it. I read that cooler
temperatures encourage penicillium infestations that I am
allergic to. Does freezing bud in a CO_2 atmosphere kill bacteria, fungi and molds?

How can you identify bacteria, fungi and molds?

MICHAEL, Internet

MARIJUANA IS USUALLY FREE of infection. Freezing stops virtually all
growth of molds and fungi and most bacteria. However, it does not
kill them. It just places them in suspended animation. Once the
material is unfrozen, the organisms become active again.

Molds and fungi can be detected by a visual inspection using a
magnifying glass or photographer's loupe. The mycellium produce
fruiting bodies that form stalks on the leaf surface.

Anaerobic bacteria, which seem to be the most likely to attack
marijuana, can be detected by an ammonia smell. If marijuana is
healthy when it's picked and is dried properly, it is unlikely to be
infected.

A FEW FINAL WORDS OF WISDOM

"DON'T LEND YOUR HAND TO RAISE NO FLAG ATOP A SHIP OF FOOLS."
—GRATEFUL DEAD

DON'T BOGART THAT JOINT MY FRIEND.
REMEMBER TO SHARE AND SMILE.

STILL HAVE QUESTIONS?

HERE'S HOW YOU CAN ASK ED

THE ASK ED COLUMN appears in every issue of *Cannabis Culture* magazine, which can be purchased at bookstores throughout North America and internationally, or viewed at www.cannabisculture.com.

If you have a burning question for Ask Ed, write to him at:

ASK ED
PMB 147
530 DIVISADERO ST.
SAN FRANCISCO, CA 94117

Or submit your question online. Just go to **www.quicktrading.com** and follow the links. Ed's site also offers additional articles on growing, the law and medical marijuana. You can also sign up for the Quick News newsletter and shop for all of the Ask Ed books, plus other great marijuana titles that are available for sale.

HAVE PHOTOS?

SUBMIT YOUR PHOTOS AND you may win Ed's Bud of the Month®, Plant of the Month® or Garden of the Month® contest.

Prints can be sent to the address listed above. Digital photos can also be sent online through the website, **www.quicktrading.com**. Just follow the instructions, and you may see your bud, plant or garden featured in *Heads* magazine, or in Ed's online gallery at www.quicktrading.com.

APPENDIX A:
METRIC TO ENGLISH CONVERSION

LENGTH

1 foot = 30.48 centimeters = 0.30 meters
1 meter = 3.28 feet
1 inch = 2.54 centimeters
1 centimeter = 0.39 inches

AREA

1 square meter = 10.76 square feet
1 square foot = 0.09 square meters

MASS

1 gram = 0.035 ounces
1 ounce = 28.35 grams
1 pound = 16 ounces

TEMPERATURE

$15°$ C = $59°$ F
$20°$ C = $68°$ F
$22°$ C = $72°$ F
$25°$ C = $77°$ F
$28°$ C = $82°$ F
$30°$ C = $86°$ F
$32°$ C = $89.5°$ F
$35°$ C = $95°$ F

TO FIGURE:

Celsius = (F - 32) x $5/9$
Fahrenheit = C x $9/5$ + 32

NUMBER OF HOURS OF DARKNESS BY LATITUDE

CANNABIS IS TRIGGERED INTO flowering based on the number of hours of uninterrupted darkness it receives. The dark period ranges between 8-12 hours for different varieties.

In order to ripen plants outside, it is useful to know the length of night, which changes based on season and latitude. Southern seasons are six months different than northern seasons, so the chart indicates northern latitudes on the left and southern latitudes on the right.

NUMBER OF HOURS OF DARKNESS BY LATITUDE

North Latitude	0	+10	+20	+30	+35	+40	+45	+50	+52	+54	+56	+58	South Latitude
June 16	11:53	11:18	10:40	9:56	9:30	8:59	8:24	7:49	7:27	6:53	6:25	5:53	Dec. 16
July 1	11:53	11:18	10:41	9:57	9:31	9:01	8:26	7:41	7:21	6:57	6:29	5:55	Jan. 1
July 16	11:53	11:21	10:46	10:08	9:44	9:17	8:45	8:05	7:47	7:25	7:01	7:33	Jan. 16
Aug. 1	11:53	11:27	10:59	10:26	10:06	9:44	9:19	8:48	8:32	8:15	7:57	7:35	Feb. 1
Aug. 16	11:53	11:34	11:13	10:48	10:33	10:17	9:58	9:35	9:27	9:12	9:59	9:43	Feb. 16
Sept. 1	11:53	11:42	11:29	11:15	11:06	10:57	10:45	10:29	10:25	10:18	10:10	10:02	Mar. 1
Sept. 16	11:53	11:50	11:46	11:41	11:39	11:35	11:31	11:27	11:24	11:22	11:21	11:16	Mar. 16
Oct. 1	11:53	11:59	12:03	12:08	12:11	12:14	12:18	12:22	12:24	12:26	12:28	12:30	Apr. 1
Oct. 16	11:53	12:07	12:19	12:35	12:43	12:53	13:06	13:17	13:23	13:30	13:36	13:45	Apr. 16
Nov. 1	11:53	12:13	12:36	13:01	13:15	13:31	13:49	14:14	14:24	14:35	14:48	15:03	May 1
Nov. 16	11:53	12:21	12:50	13:22	13:42	14:03	14:29	15:00	15:14	15:30	15:49	16:09	May 16
Dec. 1	11:53	12:26	13:00	13:39	14:03	14:27	14:58	15:36	16:07	16:14	16:36	17:02	June 1
Dec. 16	11:53	12:27	13:05	13:56	14:12	14:40	15:12	15:54	16:13	16:36	17:01	17:31	June 16

Some example latitudes:

> Memphis, Tennessee; Albuquerque, New Mexico; Los Angeles, California: Latitude 35N
> New York, New York; Columbus, Ohio, Denver, Colorado: Latitude 40N
> Australia, Nimbin: Latitude 30S
> Canada: Ottawa-Toronto, Ontario: Latitude 43N
> Vancouver (incl. Nanaimo), British Columbia: Latitude 50N
> Holland: Latitude 52N
> Malawi: Latitudes 10-15S
> Switzerland: Latitude: 47N

GLOSSARY OF TERMS

(Note: * indicates a term which is also defined in the glossary)

alleles: Different versions of the same gene.

ampere: A unit of electrical current.

angiosperm: A plant that uses flowers to produce seed.

autosome: All chromosomes except the sex chromosomes.

backcross: A cross between an F1 hybrid and one of its parents.

botrytis: A genus of fungi that includes *B. cinerea,* which causes gray mold*.

BTU: British Thermal Units.

C3 (pathway): The most common method of carbon fixation in plants including cannabis. These plants absorb carbon dioxide from the air only when they are photosynthesizing*. The availability of CO_2 is a limiting factor in the photosynthetic rate.

capillary action: The action of water as it travels through fiber using surface tension. An example is a tissue pulling moisture upward. When water travels sideways or upwards in soil it is also a result of this. Nylon rope wicks water in the same way.

cfm: cubic feet per minute.

chlorophyll: The green pigment that uses light energy, primarily from the red and blue spectrums, to loosen an electron from its structure. This sets off a chain of reactions that ends with the combination of CO_2 and hydrogen to form a three-carbon sugar* and the release of oxygen.

chloroplast: An organelle, or specialized structure, found within the cells of leaves and stems of plants. It is composed of a matrix that hold stacks of chlorophyll*. It functions autonomously and is separated from the cell that contains it by two semi-permeable membranes. This is the part of the cell where photosynthesis takes place.

clone: A rooted cutting. It has the same genetics as the plant from which it was taken.

diploid: A nucleus that contains two sets of chromosomes, one from each parent. This is the normal state of non-reproductive cells.

drip system: A method of watering using irrigation tubing with small openings that restrict the water to a very small flow. The openings are placed only where water is desired.

EC meter: A device that measures the electrical conductivity, an indirect measure of dissolved solids in water.

F1: The first hybrid generation produced by crossing two varieties. It has great uniformity because all of the plants received half their genes from each of two stable varieties. These varieties have similar alleles, or versions of genes on each pair of chromosomes. The genetic makeup of the resulting plants is very similar.

F2: The second hybrid generation produced by crossing an F1* plant to itself or to another F1 plant. The result is a population with a wide assortment of combinations of characteristics of the parental generation.

germination: The beginning of a seed's growth.

gibberellin or gibberellic acid: A group of plant hormones that regulate leaf and stem growth. Two of these, GA-3 and GA-4 are used commercially in sprays and mixes. In cannabis they cause stem and bud elongation but not enlargement and hermaphroditism.

gray mold: The mold that attacks marijuana buds. It is caused by *Botrytis cinera**. Its spores are in the air, but it thrives only under specific conditions: high humidity, 50-65° F temperatures and an acidic surface.

medium: The material in which the roots grow. It could be a block of material such as rockwool, a natural medium such as soil or compost or a planting mix using bark, peat moss, perlite, sand or other materials.

halogen: A light bulb that is similar to an incandescent in efficiency but produces a whiter light.

haploid: A cell nucleus with only one set of chromosomes. This occurs in reproductive cells. Each parent's gamete (pollen* or ovum*) contains a nucleus* composed of one set of chromosomes. They combine to form a diploid* nucleus, that becomes a seed.

hermaphrodite: A female marijuana plant that also grows viable male flowers. The male flowers may appear in many conformations including singly or all-male branches. Usually a single marijuana plant grows only male or female flowers.

HID lamps: high intensity discharge lamps. They include metal halide* and high pressure sodium* lamps.

high pressure sodium: The most efficient, commonly used lamps. They emit more light per watt and more light in the red spectrum than metal halide* lamps.

hydroponics: The method of growing marijuana using an inert medium to hold the roots. Nutrients are dissolved in the nutrient water.

infrared: Light just below the spectrum that is visible to the human eye, so called because it is just below red, which is the lowest visible wavelength of color. Infrared light is absorbed by leaves. See page 40 for a graphic depicting the light spectrum, including infrared, visible and ultraviolet* light.

Kelvin: A temperature measurement where the zero point is absolute zero, or –273° C.

lumen: a measurement of intensity of light emission. One lumen is equivalent to one foot-candle of light falling on an area of one square foot. It measures how much light reaches what you are trying to light. Incandescents produce between 5 and 25 lumens per watt; fluorescents produce between roughly 50 and 100 lumens per watt. Metal halide* lamps and high pressure sodium* lamps produce over 60 lumens per watt, and many produce over 100 lumens per watt.

meristem: a group of cells at the growing tip of a leaf or root where rapid cell division takes place. This is the tissue used for tissue culture.

metal halide: An HID* lamp that produces a white light. It is often used as a grow light.

morphology: The form and structure of an individual organism (plant).

mycorrhiza: A group of fungi that form symbiotic associations with plant roots. They enter the roots, where some live within the cells and others grow on their surface. They provide inorganic nutrients to the plants and receive energy (mostly carbohydrates) from the roots. They also protect the roots from predators.

Mylar: An extremely reflective metal coated plastic film often used to reflect light to a garden. It is often attached to walls or used as curtains in grow spaces.

nitrogen: An element essential for plant growth. It is considered a macronutrient—plants use it in large quantities.

N-P-K: The listing of minimum amounts of percentages of the macronutrients nitrogen*, phosphorous* and potassium* found in fertilizers. It is always listed in that order on the label.

nucleus: A part (organelle) of the cell that is separated from it by a membrane. The nucleus contains the cell's chromosomes.

Oasis®: A brand of planting medium made from open cellular foam that is often used for cloning.

ovum: An unfertilized egg cell. It is found behind the flower.

parabolic reflectors: A light reflector in a parabolic shape used to direct light from a vertically held HID* lamp.

perlite: A planting medium ingredient made from puffed rock.

pH: A scale of the measure of alkalinity–acidity of water or a grow medium. Zero is most acidic, 7 is neutral and 14 is most alkaline.

phosphorus: An element essential for plant growth. One of the macronutrients.

photosynthesis: The process in which chlorophyll captures light and uses its energy to create sugar. The formula is $CO_2 + H_2O$—$(CH_2O) + H_2O + O_2$.

phylum: A major division in the Linnaean classification system of animals and plants. It falls right below kingdom and before class.

plenum: A box from which air is distributed to several lines of tubing. It is usually installed to distribute heated or cooled air to several areas.

pollen: The male reproductive product that contains a haploid* set of chromosomes. When it fertilizes an ovum*, a seed is formed. Cannabis is a wind-pollinated plant so the pollen becomes airborne.

potassium: One of the macronutrients essential for plant growth. It is the third element listed on fertilizer labels.

ppm: parts per million.

progeny: The offspring of a plant, animal or human.

psf: per square foot.

pyrethrum: a concentrate of a natural plant pesticide produced by a plant in the chrysanthemum family. It is extremely effective against caterpillars and grubs. Pyrethrum is not harmful to warm-blooded animals, but can harm cold-blooded animals such as reptiles and fish. It should never be used near a stream or lake.

reservoir system: A hydroponic* method in which the plant container remains partially submerged in water.

rockwool: A planting medium made from spun basalt rock. It is often formed into cubes.

rooting compound: A topically administered compound used to encourage cuttings to root. They usually contain abscisic acid and a fungicide.

sea of green: A method of growing in which plants are placed very closely together so that little space is required for them to fill the canopy.

sidestream smoke: The smoke coming off of the burning end of a joint or pipe rather than the smoke that is inhaled intentionally through the mouthpiece. This term is used as a synonym for second-hand smoke.

sinsemilla: without seeds.

soilless: A manufactured planting medium. It is often composed of bark or peat moss as the base materials.

solenoid: A type of electrical switch.

squirrel fan: A type of fan that is often used for ventilation.

sugar: The product of photosynthesis*.

tachycardia: A speeded heartbeat. This common side effect to marijuana use usually diminishes with tolerance.

tissue culture: Cloning that begins with a few meristem* cells.

translocated: The movement of minerals from one part to another part of the plant.

ultraviolet: Light just above the spectrum that is visible to the human eye, so called because it is just above violet, which is the last color in the visible spectrum. Ultraviolet, or UV light is absorbed by leaves and is also responsible for tanning. See page 40 for a graphic depicting the light spectrum, including infrared*, visible and ultraviolet light.

vermiculite: A puffed mined mineral used as a planting medium. It is losing favor because it often contains asbestos.

volt: A unit of electromotive force, which measures potential. Voltage in North America and South America is on 110/120 voltage, while Europe, Asia and Africa is on 220 volts. Areas of Japan use 95/105 volts.

watt: A unit of electric power or rate of work. Watts = Amps/Volts

INDEX

Page numbers in bold type indicate photos or graphics.